MS: BEYOND THE RED DOOR

MS: BEYOND THE RED DOOR

Dr. Rick Yeager and
Mary Ellen Ziliak, RN

TATE PUBLISHING
AND ENTERPRISES, LLC

Published by Tate Publishing & Enterprises, LLC
127 E. Trade Center Terrace | Mustang, Oklahoma 73064 USA
1.888.361.9473 | www.tatepublishing.com

Tate Publishing is committed to excellence in the publishing industry. The company reflects the philosophy established by the founders, based on Psalm 68:11,
"The Lord gave the word and great was the company of those who published it."

Book design copyright © 2013 by Tate Publishing, LLC. All rights reserved.
Cover design by Jan Sunday Quilaquil
Interior design by Caypeeline Casas

Published in the United States of America
ISBN: 978-1-63418-550-9
Biography & Autobiography / Personal Memoirs
14.08.28

*This book is dedicated to
those whose lives are touched by
multiple sclerosis.*

ACKNOWLEDGMENTS

Residents of Yeager World, both two- and four-legged, we appreciate your unconditional love and support. Ziliaks, clan of many, your encouragement was fuel for our writing. Roger, devoted husband, you continue to amaze with the depth of your love. *Artist Way* members, Libby and Sheila, you helped grow the artist within us.

Now, Dr. Myron D. Yeager—brother, professor, tough critic, gentle mentor, kind man—you made this book happen. Thank you for sharing our vision and reading all chapters, many times over. Your knowledge, comments, and guidance with writing, rewriting, and rewriting was invaluable. You not only edited our writing, you taught us to write from the heart. You were the midwife in birthing this book.

TABLE OF CONTENTS

PROLOGUE

Rick sent me this email when I was in the middle of an MS flare-up. We both live with multiple sclerosis. "Like you, I feel like an island in the sea, watching the sea's strong waves and tide wash away a part of me at a time, with no hope of it ever coming back. It is just part of the fight." The poetry of his words and insight to what I felt at the time moved me to write this book.

—Mary Ellen

Multiple sclerosis, MS, is thought to be an illness with an inherited predisposition, where the body's protective antibodies, designed to attack invading organisms, turn to attack one's own nervous system. Mary Ellen and I were in the medical profession for decades until MS ended our careers. We have been medical professionals for years but this is not a medical treatise. This is the experience of how each of our body's attack upon itself has changed our world.

—Rick

We write to expose the unexposed. If there is one door in the castle you have been told not to go through, you must. Otherwise, you'll just be rearranging furniture in rooms you've already been in. Most human beings are dedicated to keeping that one door shut. But the writer's job is to see what's behind it, to see the bleak, unspeakable stuff, and to turn the unspeakable into words—not just into any words, but, if we can, into rhythm and blues.

—Anne Lamott *Bird by Bird*

SUGAR AND SPICE

Peering up through the spider web of IV tubing, I could spot the classic, broad grin Kim, the RN, always wore for her patients. The potent Tysabri medicine once again coursed through my veins. The IV juice was my healing water, but it also held a one in one thousand chance of killing me.

Beside me sat my good friend, Rick, receiving the same treatment. I pondered what had brought the two of us into this crazy cosmic world of multiple sclerosis (MS). He spent years being an Emergency Department physician. I prided myself in the work I'd accomplished as a director of nursing in a long-term care facility. Now here we were, two vulnerable patients, receiving treatment for an unpredictable, chronic, and debilitating disease that had taken over our lives and ended our medical careers.

As a registered nurse, I first approached my diagnosis of MS with a scientific mind. I researched every article I could find and tried to take the high road by being accepting and brave. After all, I was a licensed and practicing RN, certified in orthopedic nursing. I cared for total hip and total knee patients and those with multiple traumas. I worked rehab and cared for MS patients with great debilitation. I worked substance abuse units, medical surgical, research, and long-term care. I moved into management and loved the challenges. Why, I even survived a sailing metal bedpan flung at my head by a disgruntled patient. So surely I was well prepared to handle multiple sclerosis. Think again.

My life story and, thus, my MS journey take seed in a rural community of southwestern Indiana.

"Dad eyed Mom bending over the chicken coop and nine months later, us boys had a little sister." This continues to be big brother Harvey's version of the not so immaculate conception of Mary Ellen Klenck.

That's me, still called Mary Ellen by most, Mary by a few, born November 20, 1952, to Harold and Esther Klenck. Mom was thirty-four, Dad thirty-nine. Was I a surprise baby to the household? Maybe. Of course I tell everyone, "You always save the best for last." I'm the baby, spoiled rotten and proud of it. With three much older brothers and being the only girl, what can you expect?

Brother Harvey is eleven years older than me; Verner, now deceased, was fourteen; and Jim seventeen. With that span of testosterone-filled years, I figured I had to be special, right?

Mom's birth stories are a bit different from Harvey's. They include how my name was chosen. Version one goes like this:

"I prayed for a little girl. I told God if he gave me a girl, I would name her after the Blessed Virgin Mary." Yes, you guessed it. I am a cradle Catholic. This included eight years at St. Wendel Grade School and four at Rex Mundi High School, which means "King of the World." I wore one navy blue uniform for four years. It was so shiny I could see my face in it. Still have it too, that is if I get it back from Sheila Kunkel. At our forty-year class reunion I loaned it out for antique show and tell.

We did not have kindergarten back then. That far out in the country we didn't need no stinkin' preschool or kindergarten! Why, we didn't even need shoes from May 1 to September 1. Beginning every school year, my feet hurt for three weeks because I had to put shoes back on. Now Mom did have me put sandals on for one hour every Sunday for Mass, but that didn't count. Besides, I could wiggle them loose under the pew if worse came to worse.

I digress. But you need to know the Catholic significance of a name like Mary. It is a high honor and comes with much responsibility. Along the years, my classmates included: Mary Elaine, Mary Beth, Mary Ann, Mary Louise, Mary Catherine, Mary

Helen, Mary Rose, and a gazillion of just plain old Mary. My close foursome of girlfriends in high school included a Mary Louise Stofleth. To avoid confusion between us she became "Stof" and I was christened "Colonel Klenck." For you youngsters to understand, Google the old TV comedy, "Hogan's Heroes."

Birth story number two, per Mom's excellent memory even at ninety-three, unfolded as:

Verner, son number two and labeled "the sick one with diabetes," was dating Mary Ellen Schnarr. Of course, Verner was madly in love with her and tried to convince Mom that Mary Ellen was one heck of a good name if I was born a girl. Mom saw Mary Ellen as a swell gal and decent daughter-in-law material.

So, the second no brainer was hatched alongside the infamous chicken coop. Name the potential miracle female baby Mary Ellen and you've got a win-win situation. You've hooked a bride for Verner and you are in like flint with God, the church, and Holy Mary, Mother of God.

By the way, Verner dumped Mary Ellen Schnarr, married a Colleen, and I was smart enough to be born before I was baptized with a heathen name.

I jest about the Mary name but I like it. It has served me well and I still turn to Mary to intercede for me in my many predicaments of life. Of course, at age ten, I did beg Mom to call me by my new name of Mickey. Memory does not serve me if that was after the big-eared mouse or the many-times-married actor Rooney. Thank you God that Mickey did not stick. Seriously, Lord, I thank you.

Hopscotch, skip, and jump rope along fifty-nine years and you come to find me today—Mary Ellen Klenck Ziliak—with a full life and abundant blessings surrounding me.

My first career after college encompassed farm wife, mother, and registered nurse. My second career, after MS derailed the first, became business wife, grandma, artist, and a survivor of all the crap one sucking chronic disease like multiple sclerosis can fling at any one human being.

Multiple sclerosis. The Big MS. The big Mother Sucker. It took my mother eleven years before she could say MS out loud. Mom would whisper to me, "That disease you have."

It hurt me terribly that Mom enforced the "Do not utter MS" rule in her household. Was it denial? Did it hurt her so much that she couldn't bear to say the two letters out loud? I still don't know, even after I got the nerve to ask her on several occasions when I lost my patience. All I know was my heart squeezed a little tighter and my chest hurt every time I heard, "That disease you have." It sounded so dirty.

MS is the worst thing that has ever happened to me. MS is the best thing that has ever happened to me. And in between those two monumental discoveries, my world has been turned inside out, upside down, and every which way but loose.

I am not unique. I'll wager most people who live with multiple sclerosis have experienced the same topsy-turvy roller coaster ride. MS straps you into the train car without a ticket. You don't have to stand in line and it is definitely the roller coaster ride of your life. Your arms will fly high at the top of the hills without even trying. Guaranteed.

The saying fits, "The only thing you can be sure about with MS is that you can't be sure about anything with MS." That makes for a lifetime of surprises.

Fourteen years have passed since the MS diagnosis. I was pissed the first ten and didn't know it.

I have gleaned much medical information about MS. But looking back I see that the practical day-to-day tips of survival, physically and mentally, have served me best.

Some adaptive suggestions I read about in books, journals, newsletters, or heard by word of mouth from support groups, family, friends, and acquaintances. Many insightful adaptations I learned from my daughter Liza. This middle child is one of the strongest women I know who has dealt with her own chronic illness for twenty years and makes a heavy cross look easy to carry.

Yet the bulk of my best dos and don'ts come from living with this disease and attempting to give purpose to my life, even with the losses.

God has put it on my heart to share my story. I used to think things to death before deciding something. Not anymore. Deciding to write this book took all of twenty-four hours. I no longer have the luxury of procrastinating. And I realized I was pretty arrogant by questioning what God is capable of in me. Who am I to question? He can do anything.

So my goal is to share what I know, feel, and have experienced on my MS journey with my reader friends. I hope you find some good tips, some good insights. But above all, I hope you find you are not alone. And your quirky private symptoms are not freaky. We all have them. And our purpose in life does not always end up looking like the picture or plans in our pre-MS head. God is so much bigger than that. Sometimes we just have to quiet our hearts, open them up wide, and accept what is placed upon them.

MOJO JUICE

These days I spend about four hours, every four weeks, at the Evansville Cancer Center in Evansville, Indiana. They need to change the name of that place. Who wants to walk through the doors of a place with CANCER as the essence of its name?

I can try to be politically correct and open-minded and positive and all nursey, but sitting in the waiting room the first time, as a patient, was creepy for me. I was with strangers, many of whom looked pasty white, emaciated, and weak as kittens. My first instinct was to get the heck out of Dodge. I didn't care what miracle juice awaited me behind the Let's Make A Deal Door.

With the passing of time I have come to perceive strength and camaraderie in that same waiting room. There is an unspoken acceptance into family. Don't get me wrong; I still absolutely hate getting my IVs. Over the years I have developed a needle phobia. So I have taken friends and family with me some days for moral support. Here I am an RN and a big old wuss. It is totally different being on the receiving end of that friggin' needle.

This new treatment modality experience started four years ago. It involves taking Tysabri intravenously every four weeks. I usually take twice the standard time for infusion because I get a bad headache and some nausea as side effects. Slowing the rate of infusion seems to lessen the impact some.

The simple explanation of how Tysabri works is that the medicine is an antibody and theoretically slows down the progression of multiple sclerosis and reduces the number of exacerbations—flare-ups that is. It is not a cancer drug but is treated as one. At present, only four facilities in my tri-state area are certified to administer this drug. It must be given under strict guidelines in a controlled medical setting. A cancer center is a good fit for that.

Part of the big hoopla surrounding this fairly new drug is that several people have died taking the drug. Tysabri was, for a time, taken off the market because some patients receiving it developed a thing called PML. PML stands for progressive multifocal leukoencephalopathy. PML is a kind of weird encephalopathy—a brain infection that is serious crap. The mortality risk seems to be greater in the population that receives Tysabri, plus a second disease-altering MS drug.

When I die, I don't want PML to be the culprit if I can help it. So I put on my nurse's cap and did a lot of research on the pros and cons of the IV treatment suggested by my local neurologist. He is a conservative physician, which is one of the reasons I go to him. As my needs with MS change over the years, so do my needs with my neurologist. I see a change coming soon as to the fit between my neuro doc and me, but all in good time. I trust God and His knowing synchronicity will guide me as needed there.

I had had some very serious side effects with other modalities of treatment in the past. My doctor and I were slow to jump on any new bandwagon, much less a big one like Tysabri. We waited for some time to pass for Tysabri to prove itself when placed upon the market a second time. Then we revisited getting me started on a Tysabri once a month IV infusion and decided to give it a try. Four years later, I am still on it.

My decision to take Tysabri has been a good one. It is right for me at present. Every case of MS must be looked at on an individual basis because there is no one cure-all plan. Each patient presents differently and has different needs to get the quality of life desired. Over the years I have chosen four different modalities of treatment. Sometimes after much discussion with my physicians, my final choice is made by gut feeling and a lot of prayer. Even as a nurse there are no clear-cut right or wrong options.

With Tysabri use I have had much more energy, better balance to the point of using my cane infrequently, more cognitive clarity, and less pain. When starting the Tysabri, I used to lie flat and rest about three to five times a day. I call that my "flat time." I don't sleep but I need to be flat somewhere so as not to use even my torso muscles to hold myself halfway upright in a recliner. Sitting upright can zap my energy and make my arms and back hurt like the dickens. So, I must be flat and sometimes prop my arms up with pillows underneath to support them fully.

Now I do flat time on average about one to three times a day. I average twenty to thirty minutes each time. That is a major improvement for me. It gives me a bit more of my life back that MS has stolen from me. Take that you pesky wabbit!

I actually can tell when I am running out of Tysabri juice near the end of my four weeks. I can do this without a calendar because I begin to feel exhausted and heavy and more befuddled in my brain. It's like my battery has run out of juice or my gas tank is flashing "empty."

MS fatigue is different than regular, "I'm tired." The general public and even some physicians don't get that. So general public, please don't tell me you know how I feel. *You don't!* Your saying that really pisses me off!

The debilitation of MS fatigue is so hard to explain if you haven't experienced it. To me I think of having ten-pound sacks of potatoes on both arms and legs and then trying to walk through mud in the middle of a cow pasture on a foggy morn. Little scary how my mind works. Of course I can always blame it on my illustrious country upbringing and the big cavernous ventricles that now landscape my brain.

Even lying flat with severe fatigue sometimes makes me feel like my head and my body is sinking deeply into the center of my mattress stuffing and I will smother. It feels like I can't lift my head, arms, or legs if my life depended on it. Sure, most times I can concentrate and move myself. But sometimes Roger, my Sir Lancelot husband, has to save his damsel in distress and literally roll me over and help me rise up. That is what I mean when I say "MS fatigue."

Looking back four years to my very first IV infusion of Tysabri brings back many memories and very mixed emotions. It was "a defining moment" as good old Dr. Phil would say.

By then I was ten and a half years into my diagnosis of multiple sclerosis. We MS-ers track our years with the disease like it was a newborn baby. In a way I guess it is. But that baby would definitely be in NICU. I often get confused as to how long that time really is. There seems to be some protective mental block or a plain old sclerotic plaque blocking that accuracy. Early on I used to keep a journal of my MS symptoms, meds, labs, doctors' appointments. I could easily check dates there. A few years into my diagnosis I pitched the journals thinking they were too negative. I did not want to focus so closely on what was a downer in my life. It did not seem healthy. Now I wish I'd held onto them. I have so many gray areas in my gray matter that hinder accurate recall.

Having been a nurse for thirty years, that day at the Cancer Center, I could look back to my training and have both an RN's view and a patient's view of what I was undertaking. It is a bit like being schizophrenic in a very constructive way. One personality was Mary Ellen, MS patient; another was M.E. Ziliak RN.

I started my college career at Indiana University and graduated from the University of Evansville, also in the great Hoosier state. If memory serves me correctly, Mrs. Titzer—my UE anatomy and physiology teacher, a clinical instructor, and another Mary— hit upon multiple sclerosis in one of our classes and pretty well summed it up with, "If a patient has multiple sclerosis, we can expect them to be in a wheelchair by the age of fifty."

So sitting among some walking dead in my ugly, stiff, vinyl recliner that beautifully crisp, fall day, the first thing that popped into my head was, "Holy crap, I'm fifty-six. I'm screwed!" Please note that was the MS patient personality speaking.

My nerves were shattered that eventful IV day. There I was, hating needle sticks since I developed a bit of PTSD—post-traumatic stress disorder—after having twenty-one lesions removed in two outpatient settings by a plastic surgeon years before. Twenty-one lesions times about three local anesthetic sticks for each lesion makes for about sixty-three needle pricks. And "prick" is definitely the right phrase for that little medical step.

PTSD was the phrase daughter Liza attached to my angst about IVs and injections when I whined to her about it. What are daughters for if not for a little payback whining? She is a mental health therapist for homeless youth in Seattle, Washington. Nurse Mom plus counselor daughter add up to some knee slappin' crazy work discussions.

So there I am in the treatment room getting hooked up to an IV. I was told it would take two hours. They failed to tell me I would see the oncologist or nurse practitioner every other visit to monitor my status and report back to my neurologist. And they had no crystal ball to know I would have side effects that caused a killer headache and nausea every time so the IV rate had to be slowed down to half as fast as the norm. So my infusion visits often lasted four hours instead of the two I was told to expect. I count that as five and a half hours, a half-day, because I count shower and getting dressed and commute time when I mete out my precious energy time on any given day of my life. That is the way many MS patients view their daily planner entries. We have only so many limited hours of what I call "up time," or time that we have enough energy and strength to do physical activities. Therefore, any commitment must factor in pacing myself, hygiene, dress, commute, and rest time. There is a lot of math involved with the simplest of tasks.

Kim is a very petite and perky RN at the Cancer Center with many years of experience in oncology. Living just across the river in Kentucky, a southern drawl only intermittently peppers her quick-clipped voice. Kim has a tendency to peer over her chic, narrow-rimmed glasses and it adds to her pertness.

That first IV day I looked up to find those sparkling eyes looking over the brim of her glasses and directly at me. Kim approached and immediately began reading questions off a typed sheet in her hand. The long, formal list of queries included:

"Over the past month, have you had any new or worsening medical problems (such as a new or sudden change in your thinking, eyesight, balance, strength, or other problems) that have persisted over several days?"

"Do you have a medical condition that can weaken your immune system, such as HIV infection or AIDS, leukemia or lymphoma, or an organ transplant that may suggest that your body is not able to fight infections well?" (Personally, I am especially fond of that question. If I have suddenly developed AIDS, I am expected to acknowledge this for all the world to hear in the middle of the open treatment room with a dozen other patients, friends, and family. Yeah, right.)

"In the past month, have you taken medicines to treat cancer or MS or any other medicines that weaken your immune system?"

"In the past month, other than for the treatment of a recent relapse, have you taken any of the following medicines: Solu-Medrol, methlylprednisolone, Decadron, dexamethasone, Depo-Medrol, prednisone, or other steroid medicines?"

This list of questions must be asked before every treatment. If I have had worsening MS symptoms, my neurologist is called to okay the infusion. If there is a yes answer from me, my IV can be withheld for a month and I miss a shot of my golden liqueur.

The IV cannula is expertly guided by Kim into the antecubital space, the elbow bend, of my left arm. I feel the classic "pop" of it piercing my vein wall. It's in on the first try. My veins are good so I am seldom a "multiple stick" start as we nurses would say.

I myself sucked at starting IVs. I hated to do them and when I had to do the lab draws on all my little retired nuns at Seton

Residence—a retirement center for aged Daughter of Charity sisters—I cringed inside every time. There was just something creepy about trying to visualize the hidden vein under the skin like some vampire and then magically hitting the sometimes-rolling vein at the right angle. It is an art. Believe me. As Director of Nursing (DON) I was glad to eventually contract out that task with a local lab business. I haven't had to do IVs or draws since that time—another little blessing in life.

So Kim gets my IV running per pump at 100 cc/hr. Within twenty minutes I feel like a big, heavy stage curtain has descended upon my forehead. And with the curtain, a pressure headache washes over my entire forehead, with the worst just above both eyebrows. The first time this happened I thought it was nerves, tension of the experience, and my whole paranoia about needles. I did not know it would be a monthly experience. Just my luck. I get rid of monthly PMS and replace it with TH, Tysabri Headache.

My stomach was queasy but not much. I did not even mention the headache to the nurses. I was too busy fighting back the tears welling in my eyes. What the hell was going on with me?

The tears started to quietly trickle down my cheeks. I tried to act cool. Then a sob squeaked out. Oh, no, then came Oprah's ugly cry. Wailing began, mascara ran, people stared, and my nose got red. The whole time I'm thinking what an ungrateful bitch I am. (I'll confess that slip later.) I am surrounded by deathly ill cancer patients and I have the nerve to cry over a little IV for MS. I thought I saw disgust register in my recliner neighbor's eyes.

But the staring was short lived. Looking back, it was more curiosity I observed. I believe the cancer patients are desensitized to crying. It is part of the Big C package. They were just curious to see when it would hit the new gal on the block who had all her hair.

My diligent nurse Kim approached me with sincere concern in her eyes. "Are you okay?" she asked.

"Yeah, I'm okay. I don't know what's going on."

I was in no way prepared for this breakdown. I didn't even stress a lot about the whole new IV treatment beforehand, other than the initial stick. I was clueless.

Then I figured it was mostly the role reversal. I was used to being the nurse in charge. I consoled patients, not the other way around. I said all the right words, held the hand and reassured. That must have been it.

Well, this well of tears was deep. I could not halt or even slow the gusher. Embarrassment and shame enveloped me. I was a hopeless basket case.

Obviously the nurses agreed because next thing I know the all-powerful shrink was called in. Now I didn't know whether to be mad or grateful. *How dare they!* I thought. They did not even consult me first. I am not some sniffling, helpless broad here. I am a competent human being and a nurse to boot. My panties were in a wad for sure about this one but not enough to stop the tears.

So Dr. Dixon-Reed, later to be called Dr. Reed, appeared at my side and quickly sat next to me so as to project the correct body language. No standing, towering over the seated patient, or arm crossing will do for shrink face off. For a brief time I had worked rather indirectly as an RN with Dr. Reed on the rehab unit at Deaconess Hospital. He did not remember me. There was no facial recognition to support that.

So Dr. Reed sat and asked directly, "What is wrong?"

Oh my. That question knocked down the last wall of defense I was so desperately propping up.

I yelled, "I don't know my purpose in life!" Now where did that come from? The light bulb went on that maybe I did need someone to talk to.

I ended up having a very nice chat with Dr. Reed. It eventually calmed me and I felt my humanness was acceptable in the given situation. Sometime later I reflected back to that moment and tried to capture it in words. Here's what I wrote:

Discovering My Purpose

"I have MS but MS does not have me." So goes the mantra we people with multiple sclerosis tout. Yet after eleven
years diagnosed and twenty-five with symptoms, I still
struggle to live that mantra every day.

Intellectually I tell myself I've handled the MS well.
When being honest and true I realize the anger, resentment, and loss still smolder as embers deep within me.

My career as a registered nurse was one of challenge
and reward. I took pride in my work. The long hours and
crazy shifts were hard, but caring for others and using my
talents was gratifying. I felt blessed.

After diagnosis of multiple sclerosis at age forty-five,
progression of symptoms quickly led to my inability to
continue work as an RN. I went from full time director
of nursing to disabled person at home full time, from caregiver to care receiver. Bang, bang, bang!

Who was I now? My identity was actively wrapped up
into wife, mother, nurse, and friend. All these titles were
now chiseled into a new art form I did not recognize. My
biggest question was, "Now what?"

The defining moment," as Dr. Phil would say, came last
fall at the Cancer Center where I received my first intravenous infusion to treat the MS. There I sat, amid all these
brave cancer patients. I was the lucky one. I only had MS.
Yet I sat crying my eyes out for no apparent reason.

When the resident psychologist was sent to console me
and treat me on the spot, I blubbered, "I don't know my
purpose in life!"

Once stated as fact I gave myself permission to search
and pray vehemently for an answer—and that I did.

Months later the psychologist followed up and asked
if I'd found any answers. I shared with him: "I spent much
time praying over this. I discovered I don't have to worry
what my job is or the title I bear. My sole purpose in life is
to get up every day and be quiet and see what God puts on

my soul for that day. I don't need to know the big picture. God does that. I just need to honor Him and serve Him to my best ability every moment of the day. He takes care of the rest. Titles, careers, and paychecks don't define me. My talent as an RN is but a speck in God's plans for me."

Dr. Reed paused a long beat and smiled. He noted it was one way to look at it and he hadn't heard it put quite that way before. He joined in my joy of a prayer answered.

So now I frequently recite my favorite scripture: "Be still and know that I am God" (Psalm 46:10, KJV). That is all that is required of me to have purpose in life.

And oh what peace that discovery has given me. The peace of giving my will to God and just following His cue is a true blessing I now cherish daily.

My peace does not exempt me from bearing crosses. I still have MS. We all have crosses to bear. They are all a little different in shape, form, and weight on any given day. But the discovery of my purpose in life has made my life easier, simpler. I feel Christ's arms wound tightly around me. Thank you, God.

I no longer cry when receiving my Tysabri IV. I don't feel as out of place or troubled. I do still need support. That brings me to talking a little about my IV support circle. Smack dab in the middle of that support circle sits one Ricky Bob Thornton, I mean Yeager.

RICKY BOB

The large L-shaped room at the Cancer Center is filled with butt ugly recliners. I do not exaggerate. They are solid navy or gray or burgundy and are conveniently leather or plastic or such, so as to wipe away blood or other body fluids. Some have a small pop-up arm table on the side. If you're lucky you can nab a chair that has a slit in the seat that will conveniently pinch you in the buttocks or leg. I learned early not to wear shorts to my appointments.

Upon entering we all jockey for our perfect seat in its perfect location, a little like Goldilocks. For me, that entails a seat as far away from a blaring TV as I can get. I am stressed enough with the IV. I certainly don't want anymore screeching stimulation to put me over the edge. Sometimes the simplest little noise can overtake my thought processes and put me almost in a state of panic. I try to avoid those situations.

Last fall, while snuggled in with my geriatric lap blanket, I sensed a big, dark shadow passing over me. Upon looking up, it was not Sasquatch, but close. It was a very slow moving person, a tall, looming man, topped with thick, longish gray James Dean hair and sporting a somewhat faded blue sweatshirt with a large Purdue University logo. I tried not to hold that against him. I attended Indiana University (IU), Purdue's archrival, and two of my three children graduated from IU, the third from Ball State. Bigfoot was making a large swath with two metal canes leading the way.

Now I have this thing about boring, ugly canes. Canes are to be an extension of one's fashion sense, somewhat like a purse or scarf. They should not define a person as sick or, heaven forbid, "handicapped." I prefer my cane to say, "She has it together, right down to her matching cane—good accent, not too flashy, and very classy look." It's the little things in life that give me joy.

As an artist I have painted some walking sticks in a bright, uplifting Monet-type design. And I have applied Mehndi art to many walking canes. Mehndi is a type of Indian body art that is painted on with a henna dye. Among my many hats, one I don is labeled "henna tattoo artist." It got me started in my post nursing artist career. That is another story.

I have kept my favorite decorated canes and sold the others or given them away. I again tried not to hold this against the man that walked past me as he chose to go the utilitarian route. He had plain, old metal canes. But then, I guess men may not be as excited about intricate Indian artwork on their canes.

The slow, shuffling gait and the scooter alongside the man made me think, *Wow, he's probably like me and has MS.* It is kind of a game to pass time in the IV dungeon for me to guess diagnoses of fellow patients. It is even acceptable to ask each other, "Watcha in for?"

We all know we would not be there if not for some malfunction of our bodies requiring serious IV treatment. Privacy is out the window. It is a luxury we seldom experience after a diagnosis of MS. Inside this disinfectant-smelling institutional hole, we are exposed for all the world to see like broken, arm-missing dolls on a child's shelf. We get asked the most personal questions that could range from "How's your pain?" to "How have your bowels been?"

Needless to say I get giddy when I think I might meet another MS-er. I feel guilty enough being a sort of "imposter" there. I like other imposters with me. We are the lucky ones. We only have multiple sclerosis. They have cancer. MS seldom shortens one's life span. Cancer trumps MS. Everything is relative, right?

So I had time while Bigfoot was in the restroom to decide my opening line. I would ask him if he was receiving Tysabri. I try to read the patient first before I approach them to see if they will be easy to have a conversation with and to be sure they are not in a lot of pain and that I am not adding to that. My guideline is also to avoid big whiners if at all possible. I think everyone needs to vent their pain and frustrations, but I don't enjoy the constant whiners.

This guy gave off good vibes and he seemed at peace with himself. I gave him the green light and would talk to him upon returning to his chair. I also noted the nurses had offered to assist him with his ambulation and he politely declined saying he had his routine, it worked, and he did better taking his time on his own. "He'd be fine."

I liked that assertive but polite, "No, thanks." Independence is a must when trying to keep MS from overtaking your life. This guy got that. Points were adding up. I liked this guy. Hope when he opened his mouth I still did.

Upon mystery man's return I casually asked if he was receiving Tysabri, like me. He seemed a bit startled but quickly replied, "Ah, yes. Are you also?" The light of comrade recognition registered on a face near my age. He made direct eye contact. A confident man, who took the time to see me—me! Not just another warm body sweat stuck to a Lazy Boy reject piece of furniture. Bingo! I have someone to connect with in a room full of fearful people, all of whom bear crosses the outside world feels uncomfortable acknowledging.

We made introductions.

"Rick Yeager. Ah, let me just sit down so we can talk. Just a second. I need to do this." He shuffled the U-turn to his tagged recliner and slowly sat, positioning his legs with some help from his arms. He did the lift and move maneuver I sometimes do in the car to get my legs in and out on a bad day. Classic physical MS give away.

Seeing the difficulty Rick had getting into a simple chair was one of those scary moments of looking into my potential future. Here was a man, maybe a bit older than me, with MS, and walking and sitting were major time-consuming tasks for him. He used two canes and a scooter. He hesitated with his communication, searching for words that were hard to retrieve. Words we use every day. And standing for mere seconds was too much for him. He had to sit quickly after the marathon walk to the restroom.

That could be me. That could be me tomorrow if my body decides to have a flare-up tonight. There is always the worry that the exacerbation that puts me in bed for a week with limited mobility, double vision, confusion, and weakness may not improve at the end of the week. I could have a lot of residual. My symptoms could stay forever.

MS is the ultimate crapshoot. We don't need to go to Vegas to gamble. MS brings it to us and the odds suck, baby.

So, back to new guy, Rick. We conversed easily and quickly realized we had a lot in common. He was a physician. I was an RN. Our careers both included much time in a hospital setting. We both sensed we had to leave our medical careers early but avoided visiting that painful subject.

Rick shared with me that his family and friends called him Ricky Bob. He described himself as just a dumb hillbilly doctor. Somehow that did not seem to fit. I thought he used that opener just to put me at ease. He had to know that as a nurse, my profession is very well acquainted with the God complex doctors have. Most are full of themselves. One doctor on our ortho unit was quietly announced for morning rounds with, "God has arrived."

This new acquaintance did not strike me as the least bit arrogant. Not even close. And dumb was not a first impression I got. I bet he wasn't even a doctor. What doctor wore sweats in public to impress? I became a little bit skeptical of good old boy Dr. Ricky Bob Yeager. I'd let the jury reconvene later for a verdict of who this proposed hillbilly truly was.

Rick, a.k.a. Ricky Bob, a.k.a. Dr. Yeager asked, "So, may I ask? Has the Tysabri seemed to help and how long have you been receiving it?" He was a polite gentleman. Polite, modest, and a gentleman—I really was ready to investigate with help from the AMA.

I responded, "Oh, about two years now. It took several months before I could see a difference. I was really disappointed at first. Everyone was talking about miracle responses. Some were leaving walkers and going to canes, and others were able to get rid of their assistive devices all together, so I didn't think it was helping at first. But then I realized I went from taking my usual three to five times to rest, I call them 'flat time,' to maybe one to three times a day. And my energy is *so* much better. And I can think more clearly. Sometimes making sense of reading a cake box recipe is more than I can do. That's better most days."

With a hint of sadness in his voice, Rick replied, "Oh, I wish that were true for me. I am not so fortunate. I honestly cannot see that the Tysabri is helping me much. Perhaps a little. I have declined rather rapidly the last several months and I am questioning the benefit of continuing with this modality of treatment. My neurologist at Vanderbilt suggests I do so and give it more time. I was on the IV before and got messed up with my insurance and had to be off for a time. This is my second time around. I take Ampyra and it seems to be helping me more."

"What is that? I'm not acquainted with that drug."

"It is a type of potassium channel blocker that aids in walking."

It was refreshing to share all this talk of multiple sclerosis with another person my age who knew exactly what I meant. He not only had MS, he had the medical background that let us converse like professionals. I guess I had to return a verdict that this sweatshirt-clad man was a physician after all.

Without acknowledgment, we knew neither of us wanted to be there. Sure, no one did, but we were used to taking care of sick people. We'd spent our lives caring for the sick—Rick as an emergency room doctor, me as an orthopedic nurse. Being on the receiving end of care like this was foreign to us. So our conversation took us briefly back to our hospital days as professionals. It was great! It's like we had a secret and could talk code and pretend we were back at our pre-MS lives. I caught myself smiling broadly and did not know why at the time. It felt so good.

If not for just a moment, we weren't patients. He was a doctor in the hospital casually chatting about the efficacy of a medication he prescribed for a patient. I was the nurse he trusted to administer the med and care for that patient. Yes, if not for just a moment.

SASQUATCH MEETS MEZ

DOC'S EXPERIENCE

I parked myself on the treatment chair in the Cancer Center. It was that time of month for another Tysabri infusion. The RN made her usual multiple sticks. We both laughed because she never succeeded with the IV on the first try. Repeated attempts to start the IV were just part of the drill. Neither of us was uncomfortable about it. Finally it was mission accomplished and she left.

I turned my attention to assessing the other patients in the large room. It was part of the ritual to glean information about each of the other patients from their appearances. I think we all did it to guess who had what, who was better off and who was closer to being lawn fertilizer. When I came to a younger woman sitting across the aisle from me, my eyes came to full stop. She had a full head of hair and was not gaunt or pale. That moved her away from a cancer diagnosis. But still her eyes were a little flat. My former doctor nature coerced me to take a second glance, seeking more hints as to what brought her, but I never finished the thought. Tiredness trumped curiosity and I slumped back thoughtless into the worn recliner.

Near the end of the infusion, a full bladder put me on a forced march to the bathroom. On the way back, the gal with hair spoke to me. She asked me about the Tysabri, which caught my attention. A fellow MS-er? I checked her out more carefully. She had a pleasant, genuine smile but still it was a little reserved. She was wearing a squared blue top with sequins on the upper area. She had straight, informal black slacks rather than jeans and flat-heeled black shoes rather than sneakers—comfortable but chosen with purpose. In a few sentences, I became more comfortable; we talked.

I learned that we both had MS. The disease had taken her successful nursing career from her, and until starting Tysabri she had not done well. Her eyes were beginning to show life as she shared more. Her infusions were running slower than the norm so we talked more. She explained she had discovered an interest in Henna tattoos, which led her to painting. She said that she had painted a mural in a local business depicting Mardi Gras. Her work was titled "Blue Moon Baby." She knew what a blue moon was and that there were two uses for the term. I was enchanted at the depth she had achieved in her new passion for art after MS had closed her nursing world. We exchanged e-mail addresses. Mary Ellen invited me to join *The Artist's Way* group she was sponsoring.

Over the course of the next few weeks, she sent me images of her paintings. The mural captured the festive atmosphere of evening Mardi Gras and its quality merited display in a professional building. It was in keeping with what I thought she might do. Maybe Ali McGraw once said that there was an exhibitionist in every good artist.

Mary Ellen's next paintings truly reflected that. Her personal paintings were abstract and far from the tangible Mardi Gras scene. I don't like abstract art. I don't understand abstract art, but there was something that drew me to these pieces. I did not know what it was. To me, her earlier works depicted the darkness this disease had brought her. The paintings were overwhelmed with the oppression of her MS and her plight. But still each had some small, almost unnoticeable, vestige of hope. Suddenly she did a painting full of color and life. It was her most abstract. I believe it reflected her feeling better and finding new strength and hope.

Mary Ellen was not aware of the candor of her work. She just painted what she felt. It was unabridged nakedness. That's what made it pure art. The progressing messages on canvas reflected a partial deliverance from her struggles with MS. As well, her work became a part of that deliverance. Her paintings studied me.

I am not sure how it happened. Maybe it was the way her work had touched me. Maybe it was her genuineness. Maybe it was her inviting description of the eclectic nature of the other members. Maybe it suggested an interaction I had lost with my life in the ER. I don't know, but somehow her invitation landed me in her next AW meeting…a Sasquatch at a ladies' tea party.

After the first Artist's Way meeting she showed me her latest work, "The Red Door." It was a complete divergence from her previous works. There was a periphery with bright sky and green grass and trees. The central subjects, a stone wall and door, were imposing. She made the stone texture so real it seemed touchable. The viewer's eye then focused on a closed, roughhewn door of wood with large, wrought iron hinges.

Much later, as our friendship grew, we talked about this painting. I shared with her that I was facing a formidable, large stone structure with only one door. There were no other doors—no other choices. The door both invited me and compelled me to go through. What was on the other side of that door, I had to find for myself. I told her that I imagined forcing open the creaking door and entering. Once in, there was nothing behind. I envisioned seeing the interior of a large beautiful cathedral with white light streaming through high, ornate, stained glass windows. Or I also envisioned a stone-floored, dank mausoleum filled with grays. Maybe it was a little of both. She understood the thoughts.

I have repeatedly thought about "The Red Door." When she painted this, I don't believe she realized that this represented the present point in our MS journeys. We have no choice about going through the door this disease has presented, but we can, in part, choose what we find on the other side. Mary Ellen and I both recognize its significance now. I am beginning to understand what drew me to all her art. It was her, it was me, it was all of us with MS.

MARY ELLEN'S DIAGNOSIS

A diagnosis of multiple sclerosis is far from an easy one to make for our well-educated, well-intentioned physicians, be he or she family practice, internist, neurologist, or horse doctor. There is no one lab test, X-ray, or procedure that will definitively prove MS. That makes for some frustration and anxiety for those people with symptoms that look like MS. They are sometimes labeled "probable MS" in their medical records. Sort of makes that person a "floating head" in the family picture album.

The general public expects medicine to be an exact science. It is not! Black and white can be more like grayish blue. Those of us in the medical profession appreciate that fact. Because we too become very frustrated when modern day medicine, in all its progressive glory, still cannot assign words to the misery some people experience.

I have often sensed my patients thinking doctors and nurses are too busy or too lazy to get the right tests done to get the answers they so desperately seek about their health. I have never found that to be the case. My entire nursing career has been working alongside caring, intelligent people who truly want to help all their patients. We are in it to take away pain, not to torture or tease the patient and cause more pain. Sometimes that crystal ball we look into just doesn't show a clear picture. Medical diagnoses can often be a process of elimination. MS is usually that way. Lucky us!

The attending physician will look at how the patient presents; what signs and symptoms they are experiencing. Then they take a complete history and run the obvious tests related to possible disease processes. Symptoms can be present for decades before a diagnosis of MS is made. Or all tests can be exhausted and still have no answer to the question of, "What is wrong with me?"

Waiting to get a name to put on what are very weird, often intermittent, vague symptoms can make a person feel like they are imagining a problem or going insane. And unfortunately, their physicians will often, in frustration of a parade of negative tests, offer that same suggestion.

The scenario might sound like this. "I've done every test I can think of. They are all negative. I believe at this point we are looking at some kind of stress disorder. You have been under a big strain lately. You've had some depression and difficulty keeping up at work. The fatigue could also be related to...blah, blah, blah."

At this point we want to burst into tears. We often do. We may believe the doctor and feel guilt for spending all this time, money, and energy on something that is "All in my head." Jeez Louise. If we didn't feel bad enough before, now we get labeled as a hypochondriac, crazy person, faker, attention seeker, nut job, a weak baby, a whiny butt, a menopausal beeaatch working the system, or worse.

Well, as you may have guessed, I know some of this stuff because I lived through it. I can identify my MS symptoms twenty-five years prior to my diagnosis. I actively sought an answer to my symptoms for four years. And I was fortunate it was that short a time.

Some tidbits of my insight to an accurate diagnosis are not gleaned as a patient, but as an RN in the hospital setting for sixteen years. However I gathered these nuggets of info, I feel them in my soul. They are visceral to me.

The complex journey to MS diagnosis follows some masochistic, yellow brick road. The sequential legs of the trip are twisty curvy with a lot of roadblocks, pot holes, warning signs, and those cute, red, slow moving vehicle thingies with square points. Ever wonder why the tips of the triangle have to be square?

Being the good Catholic girl that I was raised to be, I have a confession here. Many times I have wanted to stick one of those "slow moving vehicle" signs on my rump. It would explain a little to the jerk behind me at Wal-Mart that is snickering. You know who I mean: the guy who wonders why I am holding him up slithering like a snail, wondering why I am pushing an empty cart in the parking lot; the A-hole who gives me the stink eye when I have the audacity to park in the handicap spot, and then get out of the car and not limp, use a cane on that particular day, or drool on myself.

I still want to cry when fellow MS-ers tell me their story of how they got diagnosed with MS. And never doubt for one second any person with MS does not have a story. We all do!

The MS journal I used to keep that highlighted my transition from caregiver to care receiver is long gone. It had the sequence of events for my Dorothy from Kansas story. So I have forgotten a lot of it. MS memory is sketchy at best, but just last May at the Cancer Center, I regaled some of my Big D story to my IV buddy, Ricky Bob.

By the way, Rick was legally named Ricky Bob Yeager. Catchy middle names automatically recited with first names hold the same significance in his "southern Indiana hill family" as he calls it, as does Mary in my country German Catholic clan. Rick had an older brother Merlyn Dow and a younger brother Myron Dean. I was stuck with a Jim, Verner, and Harvey. Rick wins; the Yeager boys sounded cooler.

Since our first meeting six months ago, Rick and I have tried to schedule all of our IV treatments at the same time. We did not need to discuss getting our IVs together. It just happened, as an unspoken, mutual understanding.

The Cancer Center has been most cooperative in scheduling our appointments back to back to the point of even rescheduling both of us if need be. Once one of us is off track a couple days, we are off forever. The regimen is to receive the IV every four weeks exactly, to the day. There is little leeway for adjustments. The staff jokingly gives us a hard time upon arrival each month. "Well, my gosh, here you two are again. You are quite a pair."

Rick, being a sharp-tongued jokester, usually has some quick comeback like, "Yeah, we're ganging up on you." Or, "Mary Ellen kidnapped me and made me come. I didn't want to but you know how she is. She knocked me to the ground and..."

The nurses seem to enjoy our silliness amidst such serious treatments. We are an entertaining Frit and Frat team, a bit of a novelty I think. Of course I am Frit, Rick is Frat. Scramble the letters in Frat and it spells Fart. Need I say more?

Rick and I were an easy fit to hang out together from the get-go of our first introduction. Over time, my IV buddy has grown to be one of my dearest friends. Strange how MS can give us unexpected blessings.

This particular spring day I sat in a burgundy recliner in the corner to the left of the entrance to the treatment room. That was prime location for me because first, it had a seat cushion that was not molded to look like an ass, and secondly it had an uncracked, empty recliner next to it for my sidekick who was scheduled to arrive fifteen minutes behind me. To top it all off, it was situated in the corner and gave me the option of angling it just right to Rick's so we could talk without getting a crick in our necks. We have endured a few of those with our months of gab. See how complex choosing the right chair can be?

I nested, rearranging the wooden TV tray table between chairs just so and pitching the very outdated magazines into an empty, visitor, straight back chair. Why can't medical offices receive timely, current periodicals? At $7500 a pop for the IV experience, a twelve-month subscription to "Real Simple" should be included. Aren't we patients feeling rejected enough? Must we be reminded we are second-class misfits by having year-old, torn-apart rags to read? How many times must I read that Tom Cruise is an item with Katie Holmes?

I moved the Kleenex box next, wiped off the tabletop with one of the Kleenexes, sat up my paperback, and parked my lunch tote with munchies and tea on the floor, hopefully in a spot that was not too germ laden.

My appointment was at 1:00 p.m. and Rick's at 1:15 p.m. Upon arrival of the speeding red scooter through the held-open door, the driver pipes up, "Yeah, figures you'd be hooked up already. You always get first dibs. Mary Ellen first. Poor old hillbilly has to always be last..." He was especially fast-talking with less word searching that day. I was surprised. Rick's rhythm of speech is usually slow and hesitant. He must have popped a speed pill before leaving home.

Rick plopped into the adjacent blue recliner. No nesting for him. Must be a woman thing. His butt could have been mooshed into a Purple People Eater chair and he would not be the wiser. He paid no attention to color, cracks, or sagginess. I think he was too busy assessing pallor of the other patients. Once a doctor, always a doctor. I asked, "Did you see the nurse practitioner today?" Our routine included seeing the oncologist or nurse practitioner every other visit.

"Well, uh, no. When they asked if I was due for an office visit today I happened to say no. But actually I didn't see one the last visit either."

"Ah, huh! " I replied. "Liar! You cheated! I think the visits are stupid anyway and a waste of time. All they do is take my blood pressure. Not worth it."

"I agree. Hey, Mary Ellen, did I tell you it is great to see you little sister?"

"Yeah, good to see you too." It had been a full four weeks exactly since we'd hung out with our Tysabri cocktails. Usually we were thrown together one or two times more a month since we both belonged to a "self-guided, peer-supported artist group" as Julia Cameron, the author of our book guide, put it. Doesn't that sound very artsy fartsy?

Four months earlier, I had asked Rick to join this artist's group I was forming. It followed a twelve-week program entitled, *The Artist's Way*, so the group was called that, AW for short. It took about a month for Rick to say yes after I asked. He had every excuse in the book and he swore he did not have an artistic bone in his hillbilly body. But I knew he had a hobby of restoring vintage cars. That takes an artist's vision and approach. And I had caught him describing his cars and his turn of phrases sounded very much like an artist.

The whole premise of *The Artist's Way* is that everyone is an artist in some way. We see it more easily in children before society beats it out of them in order to morph into an acceptable norm. Art is actually using any creative talent God has given you and presenting it to the world.

I believe that philosophy wholeheartedly. That philosophy has been critical in finding new fulfillment for me when I had to leave nursing because of MS. I always thought my talent was nursing, period. One of my talents is nursing but MS forced me to broaden that talent base. The physical being must embrace a talent, but so must the mind. My mind and body now embrace art.

A weeklong artist's retreat at St. Meinrad Archabbey last summer brought *The Artist's Way* concept home. Brother Martin, a Benedictine monk who led the workshop/retreat, explained it as such:

"Being an artist involves looking at something, really seeing it, then taking it into your heart and returning it to the world."

When painting, I am mindful of that visual image. It is no coincidence that my current project is painting a "St. Meinrad series." I envision this to consist of nine paintings—all inspired by scenes of the beauty I take into my heart at St. Meinrad Archabbey in southwestern Indiana. Stones are fascinating to me and hold a multitude of colors. The archabbey's private quarry provides all of the stone used in construction of their buildings on campus, some being over one hundred years old. Quite the sight.

The first of my St. Meinrad series is an acrylic sixteen-inch-by-twenty-inch canvas entitled, "The Red Door." I was inspired by the ornate and weathered wooden door accessing a turret that anchors the stoned corner of the archabbey building. It is a fabulous door of great mystery. Splintered wood with very large and intricate black iron hinges lends itself as a portal to the unknown. The door beckons to be opened, to see if it drops off into a deep black hole or if it hides a steep pile of pirate gold treasures. "The Red Door" currently hangs in the hallway of my home and draws me to its secrets. My hope is for some viewers to be daring enough to open the door and cross the threshold so their own mystery may unfold.

Number two of my series is "The Post." The post in real life anchors the base of the marbled front steps of the archabbey and is equally strong with local quarry stone. I am on painting number three at present and it touches upon stone and water in a serene garden setting on the campus of St. Meinrad. I treasure the depth of emotion these paintings give me.

Now my Mom would never have called herself an artist like I do. She didn't even pay attention to flowers growing beautifully in her backyard, much less plant one. That had been Dad's forte. He had a green thumb, the patience of Job, and an appreciation for the minutest bird, bug, or blade of grass.

Mom was a pickle counter. She would keep track of how many cucumbers Dad would cut off in one given season of cucumber plants. She was like the caped Count on Sesame Street with his jet-black, slicked-back hair. "Two hundred, two hundred forty pickles. Ah, hah, hah."

Besides being an obsessed, albeit accurate, pickle counter, Mom was one good, old-fashioned country cook from a solid German background. I recall Mom teaching me how to choose dishes to serve at a meal. She would tell me, "Now, Mary Ellen, you need to have color on every plate. Color. No one wants to eat an all white plate or all brown plate with no color. It won't taste as good. You gotta throw in something pretty and green. Make it look like you want to eat it."

Mom used the food pyramid without knowing a thing about it. Her guide was color appeal. So I considered Mom an artist with the presentation of her colorful plates that were definitely a work of art, as many St. Wendel wedding guests could attest to when Mom was the cook at the receptions. I think Esther Klenck captured the whole "everyone is an artist" mentality.

So after some well-intentioned brow beating, Dr. Rick Yeager gave in and joined three female artists in an Artist's Way club. I am a painter, Libby a writer, and Sheila a mosaic creator. A butcher, a baker, and a candlestick maker. Oh, I crack myself up.

Since three of the four AW club members live with a chronic illness, we have had to postpone a lot of meetings. We all knew that possibility upfront. Thus Ricky Bob and MEZ, as Rick has dubbed me in emails because my name is too long, had been apart for a month—too long for good friends. Rick and MEZ had a lot to catch up on.

While chatting in the treatment room, Rick received several calls on his cell. "Hello, son." It was Luke, the youngest of his three boys. "Yes, I'm receiving my IV. Yes, I'd heard about the storm coming. Thanks for thinking of me. I'll batten down the hatches. We've learned to pay attention better since that tornado, right? Take care."

The Boonville Yeagers had lived through a tornado ripping through their backyard five years ago. Within moments of the tornado hitting, Rick had family members gathering sheets to tear into strips for bandages. He was ready for triage and patient care in his living room. It does not take long for an ER doc to jump into full throttle in an emergency situation. He and his sons ended up taking injured neighbors to the Emergency Department, lying in the back of his pickup truck. Mmmm. Maybe Roger and I need to check out housing near those hop-to-it Yeager folks.

By this time, Renee, our nurse, was ready to start Rick's IV. Now Renee is the gentle, blond angel of mercy with the soft-spoken, unassuming voice. She exudes peace when she arrives on the scene of one of the occupied thirteen patient chairs that are in formation like sentries on duty.

On the TV tray table to the left of Rick, Renee set up her supplies, consisting of tape, IV cannula, alcohol swabs, and such. She moaned with annoyance, "Oh, geez," and popped up quickly, saying she'd forgotten something. That happens a lot with busy nurses. We haul an armload of dressing cart supplies with us to only plop our butts down and then realize we forgot the widget thing or, in this instance, the tourniquet.

In Renee's absence, Rick leaned over toward me and relayed a memory that flashed in his head from military days. "This big treatment room edged in recliners puts me in mind of thin smoke rising from embers of a fire long thought put out. I remember lines of beds against walls from the 70s. There were lines of young soldiers in the wards at the Great Lakes Naval Hospital where I was stationed and lines of poor lying in worn beds in Cook County Hospital in Chicago. Those open wards traded the privacy of a patient and, if he would let it, his dignity for medical care.

"You know, MEZ, some of those smoky images bring back feelings of hope and some make me laugh."

There was a long sad silence as Rick stared off in space that left me ill at ease. I could not help but think, *Wow, this guy has a lot more of these memories I'll never hear about, other images that do not make him laugh. I can imagine Rick might choose to neatly tuck away those images into a shoebox and place them behind some long discarded jock strap on the bedroom closet shelf.* MS has a funky way of awakening repressed memories and propelling us to dig into musty smelling, messy closets, only to find a moldy sock where we least expect it. Why has no one told us of this symptom?

Renee returned with tourniquet in hand and began tearing paper tape to hang neatly in a row on the table, much like, as kids, our underwear hung on Mom's clothesline for all the neighbors and travelers to see. Then and now, our privacy lost.

Rick had very fickle veins and was not always a first stick success. Renee seemed to hold the crown of expert IV nurse on this staff roster. I noticed over time that she was always assigned to the good doctor.

Nurse Renee smoothly accessed the vein. All the while she proceeded, Rick kiddingly yelped, "Ow, ow, ow, you're killing me. That hurts." Have I told you? This guy has one dry sense of humor. Takes a little while to figure out if he is a pain, a prick, or a poop in conversation. Turns out he is a harmless guy with a warped funny bone.

After we were both settled, Rick whips out his Subway footlong tuna sandwich and hands me a Diet Coke. Ever since I told him I believed the Tysabri thickens the blood and causes a vascular headache and part of my pre-IV prep for myself includes high doses of caffeinated beverages plus staggered Tylenol and an anti-inflammatory, he has brought me a canned Diet Coke. Now that is a thoughtful friend. He even had a cuddly, gray grandpa sweater if the chills hit again. When he flung the sweater over the arm of an adjacent chair, I thanked him. He responded quickly. "Yeah, no problem. And if we both get cold, we can cut it down the middle and share like the true Germans we are."

Over the octopus tentacles of tubing my bud peeks through and says, "You were telling me about when you were diagnosed. Please continue. I bet you were typical vision problems, years to diagnose, dramatic story."

I responded, "No, no, it took a while but my diagnosis involved differentiating between MS and brainy mets from a melanoma." In lay terms that means deciding between multiple sclerosis and a brain tumor stemming from a bad skin cancer.

"Aw, that's not what I'd figured. You messed up my whole vision of your story. Tell me more. Oh, and, Mary Ellen, did I tell you I am so glad to see you today little buddy?"

"Okay," I began. "I was forty-five and working full time as an RN at Seton Residence. I was at my internist's to have a small lesion taken off my left upper chest. I'd had a history of basal cell carcinoma (skin cancer). As my doctor checked me out before the excision, he asked how I was doing otherwise. He knew I'd been draggy of late.

"With my fatigue being really bad that day I told him I went to bed tired, got up tired, and had to push myself all day at work. When I got home from work I collapsed on the couch and sank deep into the cushions. I did not raise my head up unless I had to and could barely lift my arms once I lay down.

"Dr. K asked me if there were other problems besides fatigue. I shared that yes, my left arm had been numb a lot, had tremors, and I had twitching in my right eye with a little double vision, especially when the fatigue was bad."

Rick, at this point, was shaking his head yes, affirming he understood. "Yes, yes, I see."

I continued, "The internist stared at me a long time. I'd been seeing him about a year and he knew my profession as an RN and respected me as a colleague. He was always very direct and I liked that about him. After the long stare, he slowly said, 'I think you might have MS.'

"I stared back just as long. We both sensed the significance of this conversation and I replied, 'Yeah, I think I do too.'"

Rick interrupted, "Wait, wait. Why would you say that so quickly? What would make you think MS?"

"Rick, I had worked ortho/med-surg at Deaconess and we had thirty-two nurses on staff. Out of those thirty-two, two RN's already had MS and one was a very good friend of mine. I saw it firsthand. I knew it firsthand. And my friend with MS had made the same assessment when she saw me rubbing my arm because of numbness and tingling and knew it was weak and had tremors. I had suspected MS for about four years and had seen a slew of doctors. You know: family doctor, neurologist, internist, even the infection guy. Oh, you know, yeah, the infectious disease doctor. But no one had been able to pinpoint it. It took a while. The usual."

About this time, my bladder was full to the brim with Diet Coke and tea. I stalled the conversation to make the dreaded trek to the restroom. This involved crawling out of the recliner with a handle that was always hard to engage and unplugging the IV pump that was tethered to my IV, a pole, and me. All the while, I tried to make sure I didn't accidentally tug my line out of the arm or lose my balance reaching over everything to get to the plug.

I did the walk of shame to the bathroom. When a patient gets up and walks, it causes a Pavlovian-type response in all the other patients. This is when instinct, similar to what fire gawkers share, that makes everyone turn their attention to the scene at hand—the ambulating patient. Stance and weakness are assessed. Unvoiced questions run ramped through possible cancer-laden brains, like, "Are they sicker than me? How weak are they? Check out the hair. No, a turban on that one. How long have they had cancer? Or is it one of those MS people? Hmm."

Ricky Bob munched away. I wondered, *Was he watching me?*

Returning, I was again seated on my now cooled off recliner cushion. Don't you just love the similar sensation in the middle of the night when you return to bed from a two o'clock bathroom run and you flip your pillow over? That cool linen on your cheek feels like a million bucks. Sometimes cool vinyl on the arsch runs a close second.

Since my potty break, the room had filled considerably. I noticed a new, young man—tall, tanned, buzzed head. He was sporting high-tops and IU red-and-white gym shorts. You can peg the age of a guy by the length of his shorts. These shorts grazed the bottom of his kneecaps.

I guessed this guy twenty-eight, thirty tops, and noticed a toddler near him and what looked to be a hovering wife. Maybe this guy was in for testicular cancer. There was a lot of that in this age group and our "tri-state cancer valley" of southwestern Indiana. Possibility. Then I heard the MS quiz of pre-Tysabri questions, "Any steroids, organ transplant...?"

After the nurse with all the questions left, I asked sports guy, "I heard the quiz. You here for the Tysabri juice? MS?"

"Yeah," was his one-word response. He immediately looked back at his iPhone. This one was new to the game. He did not want to talk MS or look at me and Rick with MS. He was young. He did not belong here. He was trying hard to fade into the woodwork. I respected his one-word response that spoke a book.

Two hours later I watched him leave without making any eye contact. He all but ran out the door. He would have, that is, if not for his one leg dragging behind just a bit with the MS shuffle. Yeah, he was one of us.

By this time, Rick had almost finished his gourmet Subway treat. He shouted with faked surprise upon my return from the bathroom. "The MEZ! How are ya? Have I mentioned how great it is to see you today?" I love that guy.

Rick quickly continued, "Okay. When did you find out the MS diagnosis for sure? That was unusual, the way it presented, and that you were already expecting to be told MS. I never did. It never occurred to me. Never. I will have to tell you about it another time. Get back to you."

"I've been going on long enough. You know the rest. It's nothing new. Same old, same old."

"No, little buddy. I want to know."

"Whew, okay. Let me think. Yeah, I had plenty of suspicious skin lesions taken off before this chest one. I've told you that. Why I got the needle phobia and all that. Okay. Let's see. I was working as director of nursing at Seton Residence, the retirement home for Daughter of Charity nuns I told you about. Remember?"

Rick sighed. "Oh, yes. I remember."

"Oh, Rick, this is hard to remember." I don't like to remember. The wise eyes of my friend gazed up at me timidly. For once he said nothing.

"I guess the best way to do this is to take you to my desk at Seton Residence, where I worked as DON (Director of Nursing). It was the last full-time position of my career. Oh, I hated to lose that job. I loved it. We did everything possible to hold onto it. Voc Rehab, scooter, flat time in the PT room. I fought it as long as I could."

Rick remained quiet but nodded in affirmation.

I continued. "A few days had passed since the excision of that skin lesion. I had, in the meantime, had an MRI done. Dr. K was quick to order the MRI since I'd been fritzing with symptoms about four years by that time. He wanted an answer just like I did.

"So I'm sitting at my desk, working on the six-week schedule for my nursing staff. I had a great office space, which overlooked an outside fountain. I faced the hallway because I had an open door policy for my nurses.

"Anyway, the phone rings. No caller ID at that time. It's Dr. K and he tells me he has my MRI results. I knew it was bad news or his nurse would have called or I'd have received a form letter in the mail. Dr. K knew as an RN I wanted the report read to me word for word. I did not need to ask him for that courtesy and I was appreciative. He said, "I'm sorry, Mary Ellen, it's not good. The brain MRI was indicative of MS with multiple lesions, blah, blah, blah. You know the rest."

With eyes cast downward, Rick was nodding slightly.

"Rick, you can kind of guess the rest of it. Dr. K was fairly certain we were looking at MS and so did the radiologist, but we had to rule out a melanoma with brain metastasis from that skin lesion. I'd already had several basal cell skin cancers. Dr. K told me he was hoping for just MS and he would call me with pathology results as soon as he had them, to be sure it was not a melanoma. It was not."

I looked up at Ricky Bob sitting quietly beside me. He got the absurdity, just as Dr. K did after he said it, "Just MS."

How absurd. There is no "just MS." I'd label that phrase an oxymoron, right? But when I thought about it, if I had to choose between brain cancer with a nasty and often fatal disease like melanoma and multiple sclerosis, I'd embrace the MS with opened arms. What kind of psycho universe had I been catapulted toward? I was rooting for my diagnosis to be multiple sclerosis. Was I insane? This was insane. I knew the horrors of MS.

I immediately remembered a vivid scene of me trying to help one of my MS patients on the rehab unit years earlier at the hospital. This played in my head, but I chose not to share this memory with Rick.

This particular memory was vivid. I recall the uro techs had spent time teaching the woman with MS all about self-catheterization. As her nurse that particular evening I was to reinforce the technique and guide her as needed to feel comfortable with the procedure. I remember the cramped hall bathroom on Unit 5100 where this forty-ish woman and I were trying to act cool in a totally not cool situation.

On top of the sink sat this hard, plastic, six-inch tube with a slit at the end. The tube was nestled in its own cozy Ziploc bag. Self-cath was a clean technique, not a sterile one. This meant the tubing was used over and over and just washed out with soap and water. The patient was the only one to handle it so her own germs were less likely to cause infection than my germs.

So here I am trying to keep a modem of privacy for the woman in a five-foot-by-six-foot room engulfing the patient, me, a commode, a sink, and a mirror. She was seated on the commode, spread eagle, trying to talk herself through steps of placing the tube into her urethra and me giving her encouragement that she was doing fine and telling her the placement was on target.

It was a bizarre and awkward experience for her and for me that first time. Each consecutive time got easier and she gained her independence and confidence quickly.

After talking to Dr. K and hearing the MRI results, I couldn't help but think, *Was this going to be a picture of me? With my wheelchair parked outside the door of that tiny, white-tiled bathroom on the rehab unit, trying to act like it was no big deal I was sticking a plastic straw into my bladder opening to let pee drain out every day of my life?* A crazy but possibly accurate first picture to flash into my mind after having a radiology report read to me of my brain MRI. Just MS.

After jolting from my flashbacks I shared with Rick, "Not typical, huh?"

"No, not the usual story for sure. Your story was not what I had expected. Oh, Mary Ellen."

Renee came back to check on my beeping IV. She reprogrammed it for a couple more minutes. The 50cc normal saline bag that was a flush behind my IV medicine was almost finished. Another session of mojo juice was wrapping up. I'd been at the cancer center about three hours. Freedom was around the corner. The prophylactic caffeine, Naprosyn, and Tylenol cocktail minimized my headache to about a five. You know how we always have to use a one to ten scale these days to describe our level of discomfort. I was happy with my bearable five. It had been a good IV day.

MEMORY LANE

Returning home was always a relief after receiving my IV every month. That May day was no exception. My normal routine was to lounge on the couch, remain pretty sedentary, and push liquids. I went through the motions without giving thought to any of it. I felt a little dazed and could not for the life of me put what Rick and I had been talking about out of my mind. What I thought was idle chat had truly brought back a lot of troubling memories surrounding those early days of my MS diagnosis.

Over the next few days I found myself pulling out long forgotten medical files. I looked for the MRI report from my initial diagnosis. Surprisingly I found it. Fourteen years ago on April 28, 1998, that "MRI Brain With and Without Gadolinium" opened with these notations:

CLINICAL INDICATION: Vertigo, tremors, multiple sclerosis.

DISCUSSION: Multiple sagittal, axial and coronal MR images were obtained through the brain before and after intravenous Gadolinium.

There are scattered ovoid foci of increased T2 signal within the subcortical and deep periventricular white matter. This includes both frontal lobes and the right deep periventricular white matter posteriorly in the parietal occipital regions...

Reading about the scattered ovoid foci reminded me that Dr. K had said, "Mary Ellen, there are a lot of lesions scattered about." I remember trying to figure out what parts of the brain were affected by which lesions. I had wracked my nursing brain trying to remember all the anatomy and physiology that covered the brain, spine, and nerves. I wanted to connect symptoms with lesion location in the brain and drove myself a little crazy trying to get a grasp of that.

I don't think of that lesion and symptom relationship very much now. It has lost importance to me. What difference does it really make where my lesions are and which ones are causing which symptoms? What value is an MRI even if it does not change my treatment? The more important question for me now is, "What symptoms do I have, how do they affect my quality of life, and what can I do to minimize their intrusion?" That question helps guide my daily decisions at present.

My conversations about my multiple sclerosis also have less of an RN ring to them at present. I am first and foremost a human being trying to live a good life while dealing with MS in my life. I don't need to reference my discussion of symptoms with proper diagnostic-type lingo. Yes, the nursing identity naturally spills over into words chosen and gives me the advantage of having a medical knowledge base to pull upon along with practical patient experience, but my afflicted, female human being identity is the basis of greater value to me. I am like every other person with MS. I want my old life back. It's not going to happen. So what in the hell do I do now?

Every day of my life I try to figure out how to live well with the current cross I carry with the tacked on MS scroll. Some days are routine and easy peasy. Others are a trip from hell.

After some painful reminiscing brought on by my IV discussions with Ricky Bob about how he and I were diagnosed, I have tried to remember more of what my days and symptoms looked like fourteen years ago and what they look like now. I found myself asking Roger about that time because my memory is bad. I've pitched all journals or I have suppressed those painful memories for survival. I will let my mental health therapist empty that bag of broken toys to figure it all out if I ever want to go there.

It is interesting to note that when I was pulling out my MRI report, I asked Roger if he remembered the day Dr. K called and when did I tell him about the MS diagnosis. I could not remember when I told him the MRI indication of MS. He immediately said, "You called me right away that morning at the office. I was sitting at my computer and I knew it was bad, but I didn't know what MS meant. I didn't have a clue." His recall was automatic, mirroring the detailed recollection we baby boomers have of where we were the moment JFK was gunned down in Texas. When Roger shared those minute details, I appreciated more fully the jolting impact my words on the phone that day had on my husband. He too was embarking on a life that would never look the same again.

Looking back, I can recognize the more lingering symptoms while I was a full-time RN on an orthopedic-medical surgical unit at Deaconess Hospital. This was before my diagnosis some five years later at my next director of nursing position at Seton Residence.

Fatigue was a constant companion back then but I contributed it at the time to the day and night rotation I was working at the hospital and the general stress of being a full-time wife, Mom of three, and RN, who commuted forty miles roundtrip every day to work. My daily routine involved arising at 5:00 a.m. to get ready for work. It is a vivid memory, stepping with difficulty, raising my leg over the tub, into the shower, and leaning against the blue surround to hold myself up and thinking, *I feel like I haven't gone to bed. I don't feel any more rested than when I went to bed. Why?* This followed about seven hours of sleep. At day's end, returning home from work, I would head straight to the couch to crash and hope the kids didn't need something right away because I wasn't sure I could get back up.

I had held both bedside nursing and assistant head nurse roles during my sixteen years at Deaconess. Both positions held their own set of work stress. Both ends of the staff and management ladder are tough. Anyone who has worked in an acute care hospital setting appreciates the daily nonstop fast pace, the burden of being understaffed, and the weight of human life decisions. Unit 4600, with its forty-one beds, was no exception in the 80s and 90s.

I recall workdays, standing in my white, supportive hose and nursing shoes on a hard, terrazzo floor, behind my medicine cart setting up morning medicines. Even though I wore glasses I was having more and more difficulty with following the horizontal lines leading left to right. The name of the medicine was on the far left and I would follow to the right to the date and time column. Reading lines several times became habit. My vision was blurry and I had occasional double vision. The double vision presented as vertical, with one letter superimposed atop a second identical letter. I would blink a lot. Sometimes my right eyelid would begin to twitch uncontrollably to where another nurse might ask me what was wrong. My usual response was, "Oh, I'm just tired." I believed I was.

Being charge nurse many days left me with the task of assigning the next shift's nurses to the patients. We had a very large dry erase board on the wall across from the nurses' desk. It had patient names and room numbers listed in rows and columns like an Excel spreadsheet. The challenge was to fairly balance each patient assignment to the nurses, based upon the acuity of the patient. The patient assignment always took some complex thinking and the charge nurse would get some sharp criticisms from the RN's if they felt the patient assignments weren't fair to them. Some patient assignments were easy because if the RN was the primary nurse for any patient, they were automatically assigned that patient. But when a primary nurse had a day off, some other nurse needed to care for that patient.

Some days, back then, I would feel frustrated and then almost panicky to the point of tears because I would look at that dry erase board and not be able to figure out how to assign the patient load. The board was white, patient names in red, the primary nurse name next to the patient name in any color the RN wanted it to be when she wrote it down, then the individual nurses on duty were each a different color for that shift's assignment. It was overwhelming to me many days with the rainbow of colors and forty-one "beds to assign" with really sick people and not so sick people and maybe six or seven nurses on that evening shift for coverage. What used to be just part of my day became the time of day I dreaded. How would I ever make sense of that overwhelming chalkboard? And then, heaven forbid, if someone came up to talk to me in the middle of assigning because my mind would go blank and I'd have to start over. I was charge nurse. I was constantly being bombarded with questions, some serious patient care questions, others as simple as an oncoming nurse asking how the kids were.

Anyone with cognitive problems due to multiple sclerosis can understand why I wanted to cry looking at that board. It was the poster child for complex thought processes and sequential task performance. Little did I know that MS plaques were causing issues for me to process the complexities of the assignment board. I just thought I was slipping, losing it, too stressed, too dumb, too something I couldn't put my finger on. I did not suspect any disease process at the time. I blamed everything on the challenge of trying to be superwoman. Singer Linda Ronstadt called her an "eighties lady," Alicia Keys a "superwoman." Those days I felt like "super failure."

I came to realize after the fact that MS had caused some serious cognitive problems for me. Now I can recognize those early warning signs, but I did not know to look for them at the time. Why would I? "Chili soup in a skillet" is the title I've given to that particular group of signs and symptoms. Elaboration on that name-christening story will come later, friends.

Another flashing red light I can identify now in hindsight that falls under the "chili soup in a skillet" category involves my charting time at the nurses' station. Please understand, an important guideline for RNs is the saying, "If it's not charted, it didn't happen in a court of law." We nurses perform many tasks to provide good care for our patients. Those tasks include such things as passing meds, ambulating patients, prepping for surgery, debriding wounds, changing dressings, anchoring feeding tubes and catheters, and teaching. You get the idea. What's difficult is writing down every one of those big and small treatments in the patient chart. If ever in a courtroom trying to prove what we did, if that "patient ambulated" down the hall isn't charted in black and white, not blue and white (that's not legal colors), then opposing counsel wins the argument, "The patient was not ambulated." So you grasp the importance of charting.

Some charting happens immediately, like signing for a med passed. Present-day computers at bedside now support more timely narrative notations. Twenty years ago the computer was minimally used for patient care and it was cumbersome. Our general approach to writing nurses notes in the patient chart was called, CYA—"cover your ass." We were taught that in nursing school, and we had it reinforced by management in the hospital setting. CYA was properly referred to as risk management. The growing world of suit happy patients made this reality.

End of shifts at the hospital always painted a scene of half a dozen nurses busily trying to capture eight or twelve hours of care onto an eight and a half-by-eleven-inch nurse's notes page in a chart. We had to be concise and use accepted medical terminology and approved abbreviations. Nurse's notes read differently from a letter to Grandma in Idaho.

The painted canvas scene of shift change on 4600 had me at the center of the nurses' station trying to chart my day's work. I was surrounded by two unit secretaries, several doctors making rounds, six to eight RNs going off duty, plus six to eight coming on duty. On the periphery of the canvas were miscellaneous others like nursing assistants, family members, and respiratory and physical therapists. It was a boatload of bustling driven people humming like a swarm of bees.

The last detail of that painting, but an important one, was a twelve-inch round speaker right above my head, anchored in the middle of a white ceiling tile. It continuously played groovin' Muzak and every so often announced a doctor page or a Code Blue. It was difficult for me to concentrate with all the people and chatter, much less having a speaker above my head interrupting my train of thought.

I would complain about the noise to nurses at my side and they would look at me oddly. It did not seem to bother them. No one else understood my frustration with the speaker noise. It bothered me so much that eventually I threw around the very little management weight an assistant head nurse possesses and begged a cute, black-haired maintenance man from New Harmony, Indiana, to move the offending speaker three tiles further west of my head. It cost me some dumb, broad eyelash blinking and the bribe of a double-layered chocolate cake, but it was worth every embarrassing moment spent. Forgive me, Gloria Steinam, but mission was accomplished. I had one less distracting stimulation to thwart my charting concentration.

Only years later did I appreciate the significance of that MS adaptation. Cognitive issues in MS can make it almost impossible to separate two noise stimuli. Sometimes if music is playing, and I love music and dancing, I can't grasp the meaning of what someone is telling me. I can hear the music and the words of conversation and I know intellectually one noise is music and one is English communication, but I can't make sense of the words spoken. It is noise, just noise. It is like trying to understand Albanian and I don't know many words in Albanian (Liza spent a year in Kosovo in 1999, thus I know a few).

A few other physical symptoms arose about the same time as the eye twitching, vision compromise, and cognitive issues, but they presented minor problems. I had some left arm spasms that entailed my arm twitching sideways, away from my body. I saw this more at church trying to hold a hymnal. That position seemed to evoke an intentional tremor or spasm. An intentional tremor can be explained by watching me trying to hold a phone to my ear or guiding a fork to my mouth loaded with rice. My hand trembles and I can do nothing to stop the shaking. The focused task of holding my hand still to do something causes the tremors. That is an intentional tremor. You may now see me eating rice from a tablespoon.

I've shared most of these MS memories and symptoms with Rick and we have compared notes. There are many similarities we commiserate over and many symptoms unique unto ourselves. It is the way of multiple sclerosis. Doctor, nurse, caregiver, care receiver, makes no difference. We both, at times, shake our heads with amazement at the complexities of MS.

TO TREAT OR NOT TO TREAT, THAT IS THE QUESTION

Looking back to the choices I made in regard to treatment modalities for my MS, it is all a big blur. Those fourteen years entail gut-wrenching decisions with much uncertainty. My journey has been so up and down and gray in color. Back early on, the medical community had no clear solution or consensus as to the treatment of multiple sclerosis and they still don't. So I sort of felt like the pooch trying to dog paddle across the Atlantic Ocean and kind souls would occasionally throw me a bone for encouragement. Of course, I liked the stupid bones, but I was damn tired of paddling so hard.

Having been diagnosed with relapsing, remitting MS, meant I had devastating episodes of being off work a week or so at a time. My good friend Billie, with MS, was off work nine months at one time after receiving a Hepatitis B shot to initiate her series that was administered to all RNs at the hospital. The shot threw her into a crisis. Her debilitating nine months occurred when she was still working full time as an RN. At the time I didn't get it, thinking why didn't she just quit work? She struggled to walk at the time. Now I realize how naïve I was in jumping to that conclusion and how complex the decision to quit work happens to be for us.

After flare-ups I would follow with decent stretches of time that lasted up to three months or so when my symptoms were minimal and I could meet my daily obligations and get through the day. Most days were still a struggle but doable. I always had lingering symptoms, regardless of flare or no flare. The worse symptom of all was the constant fatigue that I had to endure. It is so hard to work, have a family, and a semblance of a life when your body is exhausted upon rising and throughout the day.

Back then, the ABC drugs of Avonex, Betaseron, and Copaxone were the only three drugs to choose from for general treatment of MS. All three of these disease-modifying drugs were given in a shot either into the muscle or under the skin into the fatty tissue.

Nothing cures the disease of MS but the theory behind all three of these injectable drugs was that in their own unique ways each drug would potentially slow down the progression of MS by reducing the number of exacerbations experienced over the patient's life span or limiting the destruction of the myelin sheath covering nerve fibers. Good theory.

In the past, some schools of thought were, "If it's not broken, don't fix it." That meant if the MS patient was functioning, walking, getting by, then don't worry about giving a shot. And there was no immediate relief seen even if you took one of the shots. A positive response was a subtle, very subjective judgment call months or years later.

The first year of my diagnosis, the new and more controversial thinking was that it was definitely beneficial to start one of the ABC regimens immediately, regardless of symptom status. That meant even if an MS person had no symptoms at the time, it was still strongly encouraged that he or she begin treatment immediately with one of the three shots available. The thinking was that in the long haul, we would be better off with less debilitation years down the road, but there would be no proof for that until after death. A patient must have great faith in a drug to get stuck with a needle every day in the hopes that life in twenty years might be better than if no shot were taken.

A few years after my diagnosis of MS, the National Multiple Sclerosis Society took a strong stance of supporting use of one of the available ABC drugs to treat multiple sclerosis at its early onset after thorough review and discussion with the attending neurologist. Today we are fortunate to have a total of nine FDA-approved disease-modifying agents for multiple sclerosis from which to choose from. They are:

- Aubagio (teriflunomide) 7 or 14 mg tablet, every day
- Avonex (interferon beta-1a) 30 mcg intramuscular, once a week
- Rebif (interferon beta-1a) 22 or 44mcg subcutaneously, three times weekly
- Betaseron (interferon beta-1b) 250mcg subcutaneously, every other day
- Extavia (interferon beta-1b) 250 mcg subcutaneously, every other day
- Copaxone (glatiramer acetate) 20 mg subcutaneously, every day
- Gilenya (fingolimod, FTY720) 0.5 mg capsule, every day
- Tysabri (natalizumab) 300 mg intravenous infusion, every four weeks
- Novantrone (mitoxantrone) dose varies according to patient weight, intravenously, every three months for a maximum of two to three years

Deciding on a treatment option remains a complex decision involving much discussion between patient and neurologist.

Armed with my nursing knowledge and much research, I had that first treatment discussion with my neurologist. I agreed with the thinking that it made perfect sense to somehow minimize the breakdown of myelin and keep lesions to a minimum whether we could see blatant symptoms, an exacerbation, or not.

My neurologist at the time of diagnosis had the protocol of being a bit on the fence in starting an ABC drug and would not order the drug until one year had passed and she could observe at least one for sure documented flare-up. I disagreed with the delay and won the argument at six months to start treatment instead of waiting the full year. It was never a question of my having documented exacerbations because I was yo-yoing all the time between being laid up in bed and days of functioning pretty well. I am grateful my physician honored my strong need to get the ball rolling with one of the available so-called "ABC" shots. I attribute early treatment to part of my current quality of life. Thank you, God.

Before prescribing the Copaxone for me, the doctor argued the point of why she was reluctant to begin a shot regimen. She put my MRI up on the backlit screen and pointed to several of the numerous lesions that even my untrained eye could identify as bad spots and said, "Now, I look at this one and this one and I have to ask if these are true MS activity or if they could be ischemic areas like a stroke maybe."

I wanted to scream, "I've got a boatload of stinking lesions been diagnosed with MS, still having consistent flare-ups, feel like crap, am forty-five, trying to work and have a family and a life, don't present like a true stroke patient, give me credit as an RN for knowing a bit about a stroke and you are still dragging your sorry ass and making me feel like I don't really have multiple sclerosis, it's my imagination, and maybe I have had a stroke or two and won't give me the freakin' shot!" Yeah, I was ticked. It was several years later when I realized I cried every time I had an appointment with my neurologist so maybe I should change doctors. I did.

Looking back, I also think part of the reluctance of my neurologist to order one of the ABC drugs is that she had a speckle of doubt of my diagnosis because of the results of the lumbar puncture, or spinal tap, she did on me with my initial workup. Ninety percent of MS patients have things called oligoclonal IgG bands that show up in the central spinal fluid (CSF) drawn with the tap. I am in the 10 percent of MS patients who don't have the OB bands show up.

The oligoclonal band presence reflects local B-cell response from inflammation in the central nervous system (CNS). The whole process of the fatty myelin sheath that covers the nerve fibers breaking down with plaque formation is part of this. Unfortunately, other chronic diseases or infections can mimic MS and also have these bands show up due to inflammation. I did not test positive for the typical OB bands, but my clinical presentation, history of symptoms, and positive MRI was enough to diagnose MS. It's a good thing the lesions showed up or I could be one of the wandering souls still waiting for a diagnosis because sometimes the inflammation after a flare-up decreases enough that the lesions disappear or do not illuminate clearly on an MRI. Another count my blessings moment.

During the waiting time of getting an order from my doctor to start treatment with Copaxone, I was reading medical reports, journals, newspaper articles, anything I could get my hands on to make a wise choice of treatment. It was all I could think to do. The Internet was not big on the scene yet. We did not even own a computer. There were pros and cons with each of the shot regimens so it was very difficult to make a choice. I attended every tri-state seminar with rubber chicken on the menu if it had MS in the program title.

Roger was dutifully and supportively at my side for each MS dinner presentation paid for by some pharmaceutical company wanting us to use their particular expensive drug as a regimen. Any of the ABC drugs cost thousands of dollars annually to receive. Yet the hope of decreasing expensive treatments for debilitation and frequency of exacerbations by using one of the drugs was cost effective and made sense.

I got to know who many of the specialists were nationally because there were many different ones flown in from all over the country. We don't have one locally, but MS clinics did exist and had some excellent minds at their disposal. Roger and I became well-educated with the disease called multiple sclerosis and quickly learned that there was always a biased opinion to consider with each presenter or panelist because there was much ambiguity with MS and definitely much money involved. Most expert presenters at these MS seminars were paid for by a sponsoring pharmaceutical company.

Reading, seminar jumping, support group involvement, physician input, and nursing knowledge was the best I could do to make an educated decision in regards to maintenance of the MS jalopy that I owned.

The prescription order to start Copaxone injections was called in the end of November of 1998. My soft diagnosis of multiple sclerosis by my internist had been nine months earlier in February of that year and the neuro confirmation was made on our wedding anniversary the following May 6th. I recall thinking, *Okay, I did not get started with shots immediately after my diagnosis, that is unfortunate and might cost me, but at least I did not have to wait the full year.* I wondered if my delay would mean faster wheelchair use twenty years down the road. I tried to envision Mary Ellen walking normally and Mary Ellen being pushed down a hall in a wheelchair, both at age sixty-five. Oh, there were so many questions pinball bouncing in my head.

I began the shots on January 1, 1999, by my choice of date. I wanted an easy date to remember the onset of my serious treatment regime. Odd consideration now that I look back upon it. Why was that important? Was it really a milestone to remember? Maybe. Funny, that is the only date of treatment onset or discontinuance I can remember.

The drug Copaxone, glatiramer acetate, was very beneficial for me. I felt it curbed my flare-ups significantly. The literature at the time suggested Copaxone could reduce exacerbations by approximately 29 percent. I liked that stat. It held significance for me if I could reduce my days of being laid up and off work.

I grew up German Catholic with a very strong work ethic and being off work for any reason was not okay. It just wasn't acceptable behavior for a St. Wendel girl and caused much guilt, similar to the weight of venial sins I conjured up with my grade two examination of conscience, sitting in the straight backed pews on the right hand side of St. Wendel Church in 1959.

Under the beautiful eight-foot stained glass windows I had to meditate deeply back then by hypnotizing myself with the mandala configurations of hundred-year-old one-inch tile, black, blue, white, on the chipped flooring outside the confessional. I most loved that innocent occasion because there was a Rudolph Red Nose Reindeer lightbulb shining brightly above the priest's closed middle door to invite me inside the snowy wonderland of the sacrament of Penance. My sins at age seven were small yet acknowledgeable in my child brain and held the appropriate guilt factor within the confines of Catholicism.

Back to my professional career—at one point in my work history at Deaconess Hospital I had perfect attendance for the calendar year. I was very proud of that accomplishment. The attendance policy was very strict and noncompliance could mean termination, so I worked hard for ethical and economical reasons.

My proud, perfect attendance year followed an ashamed year of poor attendance. Daughter Liza was suffering badly at the time with her chronic juvenile rheumatoid arthritis (JRA). Liza had numerous doctor visits out of town in Cincinnati, Ohio. I stopped counting number of visits to Children's Hospital Rheumatology Department at thirty something. Her treatments, meds, physical therapy, partial home schooling in the mornings, and a family rotation of driving her midmorning every day to junior high school were also big commitments.

I recall some mornings when I had worked a night shift at the hospital only to go straight home, pick up Liza, miss sleep completely, drive the four hours to Cincinnati, see the pediatric rheumatologist, the social worker, the dietician, get her lab work done, and drive the four hours back, only to go to bed and get up and have to go to work again the next day.

Once we knew what to expect a little with juvenile rheumatoid arthritis and Liza's particular needs, we could tweak the rou-
tines to accommodate the family and Liza better. It made all of
us happy. We did not have FMLA, family medical leave act, in
effect at that time. Liza was diagnosed with JRA in 1990 and
FMLA was passed by then President Bill Clinton in February of
1993 and went into effect six months later in August of that year.
The FMLA law required that larger employers provide employee,
job-protected, unpaid leave due to serious health conditions of
their own or a sick family member.

FMLA is valuable to anyone with a chronic illness and I
believe it is something we take for granted now. But Roger and
I had three years of trying to hang onto our jobs while caring
for our daughter with special needs. Our jobs were certainly not
protected against the work time we lost through no fault of our
own or hers, because of Liza having JRA. Little did we know in
1990 that eight years later I would again be grateful to FMLA for
protecting my job because I had multiple sclerosis. Oh, the ironic
surprises of living life.

Even though I was an RN at the time of decision making
for treatment of my MS, protocol to administer the Copaxone
at home daily as ordered demanded I receive instruction from
an RN. The RN came to my home and I can't recall if she was
an employee of a home health care agency or if she worked for
the makers of Copaxone, Teva Pharmeceuticals. The apologetic
tone of her manner for having to teach an RN how to give a shot
was outweighed by her extremely limited knowledge of MS. A
tinge of anger tickled my inners listening to this ironic home
health instruction.

I sat through the young nurses how tos and wherefores that
I knew better than her and thanked her for her help. I was told
to practice on the proverbial orange. The more laughable part of
this was after she left I was then okayed by the same company
to instruct my husband Roger and daughter Beth Ann on how

to administer my Copaxone injections for the times it was difficult for me to reach a site or if I was feeling too bad to give it to myself. This meant Joe Blow with MS, with thirty minutes of instructions on how to give a shot, could then teach others how to give a shot. Making sense of that protocol was never clear to me.

Initially Copaxone came in a powder form and I had to add sterile, normal saline to one of the vials so as to reconstitute it to give as a liquid in shot form. The refrigerated powder would have to be removed from the refrigerator about an hour beforehand and warm to room temperature before being mixed with the normal saline.

Later, Copaxone came in prefilled syringes and I would receive a month supply at a time that had to be refrigerated. The syringe box took up a bit more room in the fridge and it always involved shuffling some lettuce or oranges around in the crisper box.

The prefilled syringes involved less prep time and certainly made it all much easier to handle. I do recall the needle tips, for some reason, seemed duller and heavier with the prefilled syringes and that made them hurt more. The joke between MS people at the support group meetings was that the company must have put a burr on the end. I recalled a similar complaint by patients in the hospital when we started giving prefilled syringe doses of Lovenox—a blood thinner used prophylactically to prevent post op blood clots in patients who had received total joint replacements. They also "ouched" more because needle penetration into the skin hurt more. My thoughts on the matter guessed one reason the needle tips hurt more in pre-filled syringes might be cost containment. Regardless, I adapted for convenience sake and so did my hospitalized patients.

Normally I had no problem with the local pharmacy handling my prefilled Copaxone syringes. I do recall one month though when I went to pick up my monthly supply of Copaxone from the drug store and I stood in front of the pharmacy desk and watched the tech pick my box of syringes up off the floor next to other floor assigned unimportant item boxes and hand it to me.

Now, I did not want to give myself shots for thirty days from syringes that held bad, ineffective medicine because it had been allowed to get warm. I asked the tech how long the med had been sitting out at room temperature. Her response was, "Oh, I don't know. We ran out of room in the fridge so we had to sit this on the floor." I cringed.

At that point I asked to speak to a pharmacist about my concerns. Busy Mr. Attitude strolled around the corner toward me in his pressed, white lab jacket with an air of impatience blowing toward the troublemaking, time-consuming customer. I explained my concern of the Copaxone potentially being ineffective because it was at room temperature and it seemed I had no way of verifying how long it had sat out of refrigeration.

With confirmation, he uttered, "Well, that's right. I can't say with certainty how long it has been out, but understand, we were pressed for space and had no choice but to set this out."

"So, you had no other option like a cooler and ice? I don't question your need to make room in your fridge, but are you aware that Copaxone requires refrigeration, no exceptions? I go to great lengths keeping it cold to the point of having to keep it on ice while flying or with any travel."

"Yes, I am aware it is recommended to keep the drug cold." His tone mutely uttered, "How dare you question me you peon! I am a pharmacist. I am smart. You are not."

He followed with, "I suggest you look at the drug carefully before you give your shots. Hold it up to the light and if it appears discolored, yellow, or cloudy, bring it back and we will replace it."

"That is no guarantee I have a good med."

By this time the scowling man lost patience with me and made the stupid remark that poked this rabid dog one too many times. "Ma'am, it is simple to see if the drug is effective. If it works for you like it normally does, you're fine. If it doesn't, you have a problem. Call me back then."

Unbelievable! The first thought to pop in my head for comparison after that remarkably unethical statement was, "Okay, if some man came in here for medicine to prevent having a heart attack, would you tell him to try the pills and if he fell over with an MI, please come back in and we'll be glad to change your med out at that time?"

At this moment I fought for control of my own rage toward the two-legged problem standing in front of me. "It doesn't work that way!" I said between clenched teeth. "And I can't believe that is your solution. See if I have a flare-up? Obviously you know little about MS and nothing about how Copaxone works or you would not have made such an asinine remark."

I continued, "Judging efficacy of Copaxone injections is not an immediate process and can only be evaluated over a long period of time. I suggest you learn more about the drug you are trying to hand me and the MS it is meant to treat. In the meantime, I refuse to accept this shipment. Let me copy down the shipment info and the lot numbers and you order a new supply, put it in the fridge when you get it, and give me a call. I'll then verify that you didn't just hand me back the same shipment here in front of me. And if you could let me know the name of your supervisor, I will contact her tomorrow so as to clarify the obvious problem we have had today and to make sure this does not happen again to me or the next person coming in here for their MS medicine."

The man with the flushed red face and the sense of shock that his assertive customer knew such a big word like "efficacy" stood a little straighter and stared at me for clarification.

"I'm an RN. That should make no difference here. Are we clear and squared away?"

"Yes, I'm sorry I couldn't reassure you that this drug is fine. Our manager is Jane Doe. I will place a new Copaxone order for you. We should receive it in two to three days. Is there anything else I can help you with?"

At that point I gave up. This jerk still thought I had no grounds for first, questioning his judgment, and, secondly, for questioning that the Copaxone might be bad.

I left and talked to the manager the next day who knew both Roger and me because we were long-standing customers she had waited on numerous times. With our family of five, we supported her job security well. Her response included understanding and appropriate concern for the unprofessional approach of her employee. I was grateful for that.

After cooling off, I did not follow my first instinct to switch pharmacies. This one was almost in my backyard and a new one would have been inconvenient. Besides, there is always a bad apple in every peck of pharmacists like every other work group, no matter where you go. So instead, I got the new shipment of Copaxone with a different lot number, checked it, and all ended well. But all this happened after I had to stand up for myself. Being a good advocate who is ready and willing to kick a little ass and stand up for the cause is a required skill all people with multiple sclerosis must hone. If we don't stand up for ourselves, who will?

I gave myself the sub-cutaneous injections of Copaxone for four and a half years. I missed only one day in those four years when I forgot to take my med along to a cookout at Joe and JoAnn's—long-standing friends of ours—and did not get back home till after midnight and that negated giving it so closely to the next day's shot.

My routine was to rotate the recommended seven sites that included the right arm, left arm, right hip, left hip, right thigh, left thigh, and belly. The seven-day rotation meant a sub-cutaneous site was only used once a week and gave it time to heal before being stuck again with a needle.

Giving myself shots was much more difficult than giving them to patients in the hospital as an RN. Mine hurt! I think I did well psyching myself out each evening before bedtime and just "gettin' er done." I tried to make it a nondescript nonevent and would even set it up in front of my granddaughter while watching TV in the family room in my Lazy Boy recliner. I wanted her to feel comfortable, not scared that Grandma was getting a helpful shot and that it was no big deal. Overall, I think I accomplished that. I believe Mom and Dad were more wincing and worried I would traumatize the child. Kids pick up quickly if there is relaxation or tension in any given situation. Hopefully Sophie is now fine at fourteen and has no phobia of getting shots anymore than any other teenager.

My positive response to the use of Copaxone those four plus years resulted in my having fewer exacerbations. I still had many symptoms that affected me daily, but I felt strongly that my flares were overall less frequent than without Copaxone. I had faith that in the long haul, this was the right decision. I remember wanting a shiny crystal ball to gaze into and see my future with daily shots for twenty years and another vision of what my life looked like without the shots. I never got the crystal ball. I still wish for it.

People who haven't taken shots can't appreciate its magnitude. I understood the enormity of how often a diabetic got stuck with insulin shots that could be daily or several times a day for coverage, plus all the glucose testing skin pricks to monitor sugar levels.

My brother Verner took insulin shots from the age of fourteen until he died of diabetic complications as a double amputee at the age of sixty-three. Do the math. He endured many shots and skin pricks. I never recall him truly complaining about the shots and blood sugar checks. His biggest challenge discussed with baby Sis was having a productive life, fighting depression and anger. Oh, and figuring out how to swim with two below knee amputations. He never did get a handle on that one.

Over the years, Verner and I had a tumultuous sibling relation-ship. Yet we had a strong bond for as long as I could remember. I knew he was always there for me even when he wasn't speaking to me, which was often in his roller coaster life.

Our unspoken connection was made even stronger when I was diagnosed with MS. As I said earlier, he grew up being labeled "the sick one." I understood the significance of that when I joined ranks with that black sheep group of the Klenck clan. No one truly understands that club of misfits unless they wear the misfit coat of arms.

With calculator in hand, my meager four and a half years of daily Copaxone shots amounted to approximately one thou-sand seven hundred shots. I would like to say I was as brave as my brother Verner, but I am not so noble. Never was. With the passing of time and the arrival of much pain with receiving my shots, I would sometimes cry at the thought of getting stuck one more time.

After a couple years of injections, I developed very poor tol-erance at a localized skin level. Even though I faithfully rotated injection sites, my skin became scarred, bumpy, hard, dimpled, and irregular in appearance where I gave myself the shots. Roger and Beth Ann would help with my hips and arms sometimes. The sites of my shots would get very swollen, red, hot, painful, tender, and on the verge of necrosis. The juice of the shot would have to be pushed in hard with the plunger because of the hardened scar tissue and it would really burn going in.

My internist and neurologist both ordered a variety of ways to minimize the inflammatory reaction and the pain, from ice packs to use of an automatic dispenser for the syringe that could con-sistently measure depth of needle penetration to use of topical ointments to numb the sites. Eventually none of this worked, as my sites would not heal adequately in seven days time to trauma-tize the skin with another injection. I could not give a shot into a spot that was angrily inflamed already from the week before.

The tough decision was made to stop my Copaxone use at that time. It was not due to the efficacy. It was due to injection site tolerance. The discontinuance of Copaxone was a very traumatic and regrettable decision for me as the drug had served me well. For some time the Copaxone people have been working on an oral form of this drug, which would be awesome. At this time, Copaxone is not available in pill form.

One other complication besides injection site intolerance with Copaxone was muscle pain. Both of my upper arms, forearms, and legs hurt, especially in the quads. I only sat in chairs with supportive arms or with a pile of pillows strategically placed under my arms for support. Otherwise the pain was not tolerable to remain seated for any length of time.

Roger and I belonged to a card club at the time that involved rotating seats every four hands played. I had to have someone help me drag a chair around to my spot with each rotation. It was an embarrassment to me and at one point a brother-in-law honestly complained about the inconvenience it caused him to always have to maneuver around this bulky wooden chair.

Climbing stairs with the muscle heaviness and pain was also a real challenge then. We lived in a second floor apartment and by afternoons I would have to do the lift and shift maneuver to ascend the steps. I would take both hands, grab my thighs, and lift to the next rung. It was cumbersome and tiring and very handicapped looking.

I had blamed the muscle pain in my arms and legs on the MS. After I stopped the Copaxone, the muscle pain lessened immensely and I came to realize some of what I had been experiencing was in fact the drug and not the disease. This trap of blaming the multiple sclerosis for everything is a common occurrence, but we have to always entertain the idea that factors outside MS can be our problem at times. It is just so darn hard to differentiate sometimes between what is MS and what is some totally unrelated disease process. I think of my four plus years receiving

Copaxone as very difficult ones related to symptoms and quality of life and trying to hold onto work and family and play. Yet I feel I functioned better and had less flare-ups with the use of the drug. I am glad I made the choice of that ABC drug as my starting point.

While receiving Copaxone, I tried many other drugs to treat specific symptoms. This list is unclear in my mind because there were many. Some lasted a brief time, others years. I took medicine to help with tremors, numbness, pain, walking gait, memory, mental acuity, concentration, fatigue, energy, difficulty sleeping, and depression. I wish I could spew out the names of these drugs. At the time, I thought, especially being a nurse, that I would forever be able to recite them. That is not the case. Some of the limited recall of the list is just plain old poor memory on my part but a more significant part is God erasing it from my mind because it has baggage attached that in His wisdom He figures I don't need to fill my head with anymore. I trust that what He wants me to remember and relay to you as helpful information will be attainable, even in my befuddled little mind.

RICK SHARES HIS DIAGNOSIS

DOC'S EXPERIENCE

When I was a twelve-year-old boy, I would ride my bicycle over to Danny Strahley, my bud's house. We did the normal boy's stuff: dodge ball, Ollie Ollie over, and listening to vinyls like Bill Cosby's "Chicken Heart." One thing was different at his house. His father had MS. It was my first exposure to the disease or even the word multiple sclerosis. He lay on the couch powerless and drooling. When he moaned weak sounds, Danny and his brothers would stop what they were doing and help him with whatever the need might be, like just being repositioned. It appeared almost magical to me the way they understood his primal communications and instinctively fixed the problem and then went on with what they were doing, not giving their help a second thought.

Sometimes the man's eyes would stare at me and follow me with a sunken gaze. As a boy I did not know what to do or how to talk about it. Sometimes I would try to inconspicuously study him. I could not understand. I was a boy and this was different. I wondered if I should try to speak to him or even smile at him. I never did, even before I had MS, and it bothers me to this day.

In the formal study of scripture, there is a principle called "first mention." Simply put, when something is first introduced in the Bible that is how it will end. For example, the first mention of David was as a shepherd caring for the flock. The last scene was King David finishing caring for the people of his kingdom, the sheep. I suspect this boyhood recall may be my last experience with MS too. My hope is that should that time come, God will give me the supernatural strength to deal with it. Mary Ellen's and my story is not about the end, but how MS has changed our lives.

I enjoyed running but was too slow and heavy to be a competitive runner. That did not matter; I just liked it. It gave me more stamina for work. After running about ten minutes, my thoughts were preoccupied with taking the next few hills. There is no shortage of hills in southern Indiana. I usually ran at night. The night amplified the smells of fresh cut grass, the sounds of an occasional hoot owl, the chickens on South Eighth Street, and the distant tractors of farmers working into the dark to get their crops out or in. All were completely removed from the hectic world of medicine.

In October of 2001, I had a mild bronchitis, which lasted about three weeks. Fall bronchitis was normal for me and I just worked through it, but this episode stopped my running. The cough and mild aching resolved but I remained tired. I resumed running on the treadmill but wore out way too soon. In a few short weeks, I stopped running and started walking and then stopped the treadmill completely.

Things just did not feel right. I could not put my finger on it but among other differences, I did not believe I was seeing normally. I was not getting better. One evening at work I was at the computer screen and thought that there was an area in the right lower screen where the cursor disappeared. I could easily see the cursor everywhere else. There was a chance that it was just a localized retinal problem. This would be unusual for someone my age, fifty-two. Perhaps it was an insignificant change or it could be the harbinger of a worsening eye disease that could reduce vision— not a pleasant thought for an emergency room doc.

There was also a nagging thought that it could be a space-occupying lesion. That is an area of localized pressure or damage or mass or node in the brain. I tried to remain objective but it was an uneasy possibility. I worriedly reasoned that a crude, simple diagnostic check would be to see if the cursor disappeared in the same area of the left eye. If so, then it was possible the problem was a space-occupying lesion. With dread I closed my right eye. The little arrow disappeared; a little smaller area, but it was gone. I could still now almost hope that it was just an unusual retinal problem in both eyes but the probability of the worse of the two possibilities had to be faced. The evidence lay with the worse. I sensed at that moment my life would be changed.

Sitting at the computer desk, I started making plans. I needed to confirm that the localized vision loss was accurate. The first available visit with an optometrist for a visual field study to localize and verify a change was needed. A computer cursor is far from a diagnostic tool.

But I had to plan further ahead: a "Plan A" if the problem was with the eyes and a "Plan B" if it were a more serious result. Who would need to be told and what should be said if anyone became suspicious of my visual problems? Everybody knew everybody in my microcosm. Damage control needed to be in place immediately.

The next morning, Stacey Embry's optometry office quickly returned my call with an appointment for early the next week. Stacey was a good friend and would make a thirty-five minute drive to the Emergency Department (ED) anytime to help with a patient. He never bothered to ask if the patient had insurance or how he would be paid. Nor did he ever offer a negative comment on how I had managed the patient's problem. Both were happy attributes in a consultant when an ED doc needed help.

At my appointment, Stacey's pleasant office staff guided me to an exam room. I described the problem to Stacey as accurately as I could but did not bias Dr. Embry with my fears. At the completion of the exam, Stacey returned to the exam room wearing his characteristic smile and reported that my eyes looked good. There was no evidence of disease. Stacey showed me the visual field study where there were two small areas of vision loss but felt that they should not cause me any visual problems. I looked at them with Stacey. There were small areas of corresponding loss in the fields of both eyes. It was the telltale pattern of a partial right homonymous hemianopsia—a loss of vision caused by a problem in the vision center in the back of the right side of the brain or in the optic nerve after it pairs with the visual field of the left eye. Solemnly I looked up and said, "Stacey, this is a space-occupying lesion until proven otherwise." Dr. Embry's countenance dropped but almost instantly he managed to regain composure. Stacey was not aware of his brief, subtle nod of realization. He maneuvered for time by saying he would consult with his partner.

The following trip home and the afternoon were long. Plan B was now Plan A. It was already well mapped. About an hour later, Stacey called and said he had discussed it with his partner. Yes, the visual field study was suggestive of a space-occupying lesion. As caring a person as Stacey was, I was sure that was a hard phone call for him to make. Dr. Ali had been my friend for years and I considered him my family doctor. I phoned his office and asked them to schedule an MRI for vision changes. I offered no more explanation and they did not understand to ask. Next step in Plan A was to tell my family and Dr. David Vaughn, the Emergency Department (ED) director, that something was wrong but without arousing suspicion. Debbie had been a busy RN for twenty-five years and my impossible-to-fool wife for twenty of those years. David and she were both sharp. And I was a terrible liar. It was dicey. For both, I picked inauspicious times to address my problem, when their attentions were drawn elsewhere. Then I just casually mentioned that I was having a little difficulty seeing and explained I would do an MRI. I had always been healthy enough so no one had reason to think otherwise. Not mentioning my potential brain lesion to anyone else kept it low profile.

The MRI was two long days later. The vision was worsening and I began to note a slight tendency to lean right when walking. The vision was the big thing. I could only see part of words when reading. Plus I had mild difficulty going through doorways. The right side of the doorway did not appear quite where it belonged. I had a tendency to correct the leaning. The problem, whatever it was, was also reflected in my cognitive processes, thinking. Reasoning took longer. Ideas were not as spontaneous. Mental pictures were less defined. They were small and had an aura of darkness.

The MRI was scheduled in the evening. Though I had ordered hundreds over the years I had never had one. The technician immobilized my head so that I was essentially tied down flat. The narrow table on which I was lying began to raise and push me into the cream white tube. The technician slipped away behind a large, thick, protective shield and asked through a microphone if I were okay. Then the magnets began to rattle with a whirling sound. I am minimally claustrophobic and this was tolerable but far from comfortable. After the baseline MRI, the tech asked again with added interest what my symptoms had been. *This was not a good sign,* I mused. He started an IV for the follow-up contrast study. No, things here could be better.

When the MRI was completed, the tech was gracious enough to let me peek at the images. There were three lesions present with no other changes. Although the largest was only about 2cm, they looked like cannon balls in my brain to me that night. I thanked the tech and tried to not let my inner fears show. A man who had been running three miles a few months ago could now be looking at his radiographic obituary.

The dreaded report was back the next day. The MRI could only offer so much information. People often believe that a test as big, noisy, and expensive as this one should be the end all of scientific studies. No diagnosis could be too obscure, too small, or too terrible to escape it's all-knowing eye. Unfortunately, this is not true and especially untrue in diagnosing MS. The radiologist's report had all the typical fanfare of possible something's, but my flawed vision focused in on the simple phrase, "Possible metastatic lesions." There was still a real chance of a better diagnosis, but metastatic cancer was the logical conclusion.

It was time to prepare family and coworkers for this conclusion. Dr. George Caleel, the senior medical instructor in my med school, suggested that when sharing a diagnosis with a patient, always give the worst outcome first. That way if things go badly, you prepared the patient. But if things go well, then you're a hero—simple enough. This was going to be a George Caleel moment.

I called my wife and three sons together. I had been rehearsing possible approaches. There was no good way to present it. As a veteran RN, Debbie would have some understanding, but that was the nurse listening. What would Debbie the wife and mother hear? What could I say to my sons? I was Dad, the rock. Josh was sixteen, Matt fourteen, and Luke had just celebrated his twelfth birthday. There were no right words. We met in the family room. The Christmas tree was already up. Debbie loved the Christmas season and always decorated early. Before starting, I looked at the holiday displays and thought that this could be my last Christmas. Silently I prayed.

I chose the words carefully while studying their faces and proceeded. I do not remember the words but can never forget their confused, unbelieving faces. I used each facial expression to guide me to the next word. I was tiptoeing through hell. Their husband, father, was sick and did not know why. But right now it looked like it could be brain cancer. They seemed to take it well, no crying. The older boys and Deb expressed their belief and hope that things would not be as bad as they appeared now. Probably it was not fully registering. But they understood enough. Their early denial had some merit and offered some comfort.

Matt, our middle son, had accepted the family responsibility of dispatching dying and deformed Yeager World critters to the sweet zoological hereafter. He would do the burial too. Granted, he generally used a larger caliber firearm than the situation merited, but no one complained. No one else wanted that job. Matt had to leave the family room for a minute. He was headed into the direction where he kept the dispatching rifle. I smiled and called after him, "No, Matt, it's not that bad." It took a second, but the family laughed lightly.

Now I had to break the news to Dr. Vaughn. As director of the ED, David was responsible for the doctors' scheduling. David and I were stark contrasts. David was brilliant and had been a high school athlete and musician. He was an easy shoe-in from college to medical school. He trained in a busy ED in Louisville, Kentucky, surrounded by some of the best attending physicians and residents the area offered. He made the best of all they had to offer him. He was one of the best ED docs in the area and respected as such even before he joined me at Warrick Hospital. David worked with John Deere tractors when he was a boy and still likes them.

In contrast, I was near the bottom of the acceptable grade average in college. I began Purdue in engineering. At the end of my first semester, I was told that forty-four per cent of my calculus class received Ds and Fs. About forty per cent of the chemistry class fared the same. It had never happened before or since. Supposedly fifty percent of these students were in the top ten per cent of their high school class. Many of my friends, quality students, left Purdue that year. I stayed and graduated—maybe not bright but resilient and determined. Or would doggedly stubborn be more fitting?

Because I was not accepted to medical school the first year after graduation, I volunteered for the army. In my first year of the military, Chicago College of Osteopathic Medicine interviewed and accepted me for when I finished the service. I am forever grateful to them. I survived medical school, with plans to become a general practitioner. I liked all of medicine and volunteered as a part-time extern in Chicago's Michael Reese Hospital. I served a one-year rotating internship at a modest-sized Ohio hospital. There too I spent extra time in the ED. Generally at night, the ED doc and I were the only physicians available for the ten-bed hospital unit. I had to learn and do what I could quickly. The docs who trained me were limited in number but shared their minds and hearts. As a boy I worked with and liked John Deere tractors. Yes, David and I did have something in common.

I wanted David to hear the news from me directly. Despite our opposite backgrounds, David was a true friend as well as a supervisor. It was nothing for either of us to stay late helping the other with busy patient loads or difficult problems. In the Emergency Department arena, we were not only partners but trusting brothers.

I began my bad tidings by mentioning that I had told David earlier that I was having some vision problems and then went on to share the MRI findings and concerns. David offered to do anything he could to help. I then made another long journey home.

The next square in the diagnostic algorithm was a neurologist. The first available appointment with Dr. Johnson was approximately a week away. It was a long week. My problems were worsening with vision deterioration. The problem was not that my vision was failing in sharpness, but rather, that I could only see a part of the visual picture. The loss was expanding in the right eye to the point that the eye dominance shifted. For the first time in fifty years I became left-eye dominant. This made reading medical reports more difficult. I could not see the values of lab reports to the left of their subjects. I had to take a finger and go across. My balance was worsening. It felt like I was "listing" to the right and the left leg did not always go where it was directed. This, added to the vision changes, made walking difficult. It was hard to walk through doorways in the exam rooms because the right side of the doorway was confusing. A little problem granted, but as a physician I thought it was interesting.

A darker problem was insidiously developing—a difficulty in thinking. Thoughts were not as spontaneous as normal. Thinking was a little like reaching into fog. "Fog" is the same description Mary Ellen had chosen to express for this blunting of cognition. Spatial relations were not clear.

Jim Eifler, a lifelong friend, had a cousin—John Holder— who was a distinguished radiologist in a teaching university. John, an old car buff, had visited my home and we had shared old car experiences. Jim suggested that I send my MRI films to Dr. Holder where he and the oncology radiologists could review them. Jim was the age of my older brother Merlyn. Jim and I had shared each other's lives from the day of my birth. As typical of Boonvillians, our parents had also been longtime friends. Jim's only daughter, Tammy, and Danny Forston married in our living room.

Debbie was riding the bus with Jim on a church trip when she saw a new for sale sign on the property we had watched for years. It was a beautiful site for a home. Debbie called me immediately while Jim waited for her to tell me her good news. I called the real-estate agent early the next day. The agent said that it had only been on the market a few days and no one else had had the chance to bid. It would be a slam-dunk. A few hours later the agent called back and said there had been another bid. I offered a counter bid and waited pensively.

My first bid was higher than I felt comfortable with. Within another day, the other party made an escalating counteroffer and it was passing my limit. Debbie shared my worries with Jim and he looked at her with surprise. He explained that he knew we wanted the property and was friends with the owner. So Jim had been bidding on the property for us, as well as being the one bidding against us. Yes, MS is a story of friends.

I took a copy of the MRI to be UPS overnighted to John, the radiologist. I was driving north on Burkhart Road to the UPS center in Evansville when I became inexplicably confused. I felt like a small child that had been lost from his mother. Loneliness, confusion, and helplessness overtook me. I just wanted to pull the car over and maybe cry, not that it would help.

My symptoms were accelerating. I was having more trouble keeping my thoughts together. Tanya Hall was the director of medical records at St. Mary's Medical Center. Years before, I had worked with her when she was risk manager and workmen's compensation director at Warrick. She had the keen ability to immediately reduce the toughest problems to their only salient elements and offer a solution quickly. She was aware of my MRI and asked Dr. Sneed, a neurosurgeon, to review the films. The evening before my neurology appointment, Dr. Sneed ordered a CAT Scan (CT), looking for primary cancers. Tanya stayed late, walking me through the procedure scheduling by phone. These final studies completed all the material available for the neurologist the next morning.

The following day Dr. Johnson did the appropriate new patient exam but did not keep me waiting for an impression. He looked at me squarely and said, "You have multiple sclerosis." The onset was a little atypical and more tests would be required but that diagnosis was most likely. That is probably the first time Dr. Johnson ever saw a patient look relieved when he was told he had MS. I was overjoyed. Instead of spending my last Christmas with family, I now had years to live. Because of my age, gender, and onset, I had not more than fleetingly considered MS. The tests were ordered and I was scheduled for a lumbar puncture in a few hours. The lumbar puncture or spinal tap is a test using a long needle to enter into the spinal canal through the low back and draw off some spinal fluid for several studies. It is needed to rule out several neurological diseases and to find oligoclonal bands associated with MS.

Dr. Johnson had finished the spinal tap. I was lying flat for the required time when John Holder called with his radiological review of my films. Since I was not allowed to move much after the procedure, Deb held the phone close to my ear. John said that he and the oncologists had reviewed the films. His voice had just a hint of tightness. It looked like metastatic cancer to his group.

John was a radiologist and he rarely, if ever, shared news like that directly with the patient. I thanked him. I appreciated his courage. It had to be difficult for him. To me the studies were more suggestive of metastatic cancer too. There were no areas of acute inflammation or old scarring. But as I lay there I decided to cling to the diagnosis of MS rather than metastatic cancer. I did not tell Debbie exactly what he said. She had been through enough.

I called David Vaughn as soon as I left Dr. Johnson's office and told him I had MS. Nurses told me later that David went back to the ED staff area and privately cried. The thought of that still saddens me. MS hurts friends too.

TREATMENTS FOR RICK

DOC'S EXPERIENCE

I was sick. Rather than awaiting further test results, Dr. Johnson ordered home IV methyl prednisolone—a steroid to reduce the inflammation of MS. The home health IV therapist started the first infusion in the early afternoon. Danny and Tammy Forston were visiting and enjoying the early holiday activities with my family. Within just a few hours of the steroid infusion, I was amazed to be able to read several letters in a row on Danny's sweatshirt. Not the whole word but several letters were a remarkable improvement. The IV treatments continued over the next several days. There were no more dramatic improvements, but I was no longer worsening either.

Dr. Johnson shared the remaining test results on the return visit. The studies were not conclusive, but he felt the evidence was strong enough to start MS therapy. I did too.

The first line treatment of MS is a choice from the "ABCs" of MS drugs. At that time this consisted of Avonex, Betaseron, or Copaxone.

Debbie gave me the first injection of Betaseron. We waited for about two hours expecting a side effect of some kind—nothing. I went downstairs to tackle some long overdue paper work. An hour later I just did not feel well. Then I started chilling and shaking. Matt had to help me upstairs to bed. I shook so hard the bed shook. This lasted about forty minutes and slowly resolved, leaving me wasted. This was my first and worst Betaseron reaction but not the last. Over the following several injections, the reactions diminished but they always left me tired.

I resumed working. A few weeks before, Dr. Jack Bland, another of the ED staff, had a heart attack. David scheduled the two of us for the easier night shifts. I would work the first six hours and Jack worked the second half. We did this until we both were stronger. The weakness following the Betaseron injections seemed to be worse the first eighteen to twenty-four hours. I would take it as soon as I finished my last shift to give myself the most time possible between the injection and the next shift. Still, I had no strength and it was as if I were doing any activity with anvils strapped to me. This was not improving. My attempts to try to rebuild strength with exercising on the stationary bike or treadmill were worthless. Not only was I too tired but I became short of breath with even minimal exercise.

I was able to work effectively, more so than before the medicines, but it was consuming. I sought objective advice about continuing work as a physician from Carl Linge, the radiologist, at lunch one day. Carl's sister had multiple sclerosis. Carl could see my struggling but wisely suggested that I wait a little longer before making a decision. Time proved Carl's counsel to be wise. I was glad I listened.

My close friends and the physicians with whom Debbie worked wondered if there could be anything else done to help. Our friend, John Lewellyn, had seen very good success at a major medical center. He helped make arrangements for me to be evaluated in their MS department. I felt that my present diagnosis and treatment were reasonable but consented to the second opinion.

The thoughtful MS specialist examined me carefully. While sharing my history, I said that the findings were not typical but it just "smells like MS." Then he left the room to review the MRI and CTs. In a little while, which seemed much longer to Deb and me, he returned. The doctor smiled and said, "I believe I have good news. You appear to have ADEM, acute disseminated encephalomyelitis—a post viral syndrome possibly caused by your October illness. In time you should do well. We cannot be certain but it just doesn't 'smell like MS.' I will follow you, but at this point you may stop your MS medicines."

I was unfamiliar with ADEM in this setting but for some nagging reason I was not convinced. I wondered if the side effects of the Betaseron were now causing more problems than the original illness, whatever it was. I stopped the Betaseron that day.

Within a month I was running a couple of miles again on the treadmill without the earlier air hunger. The tiredness improved but still stayed with me like a shadow. I worked full time and felt more human. I was able to resume a livable lifestyle. There were some residual problems. The left leg sometimes would not go quite where it belonged. My field of vision was better but not resolved. I returned to right eye dominance.

I went to the MS specialist for a few visits over the next year or so and had not noted any new problems. I felt that the weakness in the left leg and tiredness were minimally worse. In the fall of 2005 I was doing well enough that John Lewellyn asked me if I still thought that I had MS. After some thought, I answered that it may not be classical MS, but it still seemed like some form of MS. Maybe I was going to get through this without big problems. I doubted it, but maybe it would not be wrong to hope.

That hope was squashed in the spring of 2006. I was cleaning the pasture fencerow. The weather held a normal temperature but the sun was hot. In two hours I had to quit. Although the work was demanding, I did it the year before without problems, except annoying chiggers. During the weary walk to the house I realized that the very, very small hope for a happy ending had just evaporated in the heat. It was just a matter of time until who knows what would happen next. I told Deb that she needed to sell the horses. I could not help care for them any longer.

No other big life changes occurred. I continued my prized daddy job. I worked long hours in the ED. The great folks in the department, hospital, and even most of the patients made the long hours in the ED go by pleasurably.

I still played with the hobby cars. I had the Cobra replica kit that came as a body and frame in a kit. Mike Winge had a beautiful '57 Chevy hard top, which he was converting to a 454ci Chevrolet engine with a five-speed transmission. We both enjoyed the planning, problem solving, and skill challenges the projects brought. The tiredness was worsening. Lying on the creeper would cause me to occasionally be disoriented. At times I would lie on the creeper and just rest. Once, I fell asleep on a wooden creeper for thirty minutes.

In riding my bicycle back and forth to work, I would lose spatial orientation if I closed my eyes. The busyness of a one-day shift kept me working well after dark. The darkness posed a problem. Once when riding home, I slowed down and rode into a small patch of fog south of Gravy Heine's junkyard. It seemed like just an instant later when I found myself upside down in a ditch with my bike on top of me. It wasn't until I could find some house lights that I could orient myself. I was in a ditch on the opposite side of the road. My glasses were broken but thankfully the bicycle and I were unharmed. That weekend I put lights on the bike.

These worrisome changes came to a culmination in the winter of 2006 when the diagnosis of multiple sclerosis was finally confirmed. In November the portentous fatigue sat in again. Then my left leg became progressively weaker. I had trouble even raising body weight on my heel. Dr. Johnson had long moved away and the MS specialist's first appointment would be a month away. I mentioned the changes to Dr. Ali while we were at lunch in the hospital doctor's lounge. It was an imposition on him but he was a good friend and I needed another option. Syed asked to see me stand and walk. He saw the changes were striking enough that he was concerned that I had experienced a subtle stroke. He had a personal friend who was a neurologist. His friend, Dr. Mufti, graciously arranged to see me in three days. At the conclusion of the exam, she shared that I had MS. She appeared uncomfortable as she said this. This time though, the words, "multiple sclerosis" had no real impact. It was like someone telling me it was raining outside as I walked in soaked.

In today's medicine, no good diagnosis, no matter how obvious, can go without the infliction of a multitude of expensive, time-consuming, and occasionally uncomfortable tests. It is the standard drill. Dr. Mufti wanted to repeat the routine workup. There was another MRI in which to be entombed. Tubes and tubes and more tubes of blood were to be drawn to rule out everything from anemia to syphilis and maybe even pregnancy. Who knows? Right? And of course the *coup de gras*, the spinal tap.

Before succumbing to fatigue, I had put the Cobra's all fours up on jack stands and had made arrangements to take it to the tire shop for new wheels and tires. As poor a builder as I was, choosing this important step was simple; go with whichever business was the closest. The poor car was like all my mechanical efforts. I was afraid to trust it any further than necessary. The manager of the shop told me they had an opening and wanted me to bring it in the same morning the lumbar puncture was scheduled. Kenny Parker, our anesthesiologist, had scheduled the spinal tap festivities that afternoon when the surgeries were finished. He called unexpectedly that morning and told me they had an opening. He wanted me there in less than an hour. Appreciation and courtesy obligated me to not change his schedule. Old MS saying: "One does not want to anger the man who is about to stick a big needle into the middle of one's back." I hurriedly pushed this MS-challenged bod to jack up the car and get it off the stands. John Lewellyn followed me to the tire shop and took me on to the hospital.

The officiating RN, Gail Miller, rushed me from my work clothes to the surgery table. In mere minutes, I had an IV and vital signs were done. My back was scrubbed and I was mooning

Gail in one of those ubiquitous, backless hospital gowns. Kenny painted the brown betadine bull's eye around my L4 target area. He readied a spinal needle the size of a six-inch sewer tile. Yes, I was glad I had not annoyed him. As he went straight to the festivities, he absentmindedly chanted a few of the primordial, "This will hurt just a little" and repeatedly threw in a few, "Can you still wiggle your toes?" The latter seriously caught my attention. I am sure that he and Gail were smirking. In a few sweat-filled, white-knuckled minutes the deed was done. I was free to go after a short period of observation. After all, what's a spinal tap among friends? As Mary Ellen would say, "Easy peasy." I could not help but think that few people had jacked up a car, walked into the surgery area in work clothes and car grease, had an elective lumbar puncture, and walked out in less than two hours without a hitch. One cannot be manlier than that.

I went to work the following morning. Within twenty-four hours of a big deal lumbar puncture, I was on the job full tilt. Was I not "The Man?" I made my side of the workstation "The Spinal Tap Man Cave." A day and half later I was lying at home on the couch with a major spinal headache. The big red ambulance of the Warrick County Emergency System was parked conspicuously in our front yard. Donna O'Keife, the EMT specialist, was trying not to laugh while she infused a liter of IV Normal Saline. Was I still manly? Well, I didn't cry when she started the IV.

LITTLE QUIRKS

Hearing about Rick's spatial orientation problems while riding his bike got me remembering some of the little red flags of MS that popped up through the years before my diagnosis of MS. Rick and I both had signs but their significance sure wasn't clear to this doctor and nurse, regardless of our decades in the medical profession. We just weren't used to thinking from the patient angle.

One memory comes to mind while eating at McDonald's with the kids. We all have some kind of rote memory going on with maneuvering through a Mickey D's lunch. In the middle of one of these automatic preps to sit down with a Happy Meal and my kiddos, I see myself getting a fountain drink. I filled my medium-size cup with ice, moved to the spout for Diet Coke, and pushed. Halfway through the fill up my cup collapsed in my hand and Coke splashed everywhere. I assumed McDonalds had cut costs by using thinner, cheaper, paper cups. But no, I was the only person I saw having this problem amidst the metal swivel stool crowd.

No answer then, but later I came to attribute again, muscle spasms in my hand would crush the paper cup because I had no control over how much pressure my hand exerted in holding the ever changing cup weight as Coke filled it. It was also intentional action so that issue kicked into play. Did you know how marvelously God created the complex sensitivity of our bodies to adjust to that filling cup without our ever having to think about it? Until you get MS that is. Then you better think about it and start grabbing lower on the narrow part of the cup to decrease the chance of spraying yourself and your neighbor with sticky Coke.

Spraying Coke was not my only MS challenge at the burger doodle. I found myself frequently, without thinking, raising my drink to my mouth for a sip and finding I poked the nostril of my nose instead. I'd hit the nose instead of the mouth. I aimed right; I just landed wrong, a little off. The kids thought it was funny. I never did. It hurt, inside and out. I had lost the dexterity to correctly sip a Coke with a straw. It was humiliating. My seventeen-month-old granddaughter Molly has already mastered use of a straw. Can you appreciate the irony of that?

Another nuisance could be me catching my left foot while walking down a corridor and stumbling briefly. That can be related to minor foot drop. It is hardly noticeable to someone else until I stumble or fall. I have found myself flat on my keester at the mall with the problem being the foot drop and walking from a carpeted surface at Jenny's Hallmark store out to the terrazzo floor in the mall.

Unless I look at the floor change and tell my brain it's changing, my body does not automatically adjust fast enough to the surface change and I fall off balance. Some days I use a cane and my mind registers the tactile stimulation through my hand on the cane and that helps. Wet pavement on rainy days and poor lighting exaggerate this phenomenon.

I once left a meeting at a downtown Evansville church that ran into evening hours. It had rained unexpectedly and gotten dark so when I walked out the door to go to my car, I had the sudden sensation of free falling off a cliff. I thought I was catapulting to my death only to discover my feet didn't know what to do and my brain was fogged up also. It's automatic for me now to scan my surroundings before I take any step outside any door. That brings me to spatial problems. My brain is slow to process the distance and depth and exact location of objects around me. So that also played into my near death experience in the church parking lot. This symptom also presented itself before diagnosis but has worsened to be a daily problem.

Hindsight again brings that to mind when my husband Roger, daughter Beth Ann, and I would make the many trips to Indiana University in Bloomington, Indiana. It was about a three-hour drive from Evansville to visit my son Joshua, the oldest of my three with his wife Danielle and middle daughter Liza. All three of these young adults attended school there.

If I was driving the windy, hilly trek through Terre Haute or Bedford, I would often have the feeling that the car to my right, turning left at a stop sign, was heading straight toward me and was bound to hit me. I adjusted my driving distance defensively to factor in what I thought to be crazy other drivers. But when Beth Ann, drivers permit in tow, was driving and I was a defenseless passenger, the feeling of constantly being hit by another car was huge! I would think, "This kid can't drive!" When I instinctively screamed out one time from the backseat and brought Beth Ann to tears, I realized with Roger's help that my visual of the scene at hand was seriously distorted through no fault of my own or Beth Ann's. It was a bad situation and unfair to all involved.

Moments like these hit on the whole messed up family dynamics when any chronic illness is introduced into an unsuspecting family unit. I had a social worker from Cincinnati's Children's Hospital explain the family shakeup to me after Liza was diagnosed with her systemic JRA at age twelve. She asked that I envision a baby mobile hanging above a crib that has all these perfectly balanced cute objects suspended from strings. If just one object gets weighted down it throws the whole unit off balance and they all go spinning wildly. It's hard to get the balance back.

A child with JRA suddenly becomes weighted down with pain, medicines, fear, anxiety, treatments, and all sorts of adaptations like splints and wheelchairs and home tutors. Their needs are great. They become the weighted object and it throws the whole family unit into a tailspin. Now with the MS, I had become the heavy reason my beloved family was spinning wildly out of control. I hated that realization.

Another instance: Liza was driving my little red Saturn up to Bloomington and I was the passenger and in a similar situation I thought I was dead in an impending crash and screamed and didn't know I had screamed. My instinct then was to try to explain the scream, but when Liza heard me she pulled the car off to the side of HWY 41 and told me sternly, "Mom, I know how you feel and why. You don't need to explain it to me again, but you have got to stop this screaming!"

I cried. Liza cried. But she was right. She had been adapting to her JRA since junior high and had to incorporate adjustment strategies every day of her life. She expected the same of me. And she was right. But how would I do that?

Well, I eventually learned that adaptation. If I am a passenger in a car, I prefer the backseat because I see less that way. And if I am in the front seat I often ride with my eyes closed, even though that adds to my dizziness. I turn off the radio because it adds to unneeded stimulation and anxiety. And I repeat in my head, "It's okay. It's okay. It's okay." I am into chanting mantras.

Please note, once at a management meeting in Emmetsburg, Maryland, I was in a Daughter of Charity van and in the midst of my chanting, "We're not going to hit. We're not going to hit," a big old bus hit us, square onto my side of the van. I have not been able to fine tune reality versus fantasy in my MS brain.

Son Josh was long away at college when my MS diagnosis became reality so I think the daily impact to him was not an issue. Perhaps he got off easier than his siblings adjusting to Mom at home. Instead, he had the adjustment of Mom not being quite on her game at holiday dinners and needing a written step-by-step, timed to-do list to make a meal happen. Plus I was resting a lot, used a chair lift, was not the vibrant mother he grew up with, and gave herself shots every evening in front of the fireplace. Josh and I spoke little of MS; we held tight to normalcy.

Heat sensitivity also presented itself sporadically over the years before my MS diagnosis, as far back as twenty years prior.

One such moment occurred in the middle of Kings Island outside Cincinnati, Ohio. Roger and I, plus our three children, aged about three to eleven at the time, were at the amusement park on a very hot Saturday. The heat was making me weak so I asked Roger if we could sit a while. He agreed and suggested everyone get a cold drink. Now I remember being dressed in a new short set of lavender shorts and a multi-colored, striped tank top, sitting in the shade. Roger returned with drinks and got a cold, frosty beer as a surprise for us to split. I took a sip and shortly after I felt my legs go limp. I became nauseous, weak, and hot to the point of feeling over heated. I didn't understand what was happening, but we had to cut short everyone's day and leave immediately, with Roger holding onto my arm with support to get me to the car. I felt faint, a little disoriented, and reclined my seat for the four-hour drive back to New Harmony. With time it all passed but left me feeling very drained.

Looking back, I also noted I had stopped doing any kind of hot tub at hotels or on vacations. My friends would luxuriate in the tubs and I hated the experience. My legs would become like wet noodles and I wanted to vomit. Once, a brief attempt to relax in a tub at home with very warm water and a glass of red wine ended the same way. Only after my diagnosis of multiple sclerosis did I put two and two together and realize I had some heat sensitivity. My hypothalamus is just out of whack. I still have sensitivity to both hot and cold temperatures. It is almost like when my body gets too hot or too cold, it takes forever for it to adjust back to normal. Wintertime, I shiver a long time and chatter my teeth. Both extremes leave me weak and feeling like I am heading into an exacerbation.

Being a nurse, I have wondered why it took me so long to connect all the dots with odd, sporadic symptoms. I referred to all these incidents as "my oddities," "my idiosyncrasies." No wonder so many of us think we are hypochondriacs or going crazy when we experience all this and more before we are given an accurate diagnosis of multiple sclerosis. The MS picture presents more questions than answers for years. I guess that is why most of us have a sense of relief when finally given a disease title, even if it is a life changing, sucky one. As my white-lettered, black T- shirt, given to me by good friend Libby, says, "It is what it is."

For what it's worth, I now avoid the hottest times of days whenever possible. I sip iced drinks, mostly water, when out in the heat. I always take gel ice packs along in my cooler and throw them on my chest or wrists or neck when I feel my temperature rising.

I presented quite a scene at the Posey County Fair one year when the temp hovered in the nineties at six o'clock in the evening. I would not have been out in it, but my baby girl was a beautiful sixteen-year-old in a stunning, red, haltered gown, on stage as a contestant for Miss Posey County. I would not have missed that for the world. So I rotated ice packs on my upper chest, stuck down my tank top, and had a totally wet shirt by the time she became first runner up—dang that Holly Bender for winning. I had to walk up to the stage later and embarrass Beth Ann with a sopping wet Momma taking embarrassing pictures. Please note, the cute, shy guy on stage later having a picture taken with friend Holly was named Chris and became my loving son-in-law and father of grandbabies Maggie and Molly McCutchan. Is that poetic Irish justice or what?

There are many assistive cooling devices now available for heat sensitive people, all a bit fancier than my cooler gel packs. Things like cooling vests, cooling neck scarves, etc. They are obtainable online, through companies advertised in MS magazines, at some medical supply houses, or plain old Walmart. Calling a local MS society, club, or support group is an excellent resource to find such helps.

I will have to remember to ask Ricky Bob what he explained to me at one IV session when I was preoccupied. Something about physics and what proves to be the best thing to drink or chomp on when trying to stay cool. I think eating frozen grapes was mentioned as a great cooling mechanism. He is so good at all that scientific mumbo jumbo. Doctors really do have some helpful knowledge. I just must remember not to always tune him out when he starts to spew the book smarts of physics and journals. Poor guy can't help himself when the brain balls ooze out of that mop of gray hair.

QUIRKS, LAW, AND ORDER

DOC'S EXPERIENCE

Let me explain to Mary Ellen one more time why frozen grapes or slushies or just plain ice cubes cool more than cold liquids. It is simple chemistry. It takes one calorie to cool one gram of water one degree centigrade. But it takes eighty calories to convert one gram of ice to water. In other words, converting a frozen grape to a chilled grape does eighty times more cooling than the grape continuing to cool at the same rate. Diagnosing and managing the quirks of MS is not that straight forward.

Like most MS-ers looking back, I can now recognize some vague MS quirks. In 1984, long before I developed MS, I had an episode of spots before my eyes, scotomas. They did not last a month. It was during a very busy summer and I was exhausted with activity. The thought occurred to me that this could be a harbinger of MS, but because MS usually affects more women and young adults, being male and in my midforties I dismissed the thought as quickly as it came. The demands of work let up. I felt better and the scotomas slipped away.

In my forties, when our family took a vacation or when I had a few days off, I was spending more time sleeping. It was hard to keep up with the boys doing things we all enjoyed. Still, I ran, rode the bicycle, and did a fair amount of activities. I reasoned that it was just the long hours of work and the lack of desire to push myself. But sharp-eyed Debbie suggested several times that something might be wrong, perhaps a form of chronic fatigue syndrome. All of my routine labs were normal except for elevated cholesterol from a slightly hedonistic but enjoyable diet. There is no lab test for laziness.

After I developed MS, I mentioned these problems to a specialist and he felt they were not related to MS. He was probably right. It is not a quality noted in medical texts. I only mention this because when we MS-ers get together and talk, earlier unusual tiredness or other problems are common observations—maybe not always valid, but common.

On some occasions, the vision and fatigue quirks posed challenges at work. One busy evening in the ED, I walked into an exam room. There lay a man, whom I will call Tom. He had rolled his truck in a wreck. Two buddies were with him. They said that they were in a truck behind him. He had dodged a deer and ran off the road. All three of the motley trio had the aroma of alcohol but the truck driver, Tom, was clearly inebriated and intermittently unpleasant. The truck wreck ensemble was quickly joined by two investigating county deputies. Tom denied any memory of the event and would not describe where he was hurting. These findings alone were enough to require a CT scan of the head and neck.

The staff rushed Tom back to the CT. I stayed with his two *compadres* to glean more information. Something about the story did not make sense. After a little hem hawing, they acknowledged there was no deer. He and they were racing. He lost control and wrecked. They described the ditch he had rolled into and the truck he was driving. When they described the truck, I realized it had formerly belonged to a man—whom I will call Greg, a friend of mine.

The staff called me back to CT. Tom was uncooperative, even nasty. The CT scan was important. In the past, similar patients were often found to have serious injuries to the brain or spinal cord that could only be identified with an early CT. Simple reasoning with him failed and the next step was to "drop him." That is to inject paralyzing meds into the IV. This would stop any movement including breathing. After giving the medications, I would need to hurriedly insert a tube into his airway and mechanically breathe for him or he would suffocate and die. This procedure is called intubation. It requires quick-skilled teamwork from the staff. Usually the procedure is effective and smooth, but implementing it requires navigating through several high-risk areas. The greatest of these is visualizing the trachea and sliding the tube in between the vocal cords into the air passage. The airway lies at the base of the throat, shrouded by the tongue, esophagus, and other anatomical features. When I do this procedure, my whole being is focused on visualizing an area that is no larger than a penny. The slight loss of vision and the minimally increased difficulty of coordination caused by the MS were never enough to prevent me from doing this procedure, but they did make me a little more cautious of making it my first choice.

The deputies were standing nearby, ready to assist, and I think also they wanted to see me drop him. I studied his behavior carefully and decided at least part of his annoying behavior was deliberate. I said, "Tom, the deputies don't know what you really did, but I do. If you don't cooperate, I will tell them the real story so they can take you to jail." Tom was miraculously cured. He cooperated and I completed the exam. I noticed the deputies made quick, inquisitive glances at each other but wisely remained cool.

When the treatment was finished, I whispered, "Tom, I need to know. When you were racing, were you ahead?" He answered yes. I said, "You better have been, I helped Greg hop that truck up."

POOP, PEE, AND SEX

Alrighty now. Rick and I decided these three topics of poop, pee, and sex are the ones we don't talk about in polite company, yet they are the topics we seek out first in any book on MS. Are we right? They are usually the really short chapters or the ones so medically technical we can't pronounce the words, much less understand them. I'll try to do better. I trust Dr. Yeager will do the same.

Let me cover my important nurse points first. We all poop, pee, and the lucky ones have sex. So we are all in this together. As an RN, I can also point out with observed certainty that our plumbing is all the same. Girls will be girls and boys will be boys. Girls have three holes; boys have two. We drink; we pee. We eat; we poop. And sex is sex. It fits where it fits if you want it to fit there.

Having covered the anatomy and having made any of my past anatomy and physiology teachers who might be reading this cringe with embarrassment for me, I now move onto the complexities and variations with MS in regards to bodily functions of any kind.

Multiple sclerosis is believed to be an autoimmune disease process that breaks down the myelin sheath, which covers and protects the nerves in our body and aids in nerve transmission. MS can cause any nerve to malfunction, short circuit, or just stop working because of the plaques that build up and the axon erosion due to inflammation involved.

I understand there to be about two hundred and fourteen "named" nerves, so with body symmetry that's four hundred and twenty-eight that have names. Then there is the estimation of one hundred billion neurons in the human brain and an estimate of seven trillion in our entire body. Wee doggy!

Now my simple-minded MS thinking on this is that if there are seven trillion neurons that can short circuit, we have a gazillion combinations of presenting symptoms in any two people with MS. Now my old statistics teacher at USI is probably stroking out on my mathematical skills. But really, the idea of no two people being exactly alike with MS symptoms is totally understandable to me. It makes sense.

This kindergarten approach to understanding the uniqueness of every MS patient might be insulting to the brainiacs reading this. Dr. Ricky Bob will certainly call me on the carpet for this one next month. But this is how I get my head around the massive effect MS can have on me and explain all the quirky (not QWERTY like a keyboard) symptoms I experience and blame on MS. Let me give you a few examples.

With the onset of my relapsing, remitting MS I had no bladder problems. About five years into it I noticed I was having more frequent UTIs—urinary tract infections. I would have to be put on an antibiotic each time. After a while I could not always pick up on the usual symptoms of burning upon urination and frequency. I might instead feel more run down, tired, or feverish. My sensations were impaired because of the MS. I took it upon myself to use some techniques I incorporated with my hospital patients, mostly on rehab, to make sure their bladders emptied completely, thus "avoiding some voiding" issues with UTIs.

I began doing a "triple void" technique. Every time I went to the bathroom, I would try to empty my bladder completely. I would not rush it. I would just sit there and take as long as needed. It takes longer to empty my bladder since the MS. At the end of emptying, I would again bear down like I was starting to urinate. Then I would try to go a third time. These three attempts at one sitting to empty the bladder is a triple void. I have consistently done this for years and still do it. On bad MS days, I may even lean forward and push a bit on my lower abdomen, just above the pubic bone, while on the toilet to manually help express the urine. Most days I get a little more urine out with each attempt to empty as I triple void. Any residual urine left in the bladder after going to the bathroom sets us up for an infection. Anything we can do to avoid that is good.

An interesting MS phenomenon I experience can be triggered by sitting on the commode and raising my head up and down. It is called L'Hermitte's sign. It is the sensation of an electrical shock from head to toe. The shock is indicative of lesions in the cervical spine and is most often triggered by lowering the head, kind of chin to chest. Raising my head up and down viewing canned goods in a grocery store can elicit the same response, along with dizziness and nausea.

Another technique I use to decrease my chance of infection is to urinate after sex. It does not have to be immediately, but I don't wait long. The basis for this is to again decrease the chances of a UTI. Naturally flushing urine out of the urinary tract after sexual intercourse allows the germs that might be hovering around the urethral opening to be washed away. The juices of sex and the close proximity of anus, vagina, and meatus, the pee hole, allows for a ripe place for stuff to hang out and cause a problem like germs creeping into the urinary tract that can cause an infection.

I am a very visual person so let me present the pee after sex idea in another way. Have you ever planted a big honking tree in your backyard and used the technique of sticking a hose in the base of the hole and letting it run water through after the tree is in and the hole filled with dirt? This gets the air out and waters it well. My friend Walter told me about this trick. Then you pull out the hose and it's all muddy. So what do you naturally do? You run water through the hose to wash the mud away from the opening at the end and you might take a rag to wipe off any other muddy water. Right?

Well, going pee after sex is like that. Pee flushes the germs out and off the end pretty well and toilet paper dabs off the leftovers after you're done. Same thing.

Now my other advice with the pee after sex suggestion is to not make a big deal of it. I usually just slip out of bed and say, "Be right back." There is no need to announce, "See ya, babe, gotta flush out the muddy hose." Be cool gals; just be cool.

My bladder problems have progressed more over the years. I have what my doctor describes as "a flaccid bladder." Simply put, it means the tone of my bladder is affected by plaques along the nerves that affect my bladder function. So besides the above, I also take a cholinergic drug called Urecholine to help with muscle tone in the bladder. It does help me to empty better and to empty quicker with a stronger stream of urine. If, for some reason, I don't take the med as prescribed, I can sit on the pot forever and wait for the slow trickle of urine to end. If you are in the bathroom stall next to me at Red Lobster you'd think I am being silly and deliberately dribbling my life away. I'm not. It's the best my bladder can do.

Kegel exercises are also used by some women and men. Most women with children were taught those exercises somewhere amidst their OB/GYN visits or Lamaze classes. I feel they are incorporated for me each time I start and stop my stream with triple voiding.

A healthy diet is also crucial, in my mind at least, to minimizing bladder problems or any MS problem. I eat a very balanced diet that includes a big variety of food six times a day, plenty of fresh fruit, vegetables, lean meats, little sugar, little flour, and limited preservatives. A minimum of sixty-four ounces of water daily is also apart of my diet. For the caffeine boost of energy and personal preference I still drink other things like coffee, teas, and diet drinks, but that liquid does not apply to the daily sixty-four ounces of water I consume. I believe all this water and good food helps to keep the plumbing in as good a working order as my MS will allow and supports a healthy function of my body to fight MS problems in general.

I am fortunate all these tricks have supported me not having to do the self-catheterizations I mentioned in my rehab flashback immediately after hearing my MRI results of MS. Please note, you can do every trick in the book and if your nerves have enough MS deterioration, nothing may help. It is our reality of the crapshoot I mentioned earlier.

Is self-catheterization in my future? Very possibly. If so, I'll figure out how to be cool with the pee straw in my purse and incorporate it into my lifestyle. You can bet it will definitely involve a stylin' zipper bag to carry necessities. I will include in that adjustment being totally pissed off at times that MS has taken the normal sit and pee of life from me. But "pissed off" sort of fits the whole bizarre picture doesn't it?

You are probably now wondering about urine leakage. Sure, I deal with that problem to some degree, but not every day, and not severely. Many women my age experience bladder problems like stress incontinence, and I cannot say with certainty how much of mine is MS and how much to blame on age, pregnancies, and menopause. Pantiliners are a godsend. Adult diapers are not stocked in my bathroom at this point, but I did go so far as to cut Poise coupons out for a while. That is till my youngest, Beth Ann, saw them and freaked out with, "What are you doing with these?" She was right. I did not need them at the time so what was I doing cutting them out? Everything in its time.

Moments of total shock and embarrassment have been ugly moments in my life when I would be having a bad MS day and just standing upright from a seated position caused a complete gusher of urine to soak me and run down my legs. Yuck. A few choice confessional fodder words accompany those moments. Plus the anger is jumbled up with sadness, frustration, annoyance, and usually ends with a pity party for a bit.

Bladder spasms can also be a problem for me sometimes. I notice these lower abdominal sharp pains more when I am overly fatigued, have been up on my feet a lot, or in the middle of a flare-up. When they occur, I lay flat more and address my fatigue issue that is a contributing factor and I have the option of increasing my cholinergic medicine from once daily up to three times daily. I just need to be extra vigilant with extra medicine because the increased tone of my bladder with more medicine can cross a line and cause bladder spasms with the extra tone that results. As most things with MS, it is one big balancing act.

To wrap up my MS pee knowledge, experience, and words of wisdom, I have one other very important suggestion. Ladies, always wear matching underwear! And pitch any bad fitting, elastic string hanging, stained, torn band, torn leg, butt ugly ones. I am dead serious! Underwear decorum is as important to me as having a tasteful walking cane. I feel better about myself when I know my down-undies are coordinated. No black at one end and beige on the other for me. Plus, splurge and walk or roll yourself right into Victoria's Secret and buy the lacy risqué ones you've dreamt about. What are you waiting for? Permission? Being old enough or too old or Mom's approval? And what's that you say, your butt is too big for VC? No excuse. When I was sixty pounds heavier, just a couple of years ago, I'd still hit JCPenney or Macy's and get big girl panties that were hot. Look for them and they will come. Hee, hee, nasty girl.

Apparently Mr. Florenz Ziegfeld of the Follies fame agreed with my theory of great underwear. I read that when told Irish linen petticoats for Follies dancers were far more expensive than cotton, his reply was, "I know. But Irish linen does something to their walk—remember they are Ziegfeld girls." His response spoke volumes. He believed the women would carry themselves with more confidence, pride, and grace if they knew they had the real thing on their behinds. A wise man I believe, that Mr. Z.

Heh, maybe my Ms. Z. title holds a mutual significance as the Mr. Z.'s successful business mind.

Men don't get off the hook on this point either. Oh, wow, I haven't squared off on this point yet with the good Dr. Yeager. It ought to be fun. But really men, you are not allowed to wear droop butt, saggy, faded out buzz kills. Tidy whities or boxers fall under personal choice as does color, but pay attention to how you wrap your packages. Good fit is vital! Women notice these things. The wrapping I mean, not the package. But, wait a minute; we notice that too. I digress, a common malady of an MS brain.

I joke some about the nasty pee topic. My intent is not to minimize it. Urinary incontinence, retention, or any form of dysuria can be a serious challenge to face. And when asked how we are by friends the first reply from us is not usually, "Okay, but I wet my pants before I got here and that's why I'm late." MS robs us of many things. I refuse to let it rob me of my confidence, good grooming, or sexuality. I hope you make the same choice.

Now onto the fun topic of poop, a.k.a. feces, bowel movements, BMs, number twos. Again, some people with MS will have serious bowel problems while others are not affected at all. It all depends where demyelination is occurring in our bodies.

Most days I am lucky and my bowels behave themselves. My balanced diet supports optimum bowel function along with exercise. Other days it is a pain in the butt, literally. I sometimes will lose the sensation to have a bowel movement. Days can pass and there is no stimulation close to needing to go. When this happens, I can become very constipated and get sharp abdominal pains. I have to resort to manually removing an impaction or, if I am lucky, a glycerin suppository will do the trick. The oddest sensation of all is when I experience dilation of the anus and that can cause some stool incontinence or I feel like my rectum is turned inside out and I am sitting uncomfortably on the lining inside the rectum. That sounds so odd but it is the best way I can describe it. With that irritating sensation there is always some slight stool incontinence because of dilation.

Upon arising in the morning, I have had my bowels evacuate completely, down the leg onto the floor. It is not a usual occurrence for me so I'm lucky, but I do find any stool incontinence, even light smearing, to be very disturbing for me. A little stool smear embarrasses me more than urinary incontinence. This might be because most women my age complain about bladder leakage to some degree. My gosh, even Whoopi Goldberg is advertising women's bladder leakage undergarments on late night TV. It can easily be a topic when we women pair up and make our escorted trip to the john when we are out on the town. It is acceptable conversation for the middle aged female species. We wear it like a badge of honor inscribed, "Heh, I popped out three watermelons down there, am damn proud of it, and a little dribble when I laugh is just fine."

To date I have never had a similar conversation with women friends, even MS friends, about messing my pants with poop. It doesn't easily happen. Needless to say, since starting this book, Rick and I have talked about *everything*. We agreed the scoop on poop was a must and it has been healing. Go figure—talking poop with a male MS friend.

Why is poop bathroom conversation unacceptable but pee okay? Besides the female child bearing factors I mentioned, I believe it is because there are less of us overall dealing with stool incontinence. And we are embarrassed. I know I feel childlike, even baby like, when my bowels are affected by my MS. Both ends of the spectrum cause embarrassment for me. Who wants to admit to donning a plastic disposable glove and digging for gold up your rectum or wearing a diaper to catch stinky poop? No one. Even my sexy red Victoria's Secret does not protect me from the feeling of being inferior when incontinence hits. We are human. We are proud. We are angry.

So, on those iffy, bowel-challenged days, I do what I always do: I let myself feel all the negative feelings and on occasion I cry like a baby. Both ends might as well match and flow together. Then I suck it up, count my many blessings, and do what I need to do. I throw an extra set of slacks, underwear, and a big old towel to sit on in my car when I take off on errands. Wet wipes and a plastic bag are packed. I wear my extra-long sweater or hoodie so I can cover my behind if it ends up being wet. I imagine being trendy cool if I need to tie that jacket around my waist to call less attention to my dampened derriere. I pull out extra-long pantiliners or vaginal pads. And when I have the slightest urge to go to the bathroom, I go quickly and never debate. And bad days I stay put on the padded couch and do sedentary tasks like phone calls, bill paying, or reading. Reclining a bit helps because gravity isn't pushing stool out as easily. I might also do more flat time. It helps with gravity issues and with the fatigue factor that makes matters that much worse with the bowels.

We must all be survivors in these moments and deal with the nastiness at hand. It is not noble and no one wants the task of dealing with poop, even nurses. No one pats us on the back for a job well done when we avoid poop on our cushions or in our cars. And we wish we were doing all the padding and such for our elderly Moms or grandkids, not ourselves. I try to keep in mind the gal with a colostomy bag who ties a red silk ribbon on it. If she can make a silk purse out of that sow's ear, I will attempt to do the same.

Now, before we head onto some sex matters, what you've all been waiting for, I'll defer to Rick for a bit. Our stories are different, yet the same. MS does not play favorites for male or female, for doctor or nurse. The common thread of our lives with MS weaves a thick, plaid wool of intricate detail, of mystery and intrigue; you can never be quite certain what is under that colorful, itchy kilt. But bet your bottom dollar the pattern will have a touch of red and the kilt will always be drafty.

RICK DEFINES THE DOWNS

DOC'S EXPERIENCE

Two couples had finished an evening dinner together. The men retired to the living room while the ladies chatted in the dining room. One of the men had MS and had occasional memory pauses. He mentioned to the other gentleman that he and his wife had eaten at a very nice restaurant last week. The guest asked the name of the restaurant. The fellow started to reply and the name was gone. He said, "Just a minute, it will come to me."

After a little unsuccessful searching he asked his guest, "What is the name of that flower, the pretty romantic one with the thorns?"

The guest spoke up immediately, "A rose."

The MS fellow smiled and said, "Yes, yes that's it." He then yelled out to the kitchen, "Rose, what's the name of the restaurant we ate at last week?"

Forgetfulness is a common complaint of folks with MS. A simple example is when I took my canes out of the car and placed them on the back of my scooter. I went to the other side of the car and picked up something inside. Then I looked for the canes in the car, totally forgetting they were already unloaded.

Another example of forgetfulness, I laid the cell phone on the dash before getting into the truck. The truck is a half-ton 4x4 and the ride height is high. I have a step-up, which helps. But my legs are weak and the step-up is a help, not a solution. So after sitting behind the steering wheel, it struck me that the phone was not in my pocket. I do not like to travel without it so I got back out and took the scooter back in the house and looked for the cell phone. It was nowhere to be found. I even tried calling myself with the regular phone. That yielded no ringer sound. Weighing out the pros and cons, I dared to live dangerously. I worked my way back into the truck and took off. About half way to church I heard the ring of a cell phone. With a little quick looking, I found it lying on the dash where I must have put it just before entering the truck. This forgetfulness is worse during a stressful event.

Another real downer is urine and bowel control. These problems begin insidiously. Like the proverbial frog in the pan being slowly warmed, we are cooked before we know it.

When Mary Ellen and I told the young, sports-clad man, Chris, receiving Tysabri with us at the Cancer Center, that we were considering a book, he was uncharacteristically enthusiastic. It took us several months to learn his name, but today Chris smiled and said, "Tell the ups and downs. What it's really like." A second time he reminded us, "Don't forget, remember the downs." This second time I felt he was staring squarely at me.

Chris then shared with us his MS diagnosis story. It was brief. He climbed the stairs and went to bed one night, a healthy twenty-eight-year-old man. He awoke the next morning paralyzed from the waist down. This young man knew the downs of multiple sclerosis.

What are some MS downs? Forgetfulness? Hearing the diagnosis? Losing one's career? Suffering through another spinal headache? Yes, but they are not the downs about which Chris wanted me to write. How could I communicate these downs?

Last weekend had almost arrived. Friday I went to the attorney's to have my will finished. I had to ask someone to drive me there. We set up the Power of Attorney for my health care cessation and to decide what, if anything, should happen to my body organs. I mused with the attorney that if Debbie were mad at me, she could send my body to a college as a cadaver for the entertainment of uninterested college students rather than having a proper burial in the already purchased cemetery plot. He was not used to my humor.

I signed the documents, turning the keys to our home over to Debbie. I wondered how the mortgage would be paid in the event that I outlived my disability income. I wondered just how soon that end would come. Nobody knows their future, but MS assured me that it would not be as I had hoped many years ago when I was working, running, planning vacations, and our financial future. The simple activities of the afternoon sent me home tired and pondering.

Saturday, I was still tired and slept in. The urge to pee awakened me. No problem, long ago I began keeping a urinal at the bedside so that there would be no need for an unsuccessful dash to the bathroom. I stood at the side of the bed, making a standard urinal deposit. With only enough warning to make me realize that I was headed for trouble, I sensed that I was going to poop, immediately. This was my second episode of stool incontinence in three days. In the prior episode I had made it to the bathroom, but not quickly enough. While trying to remove my slacks then, I had lost my balance and fell backward. In the fall I broke the commode seat and the toilet paper dispenser but the episode had been manageable.

This time I knew the bathroom was out of the question. Hastily I jumped out of my pj bottoms thinking that the stool could run out onto the plastic floor liner and I could clean up the mess after the movement was over. The stool was already running down before I could totally get my pants off. Then I had another round of peeing. I was a little slow in getting the urinal positioned so now there was urine on the floor as well as stool. I tried to finish removing the bottoms and fell down onto the plastic floor protector. The urinal slipped as I went down spilling more of its contents.

I struggled to get up out of the mess without spreading it around more. In the best of circumstances, getting up from the floor is difficult. This time I was trying to get up without smearing feces and urine around everywhere. The plastic liner hurt my knees as I attempted to put weight on them. My feet and legs slid as I struggled to get out of my own mire. When I tried to move my legs with my hands I found myself putting my hands in stool that had run down my legs. My hands and legs were caked in stool and slickened with urine. I was sweating and exhausted. The struggling robbed me of my remaining strength. I called for Debbie.

After some time, Debbie heard me and came. Seeing the mess, she called to the basement for Luke, Matt, and his wife Beth to help. Beth had never seen me without clothes before. Now I was lying on a floor covered with stool, urine, toilet paper, and unsalvageable clothing. I was naked and filthy.

Matt and Luke were troopers. After several tries, they were able to lift me up and wrestle me to the shower where I could begin the process of cleaning. The lifting was made worse because they were trying to avoid soiling themselves. Stool was sticking toilet paper to the sole of my foot as I tried to limp toward the bathroom without leaving a trail of more stool, not that it mattered much.

I was too exhausted to consider my pride. I was too physically and emotionally drained, to the point that I no longer considered how much I had asked of them to help me. I was helpless and pathetic. When I look for a way to describe the "downs" of MS, that about does it.

STOP AND SMELL THE ROSES

Next, let's talk about sex, baby. Let's talk about sex. This can be a fun topic. We are all equipped for it and I like to remind myself God created our sexual beings superbly with subtlety and nuances beyond what we could ever conjure up in our pea brains. He did good, didn't He? Thank you, God, for my equipment, brain, and sensations. May I never take them for granted.

That may sound sacrilegious, but I do not intend it to be irreverent in any way. Even my strict German Catholic upbringing allowed for a healthy respect for sexuality at all levels. I credit my parents for not lecturing me on being a "good girl" and having the sex talk when I asked for it at age ten. Mom and Dad never made a big deal of me holding hands with a boyfriend or making out on the dark green, nylon couch with rough nubs on a Sunday after church. Of course, in my days, making out meant kissing, hugging, and maybe a first base feel up. Mom and Dad even exchanged kisses and hugs I glanced upon on occasion next to the white-and-gold-flecked Formica kitchen counter when Dad came home from his factory work at Servel in Evansville. Sometimes sipping his quart bottle of homebrew poured reverently into the red-rimmed, white enamel pan came first, other times a proper hello to Mom was priority.

I must admit to a bit of confusion for me as a fifth grader at St. Wendel Catholic Grade School in regards to the technicalities of sexual intercourse. Father Allega gave us girls and boys a onetime gender-divided sex education class in the upstairs music room. I think we got out of geography for it. Man, sexual intercourse was much more exciting a topic than learning the Mediterranean Sea touched upon the Asian continent. Mm, maybe we were learning

the male continent touched upon the beauty of the female seas.
Not so inappropriate for geography class after all.

Did Father Allega plan that? Was it taught that way in seminary? Stick sex ed smack dab in the middle of geography class
and they won't even notice how exciting and forbidden it all is.
Put it between the Egyptian pyramids and the USSR stuff. Was
sex education even taught in seminary? I don't know.

I grew up thinking nuns were sexless and bald under that
long, flowing black dress and veil and giant, beaded black rosary.
I gasped when I actually saw Sister Julitta step into a bathroom in
the convent building next door to the school, where she was fitting me for a modest May crowning gown. I had been chosen to
be May Queen, a high honor one eighth grade girl had bestowed
upon her for May Day. This is a very big church ceremony the
first week in May, Mary's month.

But forget why I was inside the secret convent rooms where
the sisters resided. I heard an actual toilet flush! Sister Julitta,
the school principal and my Mom's beer drinking friend growing
up, was human and had to pee. Why I didn't make the beer con-
sumption human connection before I don't know. But really, red
alert! "Could she be human like me and stink up the bathroom
even though I tried to flush quickly after a number two?" And
lest I forget, I had seen a wisp of hair peek out from under Sister
Jean Marie's veil, behind her right ear while she was writing a
pretty cursive 'O' on the dull green chalkboard. I was beginning
to explore new frontiers back in that two-story convent house
and then in the music room at school.

As far as the sex education and geography sex approach goes,
I'll have to ask Roger about that theory. I stole him from the
path of priesthood to hold him captive forever with us mere lay
mortals who married, had sex and babies, and still got to heaven
hopefully in the end. Actually, Roger had returned home on his
own from Perrysburg, Ohio, from Divine Word Seminary before
we ever met. His uncle, Father Jerry Ziliak, was his mentor and

inspired the attempt at the priesthood, but it was not the right fit for my country boy.

Back to the upstairs music room—I was sitting upright in the cold, standard issue, tan, metal folding chair with my acceptable dress on as I listened closely. We did not have a uniform code but those days we wore dresses. No pants for girls allowed on church property. It was a sin. And no sleeveless tops or dresses. It was considered immodest. We measured proper dress length by kneeling on the floor and if the hem edge hit the floor, we passed, and if we showed only a modest one-inch above our knee, we squeaked by. My mom had her work cut out for her with her only daughter being five-foot-nine. I was the third tallest girl in my class of forty-eight. Only Becky Richter and Carolyn Rexing beat me out on height through eighth grade. Getting our matching pink pencil skirt dresses for graduation in 1966 would prove to be a challenge.

Now Father Allega was the enforcer of girl dress modesty and in the music room that day he did a decent but awkward job of telling us very bare essentials of sex while standing in front of us wide-eyed girls, nervously pacing in his black hassock and white priest collar. As every serious-minded girl that day, I listened closely but was unfamiliar with terminology so I missed some pronunciations. I went home that day trying to understand why boys had a "peanut" in their pants that was somehow involved in making babies. Not long after that is when I hit Mom up for more sex education and only then did I read the handout she gave me and notice the word I struggled with was "penis" not "peanut." Thank goodness later nursing school and Roger cleared me up on those fine yet important points. Points, yeah. I am so visual. Blame it on the plaque buildup that is not on my teeth.

Multiple sclerosis is naturally a catalyst for many emotional ups and downs. These highs and lows can influence our desire for sex. When a part of the body is feeling numb, we have double vision or fatigue makes it hard to move, sex can unfortunately get bumped to the bottom of our priority list. It is what it is, through no fault of anyone. This is when good communication is of utmost importance. Communication, communication, communication. Did I say communication? Regardless of your symptoms of MS, you have to let your partner in on details in order for the two of you to navigate the MS bumps in bed. We aren't princesses dealing with a pea under our mattress. We have the whole friggin' Del Monte can squished between mattress and box springs, baby.

God blessed me with a thoughtful, caring husband who knows not to take it personally when my body is not up to the rigors of sex. We discuss that openly. It took practice and being very specific with explanations, but we have gotten good at it. Paresthesia is a symptom that causes me problems. It means my skin gets overly sensitive to the point of not being able to tolerate clothing against my skin, much less a two-hundred-pound man. The softest, loosest cotton nightgown can cause my skin to burn and hurt. That is not conducive to a wild romp in the hay for sure. The sensation of having a tight band around the middle of my torso can be part of the odd sensations, along with prickly needles and pins anywhere. I try to tell Roger exactly what I am experiencing with my body and which part is hit hardest at that moment. He believes me. I feel no need to convince him. We both know I am not using the "I have a headache" bow out.

The flip side of that weird skin coin is that sometimes hypersensitivity can be super helpful in sexual arousal. There is a fine line between what feels good and what feels bad with touch. So feeling extra sensitive can mean I get extra pleasure at times.

You already know my philosophy about sexy, matching underwear. I can take that one step further and share my sex philosophy that is pertinent for life in general. Mom Schmitt, my maternal grandmother, would have coined the phrase, "Stop and smell the roses." We all appreciate the message conveyed of grabbing what life has to offer and realizing joy in any given moment. My positive philosophy for life is similar. I take the approach of, "Never waste a good hard-on." I like to think my spouse has joined me in almost forty years of appreciating that motto. But then, you'll have to ask Roger about that one.

Now, I have just taken my good friend Libby off the hook for a promise she made to me. The two of us were on an artist retreat last year near Garden of the Gods, Illinois, when I shared that motto with her. And I swear we weren't nipping Jose' Quervo at the time. On a stack of Bibles, we weren't drinking.

Libby laughed for some time after that remark, collected herself, and gave me a hug. Libby gets me and my warped thought processes. Her's are warped as well. Birds of a feather and all that stuff. I made her promise to share the philosophy with my children after I died. She imagined it to be good fodder for my eulogy. Lib, being a very creative writer and a decade plus younger than me, had the right idea. I did not feel comfortable educating the kids on that subject face to face but sensed its importance. The motto holds even more significance for those of us living with MS or any chronic illness. Father Allega didn't cover that little nugget in the 1960s music room, but I can't help but think he would approve—on religious basis that is.

RICK'S PROBLEM PICKS

DOC'S EXPERIENCE

Annette Funicello—of Mouseketeer and beach party movie fame—has multiple sclerosis. I have read that she had kept it secret for many years. She finally had to announce it publically to dispel rumors that she was an alcoholic because of abnormal walking. I have had gait changes since the onset of MS. Left-sided foot drop gradually developed. It became noticeable enough to mildly affect running by 2005. In the summer of 2006, I was running with a decided favoring of the right foot. The running shoes displayed left-sided wear and made a left-foot dragline on the treadmill. The left leg weakness, foot drop, and clumsiness were worsened with the 2006 exacerbation. I had a broad-based, short, stride-shuffling gait. Like Annette, it gave the appearance of my being publically inebriated. The poor gait and weakness of MS has caused many falls. Falls are a fact of life for people with MS.

Our son Matthew brought a new light to Yeager world when he dated and married Beth. Beth's college graduation ceremonies were held in a large stadium. Typical of MS patients, I had to make a hurried dash for the bathroom near the end. I was carefully reaching from one stair rail to the next as I descended the steps back to my seat. I missed catching one rail and fell forward striking a man with his camera raised to take a photo of his daughter receiving her diploma. I worked my way back to the seat. I am sure he watched me, thinking that I was celebrating the graduations way too early.

The team at the MS center and many friends suggested I start walking with a cane in 2007. To me using a cane would be surrendering to the disease and would be a blow to my pride. A few months after the stadium debacle, my walking was worsening. Debbie and Beth returned from a trip to Gatlinburg with a cane. They told me that Beth had picked it out especially for me and she hoped I would use it, "a little." I suspect the cane was both of their ideas, but they told me Beth picked it out because she has me wrapped around her little finger. I would do anything for my little princess. It took the edge off using the cane. I began by using it to walk to the doctor's lounge. Of course, I went in and out the back way, but I did not use it in the department where patients could see me. This worked for several months. Then I began needing it in the Emergency Department. By mid-2008, I was walking with two canes. The Veterans Administration gave me an electric scooter and scooter lift for the back of the truck in 2008.

Accepting the need for a scooter was another emotional battle for me. I used to watch Walmart shoppers walk into the store and then plop their oversized hindquarters down in a Walmart electric scooter like it was their personal entitlement. Dr. Parker told me of watching a lady on an electric scooter in Walmart drive into a large support post. She was texting. Me on a scooter was an unpleasant mental picture. I wanted no part of it. But the walking was more unsteady and demanded much more effort to the point I realized I needed a scooter to get into and around larger stores.

So I dealt with this problem like a thinking adult. Right? Wrong. I started asking friends like John, Larry, and Beth to just pick up things for me while they were in the stores. That could only go so far. Finally I yielded. I asked Larry Powers to go with me to the Walmart in a different town and swore him to secrecy. Now it was my turn to walk into the store and plop my corpulent derriere in an electric scooter. The freedom the scooter gave me was exhilarating. From then on I went straight for the electric scooter line when I entered the larger stores. Let appearances be durned.

Having a scooter of my own did not stop embarrassing falls. Last spring I was positioning the scooter to raise it into the truck bed with the hoist when my feet became entangled between the truck and the scooter. I lunged forward but caught myself on the truck tailgate. I found myself helplessly dangling with my feet on the scooter and my body on the tailgate. Of course this had to be happening at 4:30 p.m. on the town square with all the traffic passing. Not only did I look like a fool, but I had chosen a place where there was no shortage of witnesses. I realized I was stuck and the only solution was to just go ahead and fall. The fall would only be a little over an arm's length, but I would be landing on asphalt. I hate road rash. Also, the truck was parked at an angle on Main Street so I would be falling into all the traffic.

It was "Geronimo" time. I rolled off the truck. The landing was no problem. Again, like Mary Ellen says, "Easy peasy." But now came the hard part. I had to figure out how to get up. A mother and her two children came to my aid. There I was lying on the busy street after a fall with my feet playing spaghetti with the scooter. She asked the insightful question, "Do you need help?" I answered just as brilliantly with, "No, I got it under control." Yes, sometimes I still have a battle with pride. She stared incredulously and I rethought my predicament. Then I said, "Would you care to pick up the lift controller and hold it. Act like you know what you are doing with it and that everything is under control so more people won't come and stare." I know, pride still. With a little more struggling and thinking I had her lower the lift toward me. I grabbed it and held on while she raised it up. Yes, people on the square and passing cars were all staring by now. When I make a fool of myself, I make sure everybody can see it.

Last summer I went to Sears looking for a tool. They did not have it, but I found myself buying a trouble light and an electronic compass for the truck, which I did not need. Impulsive buying is one of the side effects I have while shopping on a stimulant like Adderall. The heat was oppressive that Saturday. When I got off the scooter to load it into the truck, I fell straight backward in a roll-like fall. I was not hurt except for a small abrasion from the pavement. Oh how I love that road rash. My glasses went flying and I could not see them. As I was lying on that flat, hot asphalt, two people came up and asked if they could help. I told them I was fine and would be okay. Then I asked them if they could see my glasses. They looked and could not see them. But lying flat on the pavement I could see them and the man was about to step on them. I yelled for him to stop. But he continued his step. He just barely missed them. I thanked them.

With any fall, getting up is the hardest part. After lying on that hot pavement in the sun I was weaker and did not realize it until I tried to get up. I had to ask the man to lift me at my belt loop to get on the scooter again. Yes, this had to be in the parking lot of Sears on a busy, early Saturday afternoon, but it did not stop there.

They left. I loaded the scooter and started for the cab of the truck. The distance from the tailgate to the door handle is nine feet. For someone with MS, the heat and fatigue extends that to become a perilous, painstaking mile. I was working the top of the truck bed with both hands to progress inches toward the door. A caring couple stopped and asked if I needed help. This time, with little hesitation, I answered, "Yes." I had learned my lesson—maybe for once anyway. The man was wearing a beautiful gold wedding band with a diamond cross embedded in it. I complimented it. He proudly explained his wife had made it. She made jewelry. He added that he was a pastor of Dove Church. I mentioned that during the years I lived in Chicago, I had attended an inner city church. I tried to explain that I went to Moody Church but the fatigue of the MS buried the name Moody somewhere in one of the nasty little plaques lurking in my brain. But I could tell them that I felt the little inner city church was where God wanted me. I still miss it.

When they heard that, they shared an agreeing glance with each other and then asked if they could pray for me. Each placed one hand on me and raised the other waving toward heaven. Then they simultaneously blessed our Lord and prayed for my healing and blessing. Others might not have known what was happening, but the three of us took the opportunity to approach the throne of grace together as brethren. I was delighted and thankful. Remembering this was a busy Saturday afternoon on the Sears front parking lot, I could not help but be amused, imagining what the many onlookers might have been wondering. Fortunately, I did not send them away. I could not lift my legs up into the truck. The pastor graciously lifted each foot up to the floorboard. I was grateful.

Besides falling, another problem for MS-ers is clumsiness. When our boys were young we could count on at least one spill every meal. When we sat down to eat, I would try to arrange glasses to prevent another wet disaster but my attempts failed. I thought the problem would be solved when the children grew older, but then I was having to watch out for clumsy me. The tremors, weakness, vision changes, and unsteadiness were a sure recipe for etiquette transgressions.

About a year ago, Larry Powers and I went to the Kentucky MS Association meeting about the drug Ampyra. When we sat down, a pleasant man was to the right of me in an electric wheelchair. He introduced himself as Charlie Omer. At the end of the meal, I spilled a full glass of cold ice water into his lap. Other folks at the table and I frantically began reaching for the napkins to control the spill, but nearly all the cold water went directly to Charlie's lap. By this time, everyone in the room was staring at me. I heard one male voice saying loudly, "He is trying to drown Charlie." It was very embarrassing. I glanced quickly out the window, hoping to be abducted by space aliens. The lap full of ice-cold water was not enough to quench Charlie's warm smile. He understood. He had MS too.

As noted earlier, a problem MS has given me is bladder control. For several years I had had difficulty in knowing when I needed to void. I would often spend several minutes trying to urinate, only to need to leave and return an hour or so later to try again. But I first clearly associated voiding problems with MS on Mother's Day 2005 when I was running on the treadmill and had to get off quickly to hurry to the bathroom. I wondered what I would do if this happened when I was out running, especially in a 5K race. The urgency gradually worsened and control became more difficult. The running worry never materialized. In a few months I was no longer able to run. When I was outside, I would just find a quick, secluded corner and let it flow. When I was in the truck, I would just have to pull over, if time permitted, find a more protected area, open the door, and, using the door as cover, let the poor bladder do its thing. Sadly the growing pool of yellow liquid below the door was an embarrassing give away.

One time I was at the local pharmacy drive-thru pick up. I felt that urge and began looking around. There was one area in the alley that looked hopeful. It was in full view of the parking lot, which was full, but there were no pharmacy building windows on that side and the vehicles in the parking lot appeared empty. It was public enough to be risky but the best shot. I rushed over and started to step out of the truck, preparing to use the standard door ploy. Suddenly the urgency subsided and I felt I could make it home. As I quickly turned the truck for home, I looked up and saw a Suburban full of kids with their noses pasted against the window waving at me. Of course, every one of them knew me personally.

The problem has worsened and is now associated with bowel control too. When I travel, I wear Depends. That is a difficult thing for a man to do, but it is just that way now. The VA has graciously provided a bedside commode. Now my idea of "going commando" is wearing camouflage print Depends. I wonder if that meets Mary Ellen's criteria for men to not wear buzz kill underwear? Generally I keep a urinal close. It is a good idea to make sure the lid is off the urinal when getting up to void in the middle of the night. Don't ask me how I know.

A common problem for many people with MS is gastrointestinal reflux, commonly called heartburn. This occurs when the stomach acid backs up into the food tube, esophagus, causing a burning pain. I do not know if the incidence is any higher in MS-ers, but I suspect that it could be. There are medical treatments that physicians recommend for this problem, but a universal common treatment is to simply elevate the head of the bed. Most physicians recommend that the patients raise the head of the bed six to eight inches. Occasionally the patient is warned to add elevation slowly. An easy way to accomplish the head of bed elevations is to take small, two-by-four blocks and place them under the head post of the bed. Start with one block under each post. Then in a week or two add another block to each side. Since two by fours are only about an inch and a half high, two blocks would be about three inches in elevation. Four blocks under each head post would be about six inches.

Coincidentally, I found by elevating the head of the bed, it was easier to roll over in the bed. Maneuvering into and on the bed has become a problem for me. I use a light, simple blanket over me. To help sleep, I asked for an electric bed warmer to keep me warm. I can use my cane to situate the cover over my feet. The headboard and the mattress springs serve as grips to help me get into bed and roll over. I will soon be using side rails as well.

Mary Ellen and I have found that being concerned for others is a powerful tool for dealing with the emotional challenges of MS. This concern can be expressed by listening to friends when they talk with me. I try to remember what they are interested in or concerned about and the next time when they call or visit, I ask them about those thoughts. It gives them an opportunity to share with someone who cares and has time to listen. It takes my mind off my problems. Friends are more inclined to talk and have their spirits lifted when sharing their interests and concerns—less so when listening to your same sad tales of woe. My gripes will only make their world less pleasant. But smiling, listening, and being positive makes their world better. It makes mine better too. This causes me to pray for these people and their problems. It is a way of knowing that I can help without ever leaving my confining home. In the absence of work and activities, it is easy for me to let my mind dumpster dive into a trove of unpleasant memories. A rekindled anger toward people I feel have harmed me quickly slithers out of a buried past. The most effective way I have found to handle this renewed anger is to deal with it as I have in the past. That is to pray for those I feel have wronged me. This is a lofty cure that is easier to propose than accomplish. The perceived wounds are often deep enough that I have no desire to pray for them or wish them well in any way. What has helped me overcome that resentment is to pray first for their family, especially their children with whom I have no quarrel. After that, praying for my enemies becomes easier. These prayers bring healing to old cankerous wounds and quickly pull my mind out of the self-pity trash bin.

Enough of me for now; let me turn the MS sharing back to Mary Ellen.

BUT YOU LOOK SO GOOD

My ambulation at present is very good. I have to concentrate on spatial issues and keep my balance because I have a tendency to list to the left and feel like I am walking off cliffs sometimes, but if you saw me at the new Newburgh Walmart, most days you would think all was physically well with me. Unless you catch me walking behind that empty shopping cart from car to entrance, using it for balance and support, and you wonder why?

Have you deduced by now I spend a lot of time at Wally World? It is often my lifeline to the outside social world when I am on a pity party and feel alone and miss work and co-orkers and a fully functioning, fit body. There is always human conversation waiting and that cool fat lady scooter. When those moments arise of late, I hear Dr. Ricky Bob's voice telling me in no uncertain terms to call him for Pete's sake. Sometimes I do. And sometimes I need the public fix only a quick trip to Walmart or Target can supply.

The blending in factor is both good and bad as you can guess. I love not having the "Heh, I have MS" bumper sticker on my forehead for all the world to see. Rick and I have discussed how the placement of a ramp at one's front entrance is like a flashing blue light special at Walmart. "Attention all shoppers. Crippled person inside."

I eventually tell most people I have MS as it arises, but I never like it to be the first thing people know about me. It is something I own and deal with but it is not my identity.

Near the time of my diagnosis of MS, while trying desperately to hang onto my nursing career, I had an incident when my having MS was shared inappropriately. I was at my director of nursing position and had an awesome, spunky, near seventy-year-old

Daughter of Charity nun as my very driven boss, Sister Anthony Prugger. Because the ranks among Catholic sisters were dwindling, the once all religious management team had wisely been layered with lay people like myself who were educated to the mission statement of the Daughters and could lead with the same goals in mind. Daughters of Charity is an international apostolic order of sisters who take annual vows and report to God first and secondly to their own governing body, not the bishop as other orders. That makes for some very strong religious women with business savvy to rival any corporation-running big businesses worldwide. I felt privileged to be a part of that for four brief years.

Now Sister Anthony ran a tight ship at Seton Residence on the far west side of Evansville and was a no nonsense gal with a social worker background. She expected much of me managing her nursing unit of forty-six nursing staff and sixty-four nuns scattered throughout three units. We had a St. Elizabeth Ann Seton infirmary, a St. Louise de Marillac assisted living, and a St. Catherine Laboure independent living area. Tempered with my boss' high expectations was a motherly concern on a daily basis. My diagnosis of MS was difficult for her to accept. She grieved for me.

In trying to support my ever-growing needs and adaptations, she wanted to make my load lighter and told our contracted pharmacy company out of Henderson, Kentucky, that I had multiple sclerosis. My belief is that she did so for them to have empathy for my irregular work schedule and challenges and for them to be nice to me. Bless her heart for the love behind her actions. But, "What the hell was she thinking?" quickly follows that. The sequence of those two thoughts was reversed back in the 90s when all this occurred.

I found out the pharmacy people knew I had MS when in the middle of a drug order clarification the rep on the phone with me stated, "Oh, and Sister Anthony told me. I am sorry you are dealing with MS. Let us know if we can do something with our business dealings that might make things easier. I feel so bad for you."

A hidden camera in my office that day would have captured red fireworks shooting from atop my head about then. I was furious. I resented the fact that something so personal and intimate had been shared with other professionals I worked with. Hemorrhoids would have been a more acceptable topic of discussion. The invasion of privacy and the possible loss of respect for my nurse management capabilities cut deeply. The cut was my first MS experience of feeling true pity. I did not like it in any way.

I tried to calm myself before I confronted Sister Anthony with my anger and hurt. I was dumbfounded with all of it and could not for the life of me understand how such a thing could happen. At the time it was so private to me and I had not learned to accept MS or own it in any way. I was a newbie.

Sister Anthony was quick to appreciate my hurt and the inappropriateness of sharing my medical history without my consent. She apologized and assured me it would not happen again and it didn't. We had a solid working relationship with mutual respect and moved on easily from that incident in the workplace.

I wish I could say I personally moved on easily but that would be a lie. My acceptance of my diagnosis of multiple sclerosis grew healthier with time but looking back I feel like I put on my shield of armor that day and even though I loosen it at times, it never comes off. Self-preservation is a mighty fuel in battle. And however rosy or positive we try to paint living with MS, survival instinct remains. We are warriors and do battle on a daily basis.

Everyone has a picture in their head of what a person with MS looks like and it usually has some crippled aspect to it. I want the world to see Mary Ellen first and later understand that I live with MS and it is a part of me but certainly not all of me. I know how lucky I am that I can often pull off the camouflage for a bit. Not everyone with MS has that luxury. Rick does not.

With talking about camouflage, besides Rick's crazy commando drawers, I can't help but think of the hated phrase I often hear from well-meaning family, friends, and acquaintances. "Oh, but you look so good." And I think, "Hell yes, if I was feeling bad I'd be at home in bed and you wouldn't see me. You only see me, dipstick, when I am doing well and can be out and about. Duh."

Or better yet, I gotta love the other person's comment that follows the question of how I am doing. "Well, it's good you don't have any real problems. I can see you're doing great." I hate that comment and for a split second I hate that person. I know it is ignorance forming those words that spill so easily from their well-intentioned lips. Or maybe it is fear that the tables could be turned and they could have "that disease." But comments like that hurt like a sword slicing into my belly. It places a second of doubt that perhaps I have nothing wrong with me and I am just a whiny butt imagining all sorts of ailments I don't even have. This happens less often these days but still hits and hurts. Even carefully selected words from a person interacting with me can have that doubtful inflection of speech that belays what they are truly thinking.

In the same vein, if I decide to trust the person and answer their inquiry more openly it can still backfire. Like if I mention forgetfulness or difficulty concentrating and their quick response is, "Oh, Mary Ellen, I do the same thing. It comes with age. We all feel that way." They have in three short sentences dismissed my even having MS. They are telling me it's not so bad and it's all my imagination that it is a true problem that warrants mentioning as a symptom.

I want to scream at those moments. "Shut up! It is not the same thing! Do you have to rack your brain and figure out what one fourth of a cup of water means on the back of a cake mix box? Do you read it five times? Do you search to figure out if you should be looking at ounces or cups in the red print on the side of the glass measuring cup, and oh, by the way, why is the print red and should you pay attention to the color? Does it mean something I should know already? Do you wonder if it makes a difference that you grabbed the glass measuring cup instead of the white plastic? Do you spend time trying to decide if the sequence of steps is significant or not? Like that tickling in the back of your brain that reminds you something is supposed to be added later at the same time as flour stuff and then you think no, maybe not, because it is something dry and powdery and this is liquid? Do you rack your brain to remember if you already put the water in? Do you question if you are smart enough to make a boxed cake mix?" I am college-educated and I have just spent five minutes trying to figure out what one-fourth of a cup of water means on a cardboard box. If you do that too, then yes, we are the same. It is just age.

Whew! As you have guessed, the topic of being misunderstood and dismissed can get my panties in a wad. Early in my diagnosis it made me cry. Now it makes me "madder than a wet hen" as Dad would say.

So back to my walkabout tales. When I walk along a sidewalk, Roger and I have an unspoken rhythm and technique. He falls along beside me on my left side. This is because of my tendency to sidestep in that direction. It happens more if I turn my head to look at something or make eye contact with him. I have a fear of falling into traffic because of my imbalance and dizziness. So if we are on a very narrow path and a stumble would throw me into traffic, Roger will automatically go to the protective side without giving it thought and I adjust if it is my right instead of preferred left flank. Crooking my left arm into his bent right arm creates a comfortable cane-like support. He is a mere inch and a half taller than me so it makes for an easy match with our pace of a leisurely walk. I like using him as my cane and he is always stylin' so it's even better than one of my favorite African-detailed canes.

I pay attention to what shoes I have on. If it is a gym shoe, I know the traction is strong and I must think about keeping my step high so as not to catch my left toe related to the minor foot drop tendency. If my shoe has the slightest heel I focus more on my balance. For several years I wore no heels at all and only rubber-soled shoes so as to not slip or fall. I'd had several embarrassing falls in public.

I credit Tysabri for letting me again enjoy high heels. If I plan the time and energy expenditure well, I can pull it off and it makes me happy. Another addition back to my style routine is eyeliner. My tremors were too bad for years and I could not apply eyeliner without looking like a clown. I grieved for that loss a long time. Again, I often handle the major stuff better than the small things stolen from me by the thief called multiple sclerosis.

In regards to my use of assistive devices when walking, several years back I never left home without my cane in tow. This was whether I was using it inside the house or not. Being outside on unpredictable terrain is scary business and can be dangerous. I would also carry a spare in the car trunk in case I forgot and needed the assistance of a cane.

Early on, Roger and I would be heading to a Ziliak family function that consists of the immediate ninety or so people when just Grandma, kids, grandkids and greats are invited. Festivities often take place around a big lake on the family farm in Haubstadt. The site is overlooking a west view of farmland, silos, and the home place and sits high on a hill. I attempted to capture the beauty of the spot at sunset in an oil entitled, "Up at the Lake," and it hung for years in Roger's office. Now it hangs in our living room. Amenities at the lake include a fancy outhouse, fishing, shelter, storage shed, playground equipment, fire pit, and a sanded beach and dock for swimming or paddling.

Heading to the car for the Z gatherings would usually involve some angst as to whether I bring a cane or not. It was a borderline call those days. I had more accentuated flare-ups and the pasture like setting was rough and bumpy.

My family was adjusting to my changes related to MS. So was I. I remember feeling like anyone I saw those days would look at the cane first and reels of a horror show would immediately start playing in their head. Maybe that happened, maybe it didn't. Roger told me it was my imagination and if I needed the cane, just take it already. Easy for him to say with no cane dangling from his hand.

My Ziliak family was accepting of me and my changes with MS symptoms, but they were new at it just like I was. We were flying by the seat of our pants. It is natural for someone to briefly stare at a cane when it is not always attached to a person.

Then the sticky part happens. Does that person acknowledge its use or ignore it and act like everyone walks with a dangling three-foot piece of wood attached to a hand. I always appreciate honesty and directness at those moments with a comment like, "Using a cane. Feeling worse today, Mary?" Brother-in-law Wayne would say that and was always comfortable with the direct yet caring approach comment. I appreciated his candor and voiced concern. He saw me; he really saw me. That is monumental.

On occasion no acknowledging comment is fine if the person is fine seeing me with the cane. MS can be the elephant in the room and even with best intentions of both parties can result in nervous shuffling of feet and a quick exit comment.

I was at such a bad spot back then. It falls into the time I thought I was handling everything well and instead I was really embarrassed to have a cane, felt like an imposter, and was furious I had to deal with MS. I hated it! I hated the unfairness. I hated all the deaths of Mary Ellen pieces.

I once had an elephant in the master bathroom of my two-bedroom apartment at Kenzi Estates. It was not your typical, wrinkly gray, droopy skinned kind. It was three-legged; shiny, jet black; and was topped with a wide leather-covered bicycle seat and it left no big poop piles in its wake. Oh, and caster-type rolling wheels at the end of the three-curved wide legs lent the appearance of a big spider, plucked bald with a very weak scare factor. Really, this monstrosity sat in the bathroom Roger and I shared for about three years.

A card-playing friend of ours was over one night and jokingly piped up, "Heh, Rog, what's with the funky sex toy on wheels in your bathroom? You gotta explain that one to me, man." I love our friends.

Now to appreciate the massiveness and intrusiveness of this rolling novelty, one must take in the bathroom view. We had a two-sinked, long, narrow bathroom off our bedroom that was backed by the length of a walk-in closet. It was a good size, especially for an apartment, but it allowed one-way traffic with just enough room width to push by the vanity top and the black elephant. So Roger and I plus the elephant spider were mighty tight in there. Add the stress of two humans bustling about to get ready for church or a dinner out with friends and you had a recipe for marital fireworks every time.

If you haven't figured out the true identity of the black elephant, let me explain. I worked with vocational rehabilitation on several occasions with making accommodations to my ever-changing needs because of MS. They were an excellent resource for me and kept me working a bit longer because of the great advice and adaptations they wisely offered. Keep them in mind instead of trying to reinvent the MS wheel for yourself.

Physical and occupational therapy assessed my problem of standing in one spot too long, which caused great leg pain, back pain, and a weak feeling that sometimes forced me to sit on the ground or even the sidewalk. My tolerance for walking was greater than idling in one spot. The tension of my muscles in a standing upright position was a big problem for me every day, even the really good ones.

Equipment to minimize those standing in one spot problems, along with the strain of getting up and down a lot when seated and trying to retrieve something, was ordered. Thus the black elephant was adopted into our family. It was a tall, adjustable, rolling stool. It stood tall enough that I barely had to squat to seat myself and then I could roll in front of the bathroom sink, mirror, kitchen sink, kitchen counter, dining room table, etc. I could reach for items by a quick roll to the right or left or back or forward. The caster wheels glided easily. It required a bit of a balancing act, but I got the hang of it eventually and it helped to some degree. If I'd had counters that were opened underneath and could have placed my legs under, it could have been ideal. But with my long legs I eventually found my reaching over to the counter gave me a backache. Sometimes I would open the cabinet doors under the sink and place my feet on the lip edge of the cabinet wood bottom. But even this eventually was not helpful enough to continue.

So Roger, me, and the three children—who were technically adults by then and in and out of the house—tried to get used to this eyesore burden of help. And it was one pain in the butt adjustment. The wheelbase of this thing spanned about three feet so it took up a lot of space. It was a magnet for feet passing by and often tripped even healthy limbs and caused some nasty shin scrapes or wipeouts onto the floor. We all learned to hate it, but none so much as my dear husband.

I began to notice Roger kicking the stool across the bathroom floor or across the span of the kitchen. He would curse under his breath, thinking I didn't hear. When I would point this out, he denied it. Roger is such a gentle man that this stool kicking was out of character for him. The more he kicked and denied being angry and kicking, the more I was convinced he was mad at me and the inconvenience and pain I brought into his life and our household because of the MS. I hated being a burden and now my chair was a burden too. What was I to do?

I imagined that Roger really hated me and not the chair. It made no sense that he was losing his cool over something as innocent as a three-legged stool. I cried at the helplessness I felt. I cried; Roger fumed.

I felt the need to right the wrong regardless of any benefit the chair might provide so I removed the chair from the bathroom where it had been kept, in front of my side of the vanity. Problem solved, right? No. Roger, being the all-unobservant male, meant he didn't notice or acknowledge I had acquiesced. That ticked me off. I felt I made a sacrifice and he didn't even care.

I eventually brought up the chair absence and asked what he thought of its removal. He shrugged like he didn't care. Maybe he didn't. I had so many mixed emotions that I had to talk about this and it ended in a stupid argument over the pros and cons of a big elephant spider in our bathroom.

Some days later we both came to what we thought was the heart of the problem. In simple Ziliak Pop Psychology 101, we decided that the offensive chair represented multiple sclerosis. We both hated it; we wanted to kick it aside and sometimes act like it was not one big metal inconvenience in our bathroom, in our lives. Yet I spent time and energy and learned to ride it and not fall off. The chair was ugly, forced upon us, did not fit our family or lifestyle, and we wanted it out but could not really take that step.

This led to some heartfelt discussion of our joint anger at the MS we were both living with. My having the diagnosis of MS meant he too had a spousal diagnosis of MS that was just as devastating and uprooting. We hated the multiple sclerosis, but we had to that point never let ourselves say it together out loud. When we did, it was very cathartic and healing.

The three-legged elephant spider eventually made its final swan song to the attic above our garage. It was moved because the benefits were no longer there for me, not because either of us was kicking the hell out of it. But I feel Roger and I both learned a valuable lesson about addressing the elephant in the room in a timely manner when we were able to see the elephant clearly. I believe all family units dealing with MS have similar moments. "It is what it is," as my shirt notes or as Ricky Bob and I coined, "With MS, the little things are big."

CHILI SOUP IN A SKILLET

Esther Klenck always made some good tasting chili soup. Her tidiness gene factored into her food preparation so she mashed her red beans and ground beef with a potato masher so it was somewhat pureed. The tasty balance of spices and comfort was still ever present, along with the obligatory one teaspoon of sugar that Mom swore made everything taste better and took the sharp acid taste away. Every spoonful was mouth-watering and smelling it cooking is a fond childhood memory.

Mom also called it chili soup, never just chili. I thought everyone called it that. Only when my smart-pantsed son-in-law teased me, saying chili and soup together was redundant, did I question the political correctness of Mom and the whole Klenck family in regards to this gourmet treat we relished any day of the winter week except non-meat Fridays before Vatican II.

I taught the phrase "chili soup" to my children and they later dropped it for "chili" when their high school friends teased them also. Most days it is still chili soup for me. I figure if you say "vegetable soup" and not simply "vegetable" doesn't that prove my theory? Ah well. I will save the rest of that debate to go along with my son Josh's childhood debate of how many Ding Dongs did his little sisters really eat beyond their fair share.

Little did I know as a child that chili soup would take on a medical connotation in adulthood for my family and me. Roger and I experienced a moment of pure clarity one day in our own kitchen on Galleon Drive in McCutchanville—a small north end community of Evansville. We lived there four years. It was our transitional patio home with a loft that proved to be a mountain for me to climb.

One cold, wintery Sunday afternoon on Galleon Drive I was really dragging ass. That is the technical nursing phrase I use for a bad, tired, flared MS day. Roger assumed cooking duties and made the good call of chili soup for supper. As Sundays usually evolve in our household, we ate casually that day whenever we felt like it. That is an empty nester luxury we both enjoy.

When I arose from the couch saying I was hungry, he called to me from an adjoining room, "Soup is simmering on the stove." I walked to the kitchen looking for the large soup pot on the stove. I didn't see it. I called back to Roger, "Hey, I thought you said you made chili soup."

"I did, it's on the stove."

"No it's not. I don't see it."

"Sure, on the stove."

About then I saw a deep skillet with a lid on the stove. *That's not it,* I thought. *It's a skillet not a pan for soup.* I opened the lid and saw dark, chunky liquid and it smelled good, but I knew it wasn't chili soup. I didn't know what it was. That was weird. Was Roger jerking with me?

Roger walked into the kitchen and said, "Yeah, you got it. I told you it was there."

"No, you told me you made chili."

A look of confusion crossed his face the same time anger crossed mine. I wondered why he was joking with me when he knew I felt like crap that day and it hurt to be standing so long in front of the stove.

I felt a twinge of doubt and concern that escalated into full-blown panic. I had a feeling of stupidity with this crazy discussion of soup, no soup. Roger lifted the lid off the skillet and said, "Here it is."

I still looked at the soup for several seconds before recognition registered. Then I broke down and bawled like a baby. The cognitive problems of my MS were bad that day along with the fatigue. For some reason my brain could not register that what I was actually seeing before me was chili soup because it was not in a deep pan like my brain was used to registering in my long-term recall. Soup in a skillet made no sense and there was no automatic identification that day because of the flare-up.

After some tearful explanation, Roger understood my cognitive dilemma. He had quickly grabbed a skillet for making the soup because it was handy and the usual pan was dirty.

Then he became sad and his shoulders slumped. He hated when I called myself stupid and I did that day. He would sternly correct me with, "Quit that. You are not stupid. The MS just makes it harder for you to figure out things. You are not stupid! I did not marry a stupid woman. I hate when you say that."

At that moment we could appreciate the tension often felt on flare-up days when I was more anxious about my poor comprehension. Moments like those often ended in heated arguments because neither of us recognized the problem for what it was. Multiple sclerosis. Pure and not so simple.

Since that day, when Roger and I are discussing a cognitive challenge related to my MS, we will refer to the challenge as, "Chili soup in a skillet." It is all encompassing and says it all for us.

The chili soup in a skillet phenomenon was even further clarified with a later discovery related to working on our household budget. Over almost forty years of marriage, Roger and I have sort of taken turns with who is the primary financial guru in our family. It always depended on who had more time to keep up with the bills in a timely manner.

My nursing career has been everything from full time plus a part-time job to leave of absence followed by part time with the arrival of a new child. Nursing often provides flexibility of work hours. Of course when working on the "Care Unit," which was a one month inpatient substance abuse unit at the hospital, my head nurse once called me a refrigerator nurse because of my fluctuation of part-time and full-time status. I wanted to slug him at the time.

I struggled to make wise choices throughout my career with family needs factored in as a big priority. Who did he think he was making such a derogatory statement? A refrigerator nurse is one who works only enough hours to buy herself a new refrigerator. It implies a substandard respect for the profession and substandard professional performance and advancement.

Years later I learned my head nurse at the time eventually left nursing to seek a career as a Catholic monk. Good choice. He was less likely to get hit in the face with his asinine remarks if he had Friar Tuck's brown garb on, topped with the baldy, fringed hairdo. A brown dress was fitting for that poop head. He was a super smart guy and I respected his nursing skills greatly, but his people skills left me a bit wanting.

In regards to budget work, Roger also had work commitments over the years ranging from two jobs at a time to being part time to no job. We had no sexist assignment for who paid our bills so it varied with our needs and free time. Roger now pays all our bills because it is so much easier and more accurate than I am capable of providing because of the multiple sclerosis. The story I am about to share had Roger already transitioning into that role of full time, permanent budget guy in our household.

Roger and I were in the habit for years of reviewing our budget on Saturday mornings. Sometimes it was a weekly occurrence but more times monthly. More and more I was having a hard time making sense of what he was telling me and showing me. He knows I need a visual for everything so he would talk about the budget with a yellow legal pad in hand with numbers jotted all over it. Even the legal pad wasn't helping much and in the frustration of trying to make sense of what he was telling me I often became very snippy and tearful.

One Saturday morning we were seated next to each other on the couch and I was feeling stupid and angry. I just could not follow the information Roger was showing me on that legal pad. It was Greek to me. Finally the chili soup in a skillet light bulb went on. Bright, bright! I could not make sense of the numbers and notes on the legal pad because they were scattered about, not in columns or rows. That is how Roger's brain works, fast and driven. The notations were sometimes sideways on ruled paper and my MS brain could not follow any order to grasp what they represented. There was too much unnecessary stimulation like the speaker at the nurses' station years before in the hospital. The slanted, random location of words and numbers made it impossible for me to translate sensibly and accurately. Bingo! This was chili soup in a skillet big time.

Roger and I both felt relieved to finally understand why our talking budget was such a stressful chore cognitively. My MS brain merely required more order and spatial balance for better comprehension of written information.

From then on Roger would write his notes for me in straight lines, rows, and columns. There were no longer slanted numbers or words all over the page. Many times he would just print out his notes and that made for even better recognition for me. Cursive writing is much more difficult for me to make sense of than printed word. I now ask for printed instructions and info when in meetings or medical settings. The other person thinks I am nuts but I don't care. It is an easy adaption to make in some instances and goes a long way to hanging onto some independence for me. The need for printed word was a major discovery for me that I like to share with other people living with MS.

And if you haven't already appreciated the significance of Roger in my life, I have failed miserably in talking to you. I am the luckiest woman in the world to have Roger as my husband, lover, and best friend. He will do anything for me and at the same time will not smother me with too much of a caretaker role.

Now do not assume this balance happened over night. Our learning curve was huge in adjusting to the changes MS brought into our marriage relationship. We started out thinking we had a handle on things and maybe even a false sense of cockiness because we had already adjusted to a child, Liza, with a chronic disease—juvenile rheumatoid arthritis. Granted, it did give us a leg up, but we could not fully appreciate how different it would be as a married couple versus parent and child.

Anger factored in heavily. Roger and I grieved for a long time for the loss of the me without MS—the me that did not need numbers and words in columns, neat rows, and printed word. The me that could juggle family, full-time work, and a healthy dose of play. We grieved my loss of freedom in everyday tasks and we grieved the loss of our easy relationship as a long-married couple. Simplicity gave way to complexities.

We often strained to contain the anger and hate we felt. Although we would argue with each other and be hurtful with mean words, the anger and hate was often toward the MS, not each other. That clarity makes a big difference and provides peace in its wisdom.

Counseling became a comfortable resource we often turned toward and still do so. Multiple sclerosis puts a very heavy burden on any marriage and I think we went into this believing we could be an exception, like we were too smart or too in love to have to get dirty with an army crawl in this skirmish. I now doubt any relationship can become healthy with a chronic illness without first getting very down and dirty and muddy and scratched with barbed wire. MS is humbling and leaves many scars.

BOTTOM OF THE SOUP POT

The charred beans stuck to the bottom of my soup pot include more MS symptoms like "weeble wobble syndrome." That encompasses poor walking balance and stumbling side to side like a bobbing Fischer Price toy. I look drunk—somewhat like Rick appeared at Beth's graduation ceremony. My family knows what I mean when I say, "I'm weeble wobbly today." I use a cane or grab onto a friend, family member, or nearby furniture for balance.

Weakness in my legs can mean stairs present themselves like mountain climbing. Those days I do a hand-over-hand maneuver to pull myself forward with the handrail and lifting the leg to the next rung. We once moved from an upstairs apartment to a lower one because of stairs. I felt trapped inside on days when I could not maneuver the stairs because of difficulty scaling them. Staying inside a lot added a problem of isolation from the world on top of the difficulty doing stairs. I used a chair lift at a prior home because the family room was downstairs and I was isolated from family in the evening and from the laundry room to do wash. Loneliness and feelings of abandonment are often a factor in the emotional head games people with MS face.

Numbness and tingling is most prominent in my arms, especially my left. My arm feels heavy, asleep, and I like to rub it or hold it tight to my chest for relief. The numbness can also be in my lips and tongue, especially when my head and tongue vibrate rhythmically on the bed pillow after a long day. Another head sensation involves feeling like I have a hair stuck to my cheek and I can't brush it away. Looking in the mirror, there is never a real hair there.

My arm strength is poor to handle heavy milk jugs, open restaurant doors, or to transfer wet clothes from the washer to the dryer or dry clothes to the basket. The result is swinging a jug from fridge to counter and bumping random objects, backing my body into heavy doors to open them, and transferring clothes a piece at a time. It also means sometimes I can hold a grandbaby in my lap but can't reach out safely to place the infant into the crib or retrieve them later. And family members put roasts, turkeys, or any heavy pan into the oven.

Swallowing can be difficult with solids or liquids. Sometimes I choke on my saliva in the middle of the night, have coughing and esophageal spasms, bolting upright, gasping for air, and scaring both Roger and myself. The following day I will drink with my head tilted forward a bit so as to have less chance of aspiration. I used to instruct my little old lady patients in the hospital on this technique. Guess I'm the little old lady now and less the nurse.

These random beans in my burning pot of chili can be brief sensations or more prolonged in a flare-up lasting four days to four months. And as I've mentioned before, exacerbations can be very out of the blue, unexpected, or follow stress of some kind. For years I would have a February and September flare-up on the heels of a sinus infection. The stress on my body could set me up for a worsening of MS symptoms—sometimes mild, and sometimes putting me in bed a few days. The stress can be physical or emotional.

I have no proof, but I have always believed my worsening symptoms shortly before my diagnosis of MS were related to a super large emotional trauma I had involving a family member. I found my nephew Rick, whom I felt very close to, in his home after he had committed suicide with a gunshot wound to the head. The bloody image and aftermath of that horrific event was devastating to me and resulted in some PTSD and a leave of absence from work. I include this not for shock effect but because the extreme stress on me had to factor into my following with extreme MS symptoms shortly after the suicide. Like I said, I can't prove it, but I believe if ever emotional stress is thought to be a factor in a flare-up, Rick's suicide qualified.

The worsening of random symptoms will always remind me of my lack of control due to this disease. When I am weak, Roger or my kids cut up my meat for me, put straws in my drinks, give me lighter weight glasses, and supply me with a big tablespoon to compensate for the tremors that fling my food about.

During a flare-up, bathing is put on hold or I do a sponge bath. Standing is too taxing and sitting in a tub means I cannot get myself up and out of the tub afterward. I gave up tub baths permanently about six years ago.

I had several years when I could get into the shower and sit on the stool and bathe, but I could not keep my arms raised to wash my hair. They were too weak and painful. Those times, Roger and I would coordinate his being there when I showered so he could do the step to wash my hair or dry me off. Some days he washed my entire body and rinsed me off with a handheld showerhead we installed for convenience. He later dried me.

This may sound kind of sexy and hot; it is only embarrassing and childlike. It puts both of us in unexpected and awkward parent-child roles and neither of us like it. This ritual expanded our wedding vows to include, "Thou shalt love, honor, and bathe."

Bathing challenges prompted me to incorporate some energy-saving techniques like lightweight, easy-to-open shampoo bottles; spraying oil onto a wet body; and putting on a fluffy bathrobe instead of drying and applying lotion. I eventually gave up the assumption that I must have a daily shower. It is nice but now a luxury. On bad days a shower can mean resting flat twenty minutes beforehand, pacing the shower with all the above tricks, resting flat another ten with robe and wet hair in a towel, then figuring out if there was energy to dress—be it standing or sitting on a stool or asking family to dress me.

Again, the general public has no way of knowing the details of my daily life and the assistance I require on bad MS days.

How could they? A cane or a wheelchair can prompt someone to note a physical challenge, but my use of those devices is sporadic. Wheelchairs are mostly reserved for amusement park outings and I've already given you the hit and miss use of my canes. Visuals like cane, wheelchair, or Walmart scooter can evoke empathy or the less-desired sympathy from a bystander. But what happens on bad MS days when I am out in public but don't have the benefit of an assistive device visual? Well, I can explain it better with my own Sears story. Isn't it ironic Rick and I both have memorable Sears parking lot stories? It must be the happening place.

About five years into my MS journey after diagnosis, Roger and I were at good old Sears Roebuck and Company. I was dressed in a casual slack set, Roger in a navy blazer and khakis. He was at the end of an insurance sales workday and he picked me up so we could check out a treadmill sale at Sears. We had the crazy idea we would use one faithfully, get fit, and not turn the equipment into a coat rack if we could only find the perfect match of treadmill to human. At this time in my life I was very fatigued all the time, had a lot of trouble with balance, and was using a handicap placard because I had great difficulty walking far enough in and out of a store.

So Roger and I parked in a nearby handicap parking spot behind Sears so as to be near the treadmills, which were located inside the back door next to the tools and paint. When I got out of the car and grabbed Roger's arm for support and balance on the uneven blacktop, I vaguely remember spotting a couple walking near us, about our age, a man and a woman.

We went inside and Roger got on the treadmill and was checking out the options when the same lady I saw out of the corner of my eye approached us. The man I thought to be her husband by the look on his face stood far behind her like he did not want to be an accomplice in whatever this lady was embarking upon.

The exchange went something like this.

She asked Roger directly, "Are you a doctor?"

Roger, with a surprised look, answered, "No, why do you ask?"

I, myself, already had my hair standing on end on the nape of my neck. My asshole radar was also beeping loudly. "Danger, Will Rogers. Danger, Will Rogers." I knew what was coming by the tone of this woman's voice.

She sarcastically replied with southern belle daintiness, "Oh, I was just wondering because I saw you and this woman get out of your car in a handicapped spot and I was wondering why you parked there."

Roger stammered in his gentlemanly reply and mumbled, "Uh, no, we're looking at treadmills…"

I quickly interrupted and got right in this woman's face and sternly told her, "Not that it is any of your damn business, but I have MS and that is why we parked there! Do you have a problem with that?"

About this time, a man's arm appeared from the background and firmly grabbed onto said bitch's elbow and pulled her away with, "Let's go." Smart move on the man's part. I felt bad enough and was mad enough for me and any other person with MS who had to unjustly deal with the passive-aggressive know-it-alls of the world that I was ready to deck the broad. How dare she lay a guilt trip on me. How dare she assume I was fine because I was only walking slowly, hanging onto Roger instead of using my cane that day. How dare she assume the role of moral spokesperson for the whole world and make me feel bad because the luck of the draw gave me multiple sclerosis!

Looking back on that moment, I add to my fury the idiocy of her thinking a fit, male doctor had the right to park there but not me. But do you get the whole empathy versus hostility response I refer to now?

Roger and I must also take into consideration that a handicap license plate on a car that Roger may see insurance clients with elicits a similar response when he drives up, even if not parking in a handicap spot. The whole handicap designation is one big can of worms an entire family copes with when one person has MS.

I now have secondary, progressive MS, which just means my flare-ups are usually less pronounced. With time, I gradually lose ground with my nerve function and it can be very subtle. The unpredictability of all my MS symptoms was a very difficult concept for me to accept at first. I wanted to know what I was doing wrong and how I could understand it better, maybe even prevent it. The nurse in me kept trying to figure out the whys and wherefores. I drove myself a little nuts trying to figure out if maybe I did too much or not enough or wasn't taking good enough care of myself or babying myself too much or not praying enough or being too big a sinner. I tried to explain it all somehow and got nowhere fast. There is no explanation for any multiple sclerosis path. Like I said before, it is a yellow brick road.

I used to be even more of a control freak back in my early MS days than people tell me I am now. My career as a nurse manager lent itself well to being in control and having things neat and orderly. I liked that. Then MS gave me a healthy dose of reality as far as control goes. I am in control of nothing! Absolutely nothing! Gratitude is extended to MS for that one small kernel of smarts. It is extremely humbling knowledge and I believe the insight has made me a better person by losing some of my arrogance. Heck, I was arrogant enough to think I wasn't arrogant at all. You know what I mean, Vern?

Recent bad days include much fatigue; weakness; blurred, double vision; headaches; and messed up cognitive skills. A few of the above stuck beans get scraped off the bottom of the pot now and then and end up in my bowl of chili soup. I am better at accepting the burned beans and so are my friends and family who put up with cancelled engagements and special requests of help. It's all okay. Not always good, but most days okay. Thank you, God.

NIGHT TERRORS

To wrap up the seemingly never-ending list of my multiple sclerosis symptoms, I must cover one other aspect of my personal freak show. Now I know I told you not to feel like a freak with your symptoms, but my magic wand has not worked so well on this particular symptom I have listed as "night terrors." I confess I am still working out the freak factor on this baby. The whole freaky, scary, Rosemary's baby appearance of this misfit.

Whew-ee! How do I adequately describe this? These episodes started happening about three years into my diagnosis. Maybe if I give you an example of one you might best understand.

In the middle of the night, about three in the morning, I woke up paralyzed. I knew I was awake, but I could not speak or move my legs or arms. A splitting headache bounded inside my skull and the urge to urinate was strong but with no incontinence.

When I awoke, it was after having an intensely scary nightmare that involved me walking around a bombed war zone, feeling pain and fear, and being very bloody because I was holding my severed head under my arm pit, against my torso. I remember wondering why I could still walk and breathe with my head being chopped off.

In the nightmare, I could see my surroundings, which entailed a Ferris wheel with other ghoulish people in varying degrees of agony with and without their heads. Some of these people I recognized as family members and others were strangers. A line of train cars on a track with people inside were in the background.

The nightmare made no sense to me, even inside the dream, but I had a horrible sense of doom and panic and death.

When I awoke from this scary nightmare, I had a split second of safe relief until I realized I could not move or speak. Stroke was the first thing to pop into my head, but I was too young for a stroke, wasn't I?

I had to get Roger's attention and help and do it quickly. I concentrated hard on getting my body to move and my voice to work so I could wake Roger at my side in bed. He always sleeps to my left.

So I am lying in bed, scared to death, awake, and unable to move at 3:00 a.m. Within minutes, which seemed like hours, I was able to eventually move my left index finger. But that didn't help because I could not lift my arm to poke Roger with my left index finger. Then I wiggled my left pinkie and was able to make skin contact with Roger and tickle the side of his right leg. Roger is a back sleeper. He did not stir. My fingernail wasn't long enough to be of any irritation for him.

Eventually I was able to move my left hand to poke him with my index finger about the same time I was able to mumble inaudibly. It was a sort of half-groan half-whine that escaped my dry lips.

Between the nagging finger poking him in his side and the moaning wife, Roger woke up. Now, Roger is deaf without his hearing aids in to the point he cannot hear a loud, ringing alarm clock at the side of his head. Our routine every morning is his alarm goes off and I wake him up. So when Roger woke with my prodding finger, he expected me to do some kind of sign language that is our routine and he was confused why I didn't pantomime something or scream a communication. I remember the panic and fear in his eyes when they looked into mine and he realized I could not move or talk with understandable words.

Roger scooped his arms under me and tried to get me into a seated position. That didn't work. He kept asking, "What should I do? Mary, what do you want me to do?"

Slowly I began moving more. I nodded my head side to side with a "No." I was now able to flop my arms around but not able to do much deliberate motion with my hand like a grasp. Then the language gradually reappeared for me. I told Roger I had a bad dream and he should hold me. He did until my full movement returned and I could fill him in on everything. But first I had him help me walk to the bathroom to urinate. I thought I would wet myself. The urge was so strong.

Sitting was hard and walking took all of Roger's support. I drug my feet forward with each step and felt like Herman Munster clomping about. Stroke still flashed in my head but the nurse in me knew it didn't quite fit the presentation.

The next five minutes or so had all my movements returning to almost normal. I was left oriented but very weak all over. It was like I was in the middle of a really bad MS flare-up and the following day also looked that way.

Looking back, I remember being scared to death, both of us, but after the initial scare was passed we sort of shrugged and thought, "Well, one more weird MS thing. Wonder what caused that one. Think it will happen again?" Roger and I had come to expect the unexpected with multiple sclerosis and this freak show undoubtedly fell into that category.

Not the next day, but on the next scheduled visit I told my neurologist about the night terror and paralysis I'd had. He seemed to shrug it off to something unrelated like my dream pattern. What I call night terrors continued intermittently for years and still do occur very infrequently, perhaps twice a year now.

On a recent visit to the Cancer Center for my IV, Rick and I discussed this phenomenon. Rick agreed with me that the bad nightmares with sleep paralysis could well be explained with MS plaques being in a specific area of the brain—the reticular activating system. This area normally shuts down muscles during sleep. An MS person could wake up from the dream a little early when that spot in the brain has not flipped the switch yet to allow movement. This normal phenomenon allows us to dream of running through a wheat field without our body actually moving. Neither of us has read any literature that addresses this issue with MS. Regardless, night terrors are a reality for me. They scare me, and it is just something I have learned to deal with along the years.

AND THE BEAT GOES ON

La dee da di dee…la dee da di diiiiie… I have always loved Cher. How can you not love Cher? Beautiful, chiseled, an ethnic nose worn proudly even though it borders on Abe Lincoln proportion and angle. Of course, Cher's profile begs to have an ornate, multicolored, feathered headdress top it off with Native American pride. It does not beg to be tossed for heads or tails.

And her voice, that warm, caramel topping that oozes thick and sultry and with your eyes closed gives you a hint of pause to decide if its owner is male or female. She is such a great, jumbled-up bag of contrasts and still falls out said bag looking sexy and so confident.

And when they were together, I loved Sonny and Cher. Love daggers were definitely thrown from both sets of eyes with those two. At least it appeared that way on their TV show and other public appearances. And I do not want any argument to think differently.

I never saw the two in concert, but I did see Cher solo shortly after their well-publicized breakup. Cher in concert was one of the very few concerts I attended in Evansville. She holds the ranks with John Denver in the round and Three Dog Night. One really is the loneliest number.

Thinking of those couple of hours at Roberts Stadium, my immediate flashback is of this statuesque, raven-haired beauty pacing the stage, flipping her waist-length poker-straight hair back across her shoulder and bare back of the sequenced silver gown. At the exact same time of the hair flipping, she would give the all-knowing put down yet flirtatious smirk to Sonny. But Sonny was no longer her sidekick. The stage held only her. The smirk thrown to the audience did not hold the same effect. I felt uncomfortable for Cher. She had not yet polished her solo act and I felt bad for her. I sensed her humanness in that moment. And her humanness made me love her all the more.

As a tall woman myself, I loved that Cher was always very comfortable standing tall next to her much shorter husband Sonny, or any man it seemed of any height.

All tall women know of the Murphy's height law. "Go to a dance as a tall woman. The shortest man there will ask you to dance. Guaranteed." Today's standards would not necessarily tag me, a five-foot-nine woman, as very tall. But back in the late '60s when I hit that peak, it bordered on Amazonish.

Brother Harvey has his stash of Cher CDs and tapes, pretty much every song she ever did, down on his Lake Barkley boat in Kentucky. He bounces across the reflective, sunlit waves of the massive lake with Cher blaring in the wind and grins like a possum eatin' crap as Dad would say. Harvey gets rode hard by friends and his wife Carol for that vice, but I get it. I share his admiration if not his lust for Cher.

One recommendation I must pass on to my friends here about assistive devices to use when dealing with MS is the soundtrack of "Burlesque." That movie with Cher and Christina Aguilera did poorly at the box office but not by my standards. The music was exhilarating, relatable, and definitely fell into my category of a tried and true "butt wiggler." A butt wiggler must pass my stringent criteria of making me instinctively wiggle rhythmically in my seat, no matter how hard I try to sit still. A butt wiggler gives me great joy and uncontrollable wide smiles. A butt wiggler smashes multiple sclerosis into smithereens on the worst day of the year. It is "praising the Lord in the dance" at its best.

I saw "Burlesque" at the theater with my before-mentioned good friend and dancing buddy of almost forty years, JoAnn Harris. JoAnn, husband Joe, Roger, and I have spent many nights dancing the night away on a dance floor, tripping the light fantastic. This particular afternoon, JoAnn and I grooved through

the whole "Burlesque" movie. We did the possum grin throughout the film and left the aisles at the end with a few boogie fever
moves. JoAnn gets the whole butt wiggler theory and gives it
due honor and respect. It is an integral part of our long-standing friendship.

Later that day I bought three CDs of the soundtrack. I kept
one and gave one each to friends JoAnn and Libby for Christmas.
They knew it came from the heart, as only good friends would
know. I play the CD when I want to fly high, sing loudly, dance,
or maybe even seduce my husband. Now Roger's Momma didn't
raise no fool. He learned early on that music was the way to my
heart if not my pants. Hmm, guess I need to thank Christina
for some of those bennies as she has more voice in that CD.
Regardless, those two girls belt out some soulful butt wigglers
that I rank very high on my top ten list.

I could go on and on about my fanship of Cher Bono, as I will
always think of her. She not only provided great entertainment
but she served as a sort of Gloria Steinem role model. She didn't
need to burn her bra; she seldom wore a bra, but she did blaze the
exposed belly button trail in her day.

Why Cher so vividly infiltrates my thoughts of treatment of
multiple sclerosis, I am not completely sure. But somehow her
strength, presence, allure, and adaptability fit my goals of living
with MS. I want to stand tall and confident, smiling and shiny,
flipping my hair, even in the midst of unexpected changes in my
no longer predictable life of multiple sclerosis. Cher has unwit-
tingly become a figure to model in that quest. Thank you, Cher.

Another way to cope with challenges of multiple sclerosis is
visualization. The holistic practice of visualization and imagery
took place pretty regularly in the Ziliak household many years
before, where it all began with Liza dealing with much arthritic
pain from her juvenile rheumatoid arthritis. A therapist at the
children's hospital in Cincinnati had given Liza a tape with music
and a visualization instruction to follow. The idea was to relax, see

yourself in an ideal setting, and talk yourself through relaxing all body parts from head to toe.

Liza had her own imagery that worked well. At twelve, she had a remarkable capacity to escape some pain by playing the little cassette tape, lying in her pink, flowered, little girl bed, long blond hair fanned out on pillow top, with blue eyes closed, and breathing evenly and deeply.

My own visualization routine involved me lying flat on a bed or couch with eyes closed and arms and legs lying out comfortably and symmetrically at my sides. I would do abdominal breathing similar to a Lamaze or yoga technique. Then I would find myself under a warm sun with perhaps a lit candle hovering over my abdominal area. My breath would take warmth into the top of my head; flow through my chest, arms, abdomen, and legs; and out the bottom of my feet. I would concentrate on this slow flow of breath with each inhalation and exhalation.

The setting surrounding me in my dream world was often a country scene of rolling grassed hills, dotted with gigantic clusters of multicolored, vibrant flowers, all cascading perfectly over lush, green foliage. Sweet honeysuckle smells permeated the air. The hills would ascend forever into a cloud-tufted blue sky that rose like stairs to heaven. The scene was vast yet intimate. The warmth inside me oozed out and relaxed all muscles, all body cavities. The air held miraculous healing powers and there were no cares in my secluded world.

Just writing down my inadequate description of this imaginary, Eden gives me a sense of peace and tranquility. I had a head nurse boss once who seriously practiced visualization and could tolerate some invasive dental procedures by practicing self-hypnosis with a similar technique. I had good success with visualization and still do but was never as good as Ben in his pink, starched shirt.

Another technique I have used to relax and limit pain is the reading of Psalms by hubby Roger. Roger has a radio announcer voice. His voice rings clear, low, masculine, hums a bit, and lulls a person. Our son Josh inherited the same bass voice as his dad. Their voices are so similar that at times on the phone my daughter-in-law Danielle and I have both mistaken Joshua and Roger. A couple of those times have proved very embarrassing to both of us. One time of embarrassment involved a bathroom door comment of "Can I come in?" Another involved a phone conversation opener of, "Ooh, how ya doing, babe?"

Anyway, Roger has a voice I never tire hearing. So when in the throes of pain, I will ask Roger to get a Bible and pick out some Psalms to read to me. He is always obliging and will sit next to me—be it bed, floor, or recliner—and start rhythmically reading the healing words. Now Psalms always soothe me. I try to read them most days, but I can be sporadic in my dedication to that. But when Roger utters the words, the words hold more power.

I have suggested the reading of Psalms to several friends who deal with chronic pain. Some have found similar relief with it. And my personal preference of Bible interpretations is the King James Version. All that "nee, hence, and goeth" stuff makes the poetic cadence very appealing and special to me. And long ago, while listening to books on tape, I also came to realize I prefer a male voice rather than female voice. Whatever soothes is the right choice I think.

Josh and Danielle once gave me a set of King James tapes of the Bible as a very thoughtful gift, but listening to the tapes I found the pace was too fast and it did not work the same as a human being at my side reading the words. The consolation of a human being at side only heightens the therapeutic effect of recited Psalms.

I have also found the human consolation factor true for sitting at a dying patient's side in my hospice experience. I volunteer with Deaconess Hospice Care in Evansville. As an RN in the hospital and in long-term care, I always loved being around dying patients. If a patient on the floor was dying, it was not unusual for me to be assigned that person for the shift. It is pretty clear to all nurses. You either love it or hate it, the being around imminent death. The nurses who worked with me knew Mary Ellen was one of the nuts who actually liked to be around dying people— thus, my assignments.

So it was an easy transition when I had to leave nursing to join the volunteer hospice staff. That may sound morbid and a bit warped to you, but I have always found it very spiritual to be a part of the dying process, especially when it is what I call a "good death." I define a good death as one that is as peaceful as it can be, with pain well controlled, with the dying person at an acceptance stage, and with loved ones at the person's side—be it family or friends.

I always feel special to be invited into someone's world when they die. What is more significant in any person's life besides birth and death? Everyone gets excited about birth. I happen to think death is every bit as major an event, regardless of one's faith center.

My duties with hospice involve respite care, a little in-service teaching, and Speakers Bureau engagements. I am strictly a lay volunteer. I am not allowed to administer care in any RN capacity. I cannot give medicine, even a Tylenol. That's okay. It's tough, but it's okay. My favorite responsibility is being a "comfort angel." As a comfort angel, I get called when someone is actively dying, and, in their last moments, the family wants support for the patient and themselves.

The common denominator with all my hospice assignments is that the physical presence of a human being at a patient's side will somehow lend support, with or without words spoken or deeds done. Any time someone is suffering, the physical presence of a human at a patient's side is such a blessing.

I find that true for many life experiences, not just pain or death. Ricky Bob and I can attest to that concept every four weeks when we sit side by side for our Tysabri intravenous infusions. Sometimes we gab nonstop. We are like "two old wash women" as

Dad would say. Other days we mostly say nothing, sit quietly, and know there is another person next to us who knows where we're at and what we're doing and cares. Having another human being at your side through difficult times is the best.

GOOD GRIEF, CHARLIE BROWN!

It's weird how often I have thought of the grieving process when it comes to dealing with the pitfalls of multiple sclerosis. Most people are acquainted with Elisabeth Kübler-Ross and her theories and insights to the process of death and bereavement. Her book, *On Death and Dying*, was published in 1969 and was a catalyst for negating the taboo of talking about death.

As a nursing student I was taught to utilize her steps believed to be experienced in all cases of a death. The five stages of grief noted by Kübler-Ross are: denial, anger, bargaining, depression, and acceptance. A patient or family member can work methodically through all five stages or get stuck on one for a long time. Each case is very individualized.

As Rick had noted in his email to me, MS can "wash away a part of me at a time, never to come back." When this happens, it is only natural that we experience the same stages of grief as if a loved one has died.

Our society has become better educated and accepting of this grieving process with death. Those of us dealing with multiple sclerosis, and our friends and family also, need to understand and accept this process with losses we experience through the disease process of MS.

This concept may sound bizarre to you. "How can she compare an MS loss to a death?" you might ask. But think about it. If you unexpectedly can't walk or see or drive, it's major crapola! It will make you sad. You may cry over the change. I have. The feeling of sadness will not go away over night. It is a process with great time variance, a little different looking for each one of us, just as grieving a death must be.

My experience has been that I grieve faster with the larger losses. Sometimes. Obviously the being pissed for ten years does not support that. Still, the small incidental losses usually prove more difficult for me. This isn't a consistent pattern but it always astonishes me when it happens that way. I feel like such a jerk when I get all teary-eyed and mopey over what sounds like a silly, little superficial thing.

Take, for example, my earlier note of how tremors for a while prevented me from using eyeliner. I could not steady my hand enough to apply the liner to the edge of my eyelid. The need of precise control for application only accentuated my intentional tremors. Luckily, at present, I can apply eyeliner most days. It makes me happy. Thank you, Tysabri.

That simple little thing of finishing my makeup with liner was a part of my identity. It was a teeny part of the whole picture I chose for people to view when they looked at me. My preference is to use that bottle or pencil to finish the look I like of making my eyes pop a bit more when you see me.

I realize how very vain I sound even talking about eyeliner, but my grief over its loss was very real to me. So I understand what impact the long arm reach grief can have with an MS person.

On the other end of the spectrum, my largest loss over the last fourteen years since my MS diagnosis has been my ability to work as a registered nurse. It was not a minor loss by any means. It falls under the "MS is the worst thing to happen to me" category.

I loved nursing. I was good at it. It was the talent God gave me to grow and nourish as a good steward. I expected to retire from it at an appropriate retirement age of sixty-five or so. When I had to leave nursing completely at forty-eight, I was devastated. My identity was gone!

Sure, I loved being a wife and Mom. It was a big part of who I was, but when someone met me and asked, "What do you do?" I could quickly reply with confidence, "I'm an RN." I still struggle with how to answer that question today. On occasion "RN" falls from my mouth before "artist."

And I cringe when I choose to tell an inquiring stranger, "I'm retired from nursing." Sometimes that is the simplest response that elicits the fewest nosy questions. But beware. Often the immediate response I get from that statement is a jealous chuckle and a sarcastic, "Must be nice. Wish I could quit my job so young." At that moment, I whip myself for choosing the wimpy reply that just backfired on me big time. How do I respond to that?

I fight the urge to scream, "I didn't choose to quit! I loved my job! MS chose me!" Instead, I smile and say, "Yeah, I'm lucky," and leave it at that.

Assessing a proper reply to people when it involves MS is also a skill we must learn to hone. Even family can be tricky in trying to explain what we do each day and not make ourselves sound like a lazy butt. "Oh, I lounge on the couch most mornings for two or three hours sipping coffee and doing crosswords. Then if I feel like it I might take a shower."

Translated in MS lingo that sounds more like, "I wake up slowly to see what limbs work and if my vision is clear, blurry, double, or gone. Getting out of bed, I stumble a lot at first and run into the dressers and doorway to the bathroom. Roger watches me to see if I need help or if I am safe. Then I head to the couch because I am too fatigued, slow moving, and foggy in the brain to jump into any productive item on my long to-do list. I'd love to jump into the shower and lather up body and hair like I did for years, but that may not happen today. We'll see how much energy surfaces. Instead I opt for two crossword puzzles and one cryptoquip to keep my brain firing sharply and to lay down new nerve tracks to replace the ones that the MS burned through. I look at my planner that I left out next to the couch so I would remember to look at my planner and know what I planned. Nothing much in there till after ten when my body is hopefully moving better..." You get the gist of this.

Many people with multiple sclerosis play out a similar scenario every day of their lives. Mine is not unusual but is unique because I am the only one with my particular set of symptoms. It goes back to the idea that no two people with MS are alike. I just wish there was some way of people in general knowing enough about MS to be a little empathetic and appreciate that every person with MS who answers, "How ya doing?" has a much bigger story behind their short-spoken response of, "Fine."

So grieving losses can be one honking long list. I feel a bit guilty laying some of my morning head discussion on you, but in the same token I want you to know we all share those lists of complicated choices and losses on a daily basis.

I have a friend who lumps pain, losses, and grief together as a "crap cracker." Some days it's even referred to as, "a steamin' crap cracker." Pretty fitting and much more descriptive than, "an off day." We have an understanding that we can be WWWH (women with whiny hineys) and message each other with our quick gripes, just so we feel better giving the crap cracker an identity, and, in return, we expect nothing more than an "Uh huh." That exchange works miracles some days and I am grateful I have a close friend with whom I can be that totally honest. It doesn't take long, but it validates our quirks on that given day without any judgment or expectations.

A short, uncensored list of "crap cracker" complaints from WWWH might include:

- My right ass cheek burns.
- That dang right eye is all blurry again and doesn't clear up.
- My left arm is numb.
- It's a very flat day.
- Clothes hurt today.
- I haven't had a shower in six days.
- I got brain _____ today. (I had to censor that in case a grandkid reads it.)

- These steroids make me crazy!
- How do I tell them I can't make it?
- I am sick of being sick.

I am willing to bet that everyone reading this could add a lot to the list. Rick and I each have our lists. We all have a list. My point is that the lists are all different. They all include valid complaints. I believe we need to acknowledge the complaints to a select, trusted few people in our lives and then move on to living life to the fullest around the encumbrances they present.

Live life to the fullest. Just because we have a loaded crap cracker on some days doesn't mean we have the luxury of not living our lives well.

I really believe that concept with my heart and soul. It is actually a faith belief for me. I believe God gives all of us gifts of time, talent, and treasure. He expects us to be good stewards of all that entails. We may be clueless for a while about what that picture of a good steward looks like, but with time, faith, and an opened heart I believe God shows us the way.

I am a believer in the Holy Trinity. I pray to the Holy Spirit to fill me with wisdom of what steps to make on any given day. That step may be executed flat from my bed, but it is still a step God expects me to take.

Friends tease me when I lead a heart prayer and include something like, "Holy Spirit, fill me with your wisdom. I don't know what I'm doing. And, could you make it real clear exactly what I am supposed to do? Sometimes I need You to knock me upside the head so I get what you are telling me. Thanks."

God knows what's in our heart before we speak it. That gives me consolation with my human inadequacies. He knows what I want to say even when I don't. What a relief.

FLORENCE NIGHTINGALE

My nursing education began with a year at Indiana University. And yes, I will be the first to admit it upholds its reputation of a party school. But it is also an excellent school on a gorgeous, Midwestern campus.

Then I got a job at Mead Johnson in Evansville, a nutritional company, working as a lab technician. It started out as a summer job, but when I was offered full-time position, I could not pass it up. I was already dating Roger at the time and we were becoming serious. Love for him was never ambiguous. So he also factored into my decision to leave IU.

Long story short, I married young at nineteen, Roger being twenty-one. Joshua Edward came along at twenty-one, and as part time was not an option with my position, I quit Mead and did full-time Mom and farm wife. After one year I went cabin crazy talking to only a baby and cows, went back to school, and several years later graduated at twenty-eight with an associate's degree in nursing from the University of Evansville, and, by that time, I had a second child—Liza Marie.

I graduated as a late bloomer at the ripe old age of twenty-eight. Marching with my classmates to receive my diploma, I felt old. Looking back, I was a baby.

With crisp new degree in hand, I interviewed for a nursing position. I liked acute care so I applied at the three area hospitals—Deaconess, St. Mary's, and Welborn. Welborn has since been bought out by St. Mary's.

My greatest likes were Psych and Ortho. In 1980, jobs for nurses were plentiful and I was offered positions in both fields of specialty. I chose full time on Unit 4600 Orthopedics at

Deaconess Hospital. If memory serves me well, and it usually doesn't, my pay was $7.22 an hour.

My nursing career at Deaconess encompassed full time, part time, ortho, med-surg, rehab, and substance abuse. I climbed the career ladder, obtained my ONC (orthopaedic nurse certification) designation, and moved into nurse management as an assistant head nurse.

After fifteen years, I made the major switch to long-term care as DON for Seton Residence. I had a nursing staff of forty-six at the time, consisting of RNs, LPNs, and nursing assistants. We provided around-the-clock care for our twenty-four retired Daughter of Charity sisters in our infirmary and totaled about sixty-four with two other assistive and independent units housed in the same building. Most buildings and meeting rooms on campus were named after some saint; most were somehow involved with the life and times of St. Elizabeth Ann Seton— the founder of the apostolic order of Daughters of Charity. Now, there was one adaptive, strong woman. Research her and you will find another wonderful role model that we can hope to copy with our needs to cope with multiple sclerosis.

Our fairly new building sat on the outskirts of Evansville, in very western Vanderburgh County, atop one hundred plus acres of rolling hills. The grounds included a beautiful lake with many geese afoot.

Working for the Daughters of Charity at Seton Residence was a plum job for me, and, being in my forties, this job being two miles from my home was ideal. My plan was to stay there and do the best job I could until the day I retired. That day arrived much sooner than anticipated.

The first year at Seton, I continued to work as supplemental staff at Deaconess in order to hold onto my seniority should I not be happy in my new position. I quickly knew I was staying put with the nuns.

The responsibilities of DON were heavy at times and kept me very busy. The nuns ran a tight ship, which I greatly admired, but by the same token they had very high expectations of their management team. The retirement home for their nine state Mater Dei Provincialate province was promised to be a fitting place to finish out the careers of the retiring sisters in blue.

The fatigue I had felt for years while working at the hospital lessened a bit when I cut down my work commute time and lessened the evening and night shifts. Plus I had more control over my work schedule, which helped my energy somewhat. But fatigue and heaviness left me struggling to walk the long halls and talk business when I passed someone in the hall. Standing in one spot was much worse for me. I would have extreme pain, weakness, and burning in my legs, which would force me to find a chair or have to excuse myself from meetings or rounds. I once sat on a pallet in a storage room and got some weird stares from three other managers, but it was the best I could do. Sitting on the floor would have been the other option.

The other symptoms of blurred vision, tremors, and numbness that seemed to jump willy-nilly over my entire body were still there but were manageable for the first three years.

I eventually found myself more and more not being able to read charts or make sense of office memos. Sometimes the dizziness and nausea accompanied the impaired vision and forced me to go home. Cognitive issues became big concerns for me. I would read documents several times and have to jot notes to understand what the typed words in front of me meant. I began to put post-it notes on everything to jog my memory on how to do tasks I'd done for years like employee evaluations and budget lines.

When opening my standard gray file cabinets I would be greeted with all kinds of fluttering, yellow confetti glued to manila file tags. When Jan Weiss, my assistant head nurse, assumed my position a year later, she thanked me for being so thoughtful as to give such detailed instructions on my documents. Years later

I told her it was the only way I could make sense of what was in those file cabinets. It was not thoughtfulness. It was survival of an experienced, middle-aged nurse trying to hold onto a job she was not ready or willing to give up.

A little over three years after I started my career at Seton, I received my diagnosis of MS. I had already been adapting to limitations but the diagnosis and worsening symptoms made the need to adapt more urgent. It was now the question, "How do I keep working when my body and mind are not working right and I have no energy and walking is a challenge?"

Boss lady, Sister Anthony Prugger, bent over backward to try and accommodate my deteriorating status. I found all levels of administration to be helpful and accommodating to my ever-growing needs. Sister Anthony arranged for me to have a scooter at my disposal and I used it daily to maneuver the very long halls of Seton. I charged it in the hall outside my office. I had two swinging doors that led to the hall outside my office. They were cumbersome so I had a bit of a walk to get to the scooter I parked just outside the doors, but it still saved many steps.

Seton Residence consisted of one big circle of resident rooms on one floor with front offices and a kitchen and dining room for the ambulatory nuns. It had a basement with meeting rooms, more offices, laundry, supplies, and an employee break room and canteen area. Saving those many steps saved me much energy and allowed me greater accessibility to patients, staff, and administration. I quickly found out that there was one caveat. A scooter saves walking energy but takes additional energy to get on and off the seat at a side angle. There is always a trade off. But the use of the scooter was a lifesaver.

Rick Nelson was a sight for my sore eyes at about this time. Rick, a rehabilitation engineer referred to me by Vocational Rehabilitation, assessed my home and workspace on several occasions. He observed me working like a DON at my desk at Seton. He had some wonderful suggestions of ergonomically correct office set ups that would conserve energy. He did the same for my home environment. I am grateful to him for his help and still use some of his suggestions and equipment he helped me to incorporate.

A highlight of what he had me do was to set up my space behind the desk in such a way that I could easily roll from desk to computer to file cabinet in one big U-turn. With use of a plastic rug protector, my office chair glided easily.

Earlier my office chair at Seton had been anything I could get my hands on in the storage room for cast offs. Daughters were frugal and wasted nothing. They recycled before it was a cool concept accepted and supported by society. So I relied on friend and fellow manager Steve Wingert from housekeeping to give me a heads up when he had a discarded chair with some life left in it. I had swapped out several chairs that way over the years.

Lucky for me, one suggestion from Rick Nelson was to get an ergonomically correct chair that actually supported me in every way so as to conserve energy and take care of my many body parts, especially the ones affected by MS. The awesome ergo chair was ordered and it fit like a glove. I was surprised how much relief it gave to my spasms in legs and arms and the support it supplied to my torso in keeping it upright with less energy required from me. I've already shared with you how difficult it can be just to sit upright at certain times because of generalized weakness. I became a believer in the benefits of the right chair. I have made good use of that chair at work and now in my office/studio set up at home. Thank you, Rick Nelson and Voc Rehab.

Rick and his OT (occupational therapy) and PT (physical therapy) teams also set me up with a couple of other items that made my life fuller and easier.

Living at our Parker Settlement home just on the Posey and Vanderburgh county lines, we had a great ranch home on a two-acre lot, next to a winding tributary of Big Creek with a full, finished basement. The basement held our large family room with fireplace that led to a walk out patio. Our laundry was down there and a second bath. Josh had his bedroom down there until he hit IU, and then for a year our beautiful exchange student daughter, Renata Ribeiro from Sao Paulo, Brazil, lived there. I miss Renata. She is an exotic-looking dark-haired model type, Portuguese speaking, with great intelligence and grace—a year older than our youngest beauty Beth Ann. Renata looked so much like Beth Ann that people often assumed she was our fourth biological child.

Now I might be prejudiced here, but God gave Roger Dodger and Mary Ellen some really good baby-making genes. So Renata fit right in our family on every level.

God blessed us with Josh who is a smart, six-foot-four-inch, handsome man with blue eyes and blond hair turned auburn and thinning, but that's okay. Josh graduated IU with a journalism degree and is now married to equally-smart Danielle. Josh makes an excellent Daddy and provider to five children, ranging in ages from fourteen to three. They are Sophie, Esther, Jude, Olive, and Ruby. Oh, and I must not forget Sophie's spoiled, rambunctious beagle, Sampson.

I have already filled you in a lot about Liza, who also graduated from IU. She continues to be my petite, Northwestern blond, blue-eyed beauty that kicks butt on the streets of Seattle. The strong Christian man I see in her future family has not yet been gleaned by God. I pray for that blessing if it is in His will.

Then baby girl Beth Ann has grown into a five-foot-eleven brunette that must provide teacher crush material to the teenage boys she helps teach and raise every day at her high school. She is my theater/English major from Ball State. Chris, her equally tall and good-looking firefighter husband, is kind and gentle and helps raise their own Maggie and Molly, ages four and two.

Yes, I just had to brag a bit about the children, in-laws, and grandchildren that I love with all my heart. I realize how blessed I am to have them in my life. I mention them here because they are whom I often visited when I descended the stairs into my basement family room at our Parker Settlement home. They were the reward at the bottom of the staircase. I wanted you to appreciate a bit of what I missed when I could no longer descend the stairs of my own volition because of limitations imposed upon me by multiple sclerosis. Voc Rehab helped me with that problem also.

A chair lift was installed, going from our main floor to the basement. We had a straight stairway with no turns so it was a fairly simple application.

I was embarrassed at first to use the lift. Only old people and crippled people used a chair lift, right? That wasn't me. Common sense won out because the freedom the lift gave me was worth the cost of my pride. I used the lift to hang out with family, watch TV, do laundry, etc. I initially thought it was frivolous to put the lift in and a waste of money. Rick Nelson helped me accept the support offered in a lift chair. He pointed out how isolated I was feeling because I was physically cut off from my family. They were often downstairs and I was up because I did not have the strength to do stairs.

This family room time often was in the evening after I had already pushed myself through a day at work. He was so right. I had not fully appreciated the isolation I felt. Isolation is another problem experienced by many with MS. Through no fault of our own, we are cut off from the ones we love and activities that make us happy. It is never frivolous to do whatever it takes to get quality time back whenever possible. That time is of benefit not only to us but also to our loved ones. Again, thanks, Voc Rehab.

One other piece of equipment was added to the Ziliak household that proved helpful. I started using a rolling, two-shelved, lightweight cart in my home. I used it everywhere I could. In the kitchen, it helped with the chore of getting dinner on. For example, I would load dishes, silverware, napkins, salt, pepper, and anything else I needed to set the dinner table. Then I would wheel it over. Pushing the cart gave me support and balance and at the same time saved steps and lifting. Or I would load it with pot or pan, paring knife, and a sack of potatoes. Having all my stuff at hand at the table allowed me to sit and again saved steps and prolonged lifting and toting.

The cart is an easy thing to add to a household and need not be expensive. The biggest prerequisite is that it be easy to roll and maneuver in the area needed most. I also used a cart at work to move files and charts.

Getting back to a few other adjustments at work that kept me going included adding some of my "flat time." Flat time was time I took every day, about twenty minutes at a time, to lie flat and get "re-juiced." Three to five times a day is what I needed most days while receiving the Copaxone and working at Seton. Sister Anthony okayed my suggestion to utilize our physical therapy room as we only utilized it for the nuns on a very part-time basis.

So at convenient times of the day, usually mid-morning and mid-afternoon, I would fit a few minutes into my nursing schedule to lie flat on a PT matted cot thingy with wooden legs and shut my eyes. Those downtimes always helped a little, never a lot (reminds me of the Dr. Seuss, *A Fish Out of Water*, book—feed the fish always a little never a lot or something will happen you never know what), but as you can guess it was not easy to fit these moments into a busy work day. I was fortunate to be in management and have control over my appointment times and schedule. Had I still been in bedside nursing, the luxury of flexibility would not have been available. God took such good care of me. He guided me to a job that fit so well for my adjustments to this MS-laden time in my life.

A year after my diagnosis, I found myself sinking at work. No matter how I tried, I could not meet my full-time commitment as DON. I was off work more than at work. There were no more adaptations to try. I had an ideal, office work environment and understanding bosses and the work ethic of that little girl from St. Wendel. Wrap it all together and it was still not enough.

I talked long and hard with Roger and close friends about what to do about work. Questions in my mind at the time included:

> Should I quit work completely? Should I take a long leave of absence? Should I try part time? Can I try part time as a DON? Should I look harder for ways to adapt? Am I a wuss? Am I not trying hard enough? What is wrong with me? I know people my age with MS who are making it work, why can't I? Am I holding my own at work? Is every-body waiting for me to quit? Am I a burden to work with? Does everyone hate me? Are they talking about me behind my back? Am I being fair to my nurses? Am I making wise decisions for my patients? Does everyone pity me? What do the sisters want? Will they soon ask me to leave? How can I be in this situation? Can we pay bills if I don't work? Will we lose our house? Is this fair to Roger? Can we still send the kids to college? What will I tell people if I quit? Will they look down on me? Will they think less of me? What should I do? God, why aren't You telling me what to do? Have I not been good enough?

I had counseled nurses at the hospital on what to do in similar circumstances. This was different. It was me. I was at a loss as to what was the right thing to do.

The human resources' person from Seton, Carol Orth, had become a friend of mine over the prior four years. We worked closely together as we hired an average of one and a half nurs-ing personnel a month. We turned over a lot of RN, LPN, and NA applicants in those four years with many interview hours, so Carol and I got to know each other well. Plus Carol was also a hard-working gal from St. Wendel. She had been a few years behind me in grade school. We had an unspoken deep respect for our shared upbringings.

Long-term care is a tough gig and although we were a pri-vately owned facility and made our own rules and had the best nurse-patient ratio in the long-term care community, the work was still demanding and pay was low for the job of caring for an aged population in an infirmary. Carol and I talked many times about my job situation and I felt great empathy and compassion from Carol both personally and professionally.

I sensed some uncertainty from Carol as to what she thought my work decision should be, but in the end she was carefully guiding me toward the tough yet obvious decision of resigning my position. Carol had her job to do as personnel director. Although it was difficult, she had to wear her HR hat and represent the Daughters of Charity's position in the matter first while respecting my position as an employee of the Daughters.

I talked some more, prayed some more, cried a lot more, and still didn't know what to do. The last year had proven I was unable to keep working in my job for both physical and cognitive reasons. Even if I could keep my body upright and moving, I still had to be able to have a sharp mind to perform my duties. Some days I could not make any sense of a simple document put before me. I could no longer lead my great nursing team and I could no longer be a competent nurse for my patients. I felt my world had ended.

THE BIG DECISION

How had I landed on this unrecognizable planet? Why was I wearing the clear donut ball helmet on my head and why was a white dryer vent hose dangling off my ass? These were deep crater holes like the moon I saw before me. I was doing the zombie walk and tripping and I was the only one on this barren planet of death.

"That's one small step for man…one giant leap for mankind." Yeah, right. I did not feel noble in the least bit. I got catapulted to this planet. I didn't volunteer and I didn't get glory picked after grueling years of learning and training. There was no glory remotely attached to MS.

This is how I felt the day I decided to quit work. I don't remember the exact day I decided to resign from director of nursing at Daughters of Charity Seton Residence or when I turned in the typed one pager. I don't want to give value to that day by acknowledging it with a calendar square. I do remember feeling a deep, gut-wrenching tear of grief comparable to Mom calling me at IU and telling me Pop Schmitt had died. I grew up next door to Pop and Mom and walked the gravel road, barefoot, when warm enough, to see them every day. They were a cornerstone under my life hut, as was being an RN.

My tender of resignation read appropriately short, sweet, and business like. I downplayed my leaving as much as possible when my nurses and aides became teary-eyed and insisted on hugging me. They were good, solid people, many of whom I had hand-picked over the last four years. They were my work family. Many days they saw more of me than my own family. I loved them all and did not want to leave them. I trusted in them; they relied upon me.

Once I had decided to quit work, I wanted the fall of the guillotine to be quick and painless. Do you think Anne Boleyn would report that post-beheading critique back to us as a possibility? Quick and painless? Regardless, I aimed for that goal.

My last day of work was in November. I remember thinking I was due for an annual evaluation in December and would be leaving on a higher pay scale with the expected raise if I waited until then. Daughters' disability pay, if approved, would be based upon my departing salary. My social conscience told me not to be greedy so I submitted my resignation immediately and agreed upon a last day with administration, thus forfeiting any pay increase earned over the last year.

A heavy weight of guilt sat atop my shoulders. I was now officially "disabled" and therefore secretly christened a burden to society. An added burden of being labeled a bigger moocher by getting a pay raise right before my leaving due to MS was not acceptable. There is a caste system in disability and I was already fighting for an upper caste level. So my decision to not wait for my pay raise in a few weeks was a quick one. That is not to say years later I didn't wonder if bills could have been paid just a little bit easier if I had made the other choice and over the course of years received more disability income. Disability is one shiny, double-edged sword.

The DON work transition related to my Seton departure was smooth and seamless, largely due to my assistant head nurse, Jan Weiss. Jan was chosen to replace me as DON. This was a logical choice that I fully supported.

Jan had done a bang-up job with filling in for me much of the prior year as my multiple sclerosis worsened. She had also been an assistant head nurse with me on ortho at Deaconess. I had been a part of her hospital interview process for that management position years before. Jan was quick spoken and smart in every way, with a belly laugh that echoed off corridor walls. She would do a bump shoulders move when getting to a punch line of a joke and it would sometimes send me stumbling across the nurses' station, trying to grab onto something or someone so as not to fall completely on my face. Literally, she knocked me over. Jan was a tall, large-framed woman like me and her bump had a lot of bump behind it.

Jan mourned my resignation with me. She was not only a colleague; she was a trusted friend and mutual dance partier. I had celebrated several New Year's Eves with Jan at my side, both of us practicing our butt wiggler moves with enthusiasm and due diligence. My resignation as DON was a loss that could not be discussed without including note of a big gain for her. I stepped down; Jan stepped up. I was happy for her in my sadness. She was sad for me in her joy.

Embarrassment is the word that comes to mind first when I think of that horrible time in my life when I quit work. There was a myriad of other emotions that wreaked havoc in my life back then: confusion, anger, regret, resentment, pity, jealousy, indignation, blame, relief, depression, and sadness. I still tango with some residual negativity from that fallout of grief and loss. But, for whatever reason, embarrassment topped the list at that time in my life when my identity was stolen by the masked villain MS.

I was embarrassed that I had failed at life and dropped the ball. My tiny view of the world had everyone working shoulder to shoulder, doing God's will and pulling their own weight. It went back to my belief of good stewardship. God did not expect us to breeze through life. He gave us time, talent, and treasure, and as good Christians we were to do our part to be good stewards of those gifts from God. We all had our work to do. God expected it. Nursing was one of my talents, my biggest talent. How could I be a good steward and not be a nurse?

Wearing my embarrassment like the hair shirt it resembled, I just knew everyone that looked at me saw the failure inside me. It was shameful. I was less than completely human, a misfit, an untouchable. People would begin to avoid me because they knew just associating with me would shine a bad light upon them, regardless of their present stature and success in life.

The concept of failure was reinforced every day when I awoke and had nothing of value to do for the day. The failure was most solidified when I was introduced to people or ran across an old acquaintance I hadn't seen for years. Invariably when the question was posed, "What do you do?" I would stand there, mouth gaping, with no answer in mind. I honestly did not know how to answer that.

I no longer worked. There was no paying job and no volunteer job. Out of necessity, I had slowly and methodically dropped the few volunteer jobs I did through my community or church. My kids were all grown and the youngest, Beth Ann, was at Ball State in Muncie, Indiana. Roger worked full time and did most of the housework and cooking. My job was to try and keep myself clean by getting a shower on my own and some days I made one trip to the dumpster with trash and a bit of housework. There was an occasional trip to the grocery store, but my limitations with the MS at the time kept me very isolated. So how should I answer, "What do you do?"

What I wanted to answer to the posed question was, "Nothing. Absolutely nothing! I don't work anymore." That answer made the most sense and the warped feelings that held that thought up like concrete blocks was that I was damaged goods, one of those disabled people you hate to lay eyes upon and that make you squirm uncomfortably, the people you talk about and judge severely but in the next breath say something nice about to prove your political correctness. We all do that. We are human and deep down we are all scared to death of ending up like the crippled man in front of us in the Target checkout line who is taking forever and making the rest of us wage-earning people wait.

I would love to report that I snapped out of that pity party *el pronto*; I did no such thing. Oh, on occasion I almost had myself convinced I had my crap together and was gracefully accepting my lot in life. That was my big ego puffing its chest out under the silver breastplate. My battle armor protected me from death, but I still took many arrows while on the new battleground, which I found my sandal-clad feet tripping upon.

No, human, damaged Mary Ellen Klenck Ziliak sludged along in survival mode for a long time. The year of being diagnosed with MS and trying to still work topped what I had referred to earlier as my being pissed off for ten years. I had ups and downs of partial acceptance and insight through those years that fell under various stages of grief and loss as explained by Kubler-Ross in death and dying reference. It took the full ten for me to get to a good place and lose the chip on my shoulder I blamed God for strategically placing. I thought God had a sick sense of humor and a mean streak in Him. I know how bizarre and sacrilegious that sounds, but I was really mad at God. Why did He put this big, heavy splintery cross upon my back?

I was so arrogant. I had the crazy notion that since I was an RN and had twenty years experience of caring for people and helping them deal with life's tragedy and pain that I had a "Get Out of Jail" card I could redeem whenever I liked and avoid that messy road the regular Joe had to walk down.

When I worked the substance abuse unit, we sometimes admitted patients off the street who had been on a long binge of drugging. Many arrived to an intake interview drunk, high, or strung out. Binging often meant no time or priority for bathing so the breath reeked and the body stank. We nurses quickly established an admission policy that automatically involved an "admission shower." It was the best idea we'd ever come up with. It was a win/win/win for patient, staff, and other patients on the unit.

My nursing approach to the disease process of addiction involves acceptance of where that person is in his journey of life. I don't believe alcoholism is an inherited gene, but I do believe risk factors in a family exist that makes a person more vulnerable to have an addiction. Ironically, it is the same philosophy I have with contracting multiple sclerosis. We don't have a gene to point to, but we can easily look at other autoimmune diseases in our family tree that could predispose us to have a higher risk factor to develop a chronic illness like MS.

I taught my addiction patients that it was their responsibility to educate their children on the higher risk factor they had by virtue of being a child of an alcoholic. We owe the same explanation to our own kids in regards to MS and other autoimmune diseases. Talking to them about a chronic illness predisposition may not change the outcome, but I believe we give our kids knowledge, options, and thus power by educating them.

Aftercare often involved follow-up meetings like Alcoholics Anonymous and Narcotics Anonymous on our substance abuse unit or on the hospital campus. So I could follow a patient's recovery for months. As I cared for my patients and watched their progress, I rejoiced in their individual accomplishments and got to reverently palm many chips signifying months of sobriety. I felt blessed to be a part of their celebrations that usually followed years of hell for them and loved ones. Success rate, meaning those in recovery of an addiction, was low compared to other chronic afflictions. But, man, the successful outcomes were ones to celebrate big time. And we did just that. We celebrated new life!

Looking back, there was a piece of Nurse Ziliak that thought she floated a couple of inches above the visceral pain of that group of people on our unit. I knew I was no better than anyone there, no different from them. I had alcoholism in my family and knew but for the grace of God it could be me warming a seat at local AA or NA meetings.

I registered that vulnerability in myself. I shared my risk factors when appropriate in group sessions with my patients. But upon honest reflection, I think there was a part of me that still held out, that somehow felt protected from truly being one of the down and out who could hit rock bottom. Like my being a nurse and having all that medical knowledge gave me some kind of a leg up or the very least a bit of protection from the nasty nasties. Well, we both know that isn't so. Mary Ellen bleeds and gets knocked down like the rest of them. No one is exempt. The nursing degree tucked into my back pocket just provides a tad bit of padding when I hit the ground.

Resigning from my nursing career was a definite hard knock to the ground. Intellectually and ethically, I understood the decision to quit was the right one. Emotionally accepting that decision proved to be one of the hardest journeys to travel.

The months immediately following my resignation as DON at Seton Residence were a time of recuperation for me. I had pushed my body and mind to the limit the difficult year before in trying to make a job and MS coexist without killing me in the process. So I rested a whole lot and took better care of myself because I now had the time. And I gave myself approval to do so.

A healthier, supportive lifestyle that was holistic in approach worked wonders. Multiple sclerosis did not go away by any means, but it was manageable and I, overall, felt better because I had less pain, spasms, and fatigue.

I reintroduced walking into my life. My version of power walking became a two-or three-time-a-week routine. The gracious nuns at Mater Dei Provincialate had extended privileges to me to have access to their grounds, which included wonderfully, blacktopped, winding roads through scenic, tree-filled acres around the lake. And the drive there was a mere five minutes from home.

Along the walking path, there was a walking "Way of the Cross" that I enjoyed making. That's a Catholic thing we like to do. The Way of the Cross supports meditation of the persecution, carrying of the cross, and crucifixion of Jesus Christ.

The artwork of the fourteen stations was strategically placed along the edge of a woods and each stood about five feet high. They all looked a little like a Dreamsicle ice cream on a stick with the stick end stuck in the ground. The savory confections were a perfect complement to the rustic surroundings.

One day while taking one of my walks, I passed some people entering the front of the main office headquarters at Mater Dei. I paused and talked to one of the nuns who was a very big, muckety muck. We caught up on gossip and each other. During the entire conversation, I noticed this sister checking out my purple leggings, the athletic shoes, and the sweat glistening on me. And I noticed I was fielding more than a polite few questions about my health, the MS, my limitations, and my capabilities. Now, this particular nun would have been a part of the discussion for approval of my disability benefits through the private insurance Daughters carried.

About then the lightbulb went on in my head. Sister was assessing whether or not I was truly disabled. Looking at me that day, I appeared fit to the untrained eye. I sounded good; I was smiling and high on walking endorphins; and I had worked up a sweat with exercise. I was not using a cane or scooter that she was used to seeing me with on the nursing unit or in management meetings. Sister could not help but wonder if she had made a mistake sanctioning my claim of disability and if she was being a good steward of the money entrusted to her.

My shoulders immediately drooped with the awareness of this sister's concern, doubt, and judgment related to my MS disability. The fun of the walk came to an abrupt halt. I understood the concern. I had been on the management side of this sort of dilemma; now I was on the employee side. Her skepticism seemed only natural to me. I could appreciate the perspective of a management person trying to do their job. This was part of the job.

But my guilt and shame returned full force after that brief encounter in front of the doors of the Mater Dei Provincialate office. I stopped walking the campus grounds. I stopped visiting the sisters for some time. I had enough guilt of my own without the shining dose of judgment I now could see in the eyes of one nun. One nun or one hundred nuns. It made no difference. My doubts and embarrassment were back, and, for my own good, I had to avoid any situation that made those feelings worse.

WHAT IS DISABILITY?

The three years after my DON resignation saw me coming to grips and some acceptance of my limitations due to multiple sclerosis. But it was an up and down, confusing time involving periods of no work and part-time work—nursing related and non-nursing related jobs.

Yes, I had been quickly approved for disability with the first filing with the third party administrator hired by Daughters of Charity to manage their long-term disability program for their employees. Carol, the HR person at the time, shared with me how rare an occurrence that was. Any disability claim requires great skill in jumping through many fiery hoops, sort of like the brave circus dogs performing under the big tent. And I appreciate the need to be thorough. I do not want my company dollars or tax dollars abused by a capable person who might claim to be disabled and in actuality is working the system for financial gains.

Carol worked so closely with me and held my hand through the tears and red tape process of filing for disability. I appreciated her caring approach as she equally appreciated the stress, if not the magnitude, of decisions I had to make along the way.

Carol pointed out that my cognitive problems in performing my DON duties weighed more heavily in the approval decision than my physical limitations. As you might recall, my difficulty with comprehension and concentration was at the heart of those cognitive issues. So she was saying that fatigue, pain, falling, double vision, numbness, or my needs of a scooter, walking cane, adaptive office equipment, and the need to lie flat in the PT room was not what swayed the insurance company to approve my disability claim. Better put, "No company wants a DON in their employ who doesn't have the wits about her to read a silly Betty Crocker recipe."

During the disability filing process, I had answered routine questions and given some narrative explanations of my current health status at the time and my ability to perform at work, but it was Carol who worded much of the actual application and submitted the paper work to the third party insurance carrier. Several detailed and complex documents from my neurologist and internist were attached to the claim to add clarity to my abilities and inabilities related to the multiple sclerosis.

A recurring question on the app was if I could perform my duties as Director of Nursing as listed in my job description. If the answer was "No," the next question asked was if there were any comparable jobs available with Daughters that was on the same level as DON. I was more than willing to change to another position, even with less pay, if it meant I could keep working but that answer was also a clear, "No."

So as noted earlier I resigned and shortly after my resignation I was approved for disability with the company I worked for, Mater Dei Provincialate. When that approval came through, Carol immediately informed me she would help me with next applying for my Social Security Disability, SSD.

My mouth dropped open. What in the hell was she talking about? I still believed in my heart that somehow I would be able to work in the near future. I figured I needed to recoup and regroup; get the right MS drug in my system, give it some time, and I would be almost good as new. Yes, you are right. I was smack dab in the middle of DENIAL.

My initial response to Carol was that I was not ready to apply for SSD. I did not completely understand what it meant and as time would prove, it took years for me to understand the full impact of being on SSD. Again, my big DON ego thought I was smarter than the average bear. I was not in oh so many ways.

I felt pressure to file for SSD. I was told by my employer I "had to." I was not ready for the permanency of being on SSD. Once again, I had to make a big decision and felt confused. I wondered how other people did this. There was no one who really seemed to be able to help me. I tried discussing my dilemma with MS support group members, with friends and family, old coworkers in management, with the doctors, and even with Social Security people. Nothing like real help surfaced from my outreach.

Carol and I had more informative chats—some easy and some strained. She stressed the point that the insurance company and the Daughters both expected me to file for SSD. To them, disabled was disabled. Done deal. They would agree to pay me disability benefits, which meant a percentage of my departing salary, but in return it was assumed I would immediately file for Social Security Disability. They understood once SSD was approved, the bulk of my disability paycheck would be paid for by the government; and if there was a remaining amount not covered, they would make up the difference.

Now, Social Security figures disability pay totally different from how the third party carrier did for Daughters. The government looks at my work history and income over the years to come up with a fair figure to pay me disability. An employer like Daughters looked only at a set percentage of my salary when I went on disability. I took a substantial cut in pay when I went from management in a hospital setting to management in a long-term care facility. The calculation still left a deficit between SSD and my Daughter disability benefits. It was up to Daughters to pay the difference.

Ding, ding, ding, the bell rang! This discussion of filing for Social Security benefits was all about the almighty dollar! I may have been working for a religious group who were upright and ethical, but in this instance they were working like the big business they were.

I did not understand that concept of passing the disability buck until after I had left my DON position. No one had fully explained to me the ramifications of filing for disability with my employer. To them it was a given, "File for our disability, get approved, and then you file for government disability and get off our backs."

That sounds cold. Maybe it was. I don't know. What I do know is my employer treated me with respect and dignity at the time I went through all this. But business reality shoved harsh steps into the whole process and I experienced great pressure and pain.

It crushed me at the time. How crushed does someone get who steps through all this with less respectful employers or even less knowledge base than I had at the time? I had years of management in this field of medical care and I was dumb as a doornail as to what I was stepping into. How does Joe Schmoe off the street with no knowledge base fare with all this?

Writing this now I still feel confused trying to explain how I arrived at my decisions back then. I felt I was approaching each step with adequate research, prayer, and consideration, but there was never a glaringly obvious solution to any of the choices I was forced to make related to work. The best I could do was to go with my gut and hope for the best.

With great reluctance, I filed for SSD as I was told I "had to do" by my employer. At the same time, I tried to get healthier and more stable and looked in the want ads every Sunday to see what nursing job I might still be able to perform in some capacity and not kill a patient or myself in the process.

Most Sundays left me in tears of frustration and depression. I so wanted to continue being a nurse. On paper my resumé qualified me for many nursing positions. In reality I could not do any of them at the time because of MS. Those Sundays, Roger was often left consoling me and shaking his head. He knew I could not work, but he had to be patient and let me come to that conclusion on my own. In those moments, Roger would frequently ask with a furrowed brow, "Mary, why do you keep putting yourself through this?"

My job search Sundays eventually resulted in my taking advantage of the employee handbook clause at work that allowed me to try and *rehab* myself back to work and at the same time not lose my disability benefits for a while. I eventually got stable enough to try a very part-time job. It was a demeaning job for me that entailed white lab rats.

I knew I could not ethically put myself into a nursing position that might jeopardize the safety or life of a patient. The country girl in me had less concern over putting unsuspecting lab rats in peril. So I accepted a job (not a position anymore) working in a local university research lab setting. I worked a couple of days a week, four hours a day, conducting experiments with white lab rats.

Although I grew up in good, old countrified St. Wendel, my life experience had never included touching rats so I had a learning curve just to know how to handle the rodents. I quickly learned from my employer how to pick rats up at the base of the tail for better control and minimal discomfort to the rat. My sharp mind on its own figured out that the long sleeves of a lab coat pulled down over my wrists also helped to minimize the scratches I got everyday from the clawing beasts.

People have been known to say how cute those little white mice are. First, they are not little mice in that lab; they are big rats. Secondly, believe you me; fat white rats are as ugly as fat white rats. Using the word cute in the same sentence as rat should be outlawed.

The study at the time called for me to weigh each rat then place two separately in opposite ends of a clear Plexiglas tunnel. I would start a stopwatch when I released the rats and see how long it would take them to run to a centered bowl of milk and drink it empty.

I wish I could remember the whole premise of the tests, but it somehow involved measuring appetite suppression due to depression related to an encephalopathic disease process. Between tests the doctor overseeing the research study let me read the articles related to the study. To my surprise the study was peripherally tied into the disease process of multiple sclerosis. MS in humans is often studied by comparing encephalopathy in rodents. Talk about coinkidinks.

The further irony in this experiment story is that somewhere out in the vast universe floats a published research study in some journal that has under its title the contributing people providing this data. My doctor boss would be the first noted but probably at the end, without RN or ONC behind it, would be "Mary Ellen Ziliak" because I was part of conducting this experiment and compiling data. Go figure.

With great difficulty because of my MS fatigue and pain, I made it through a few weeks of work there. Then I could no longer ignore the allergic reaction I was having to rat dander. I had to take Benadryl just to tolerate the sneezing, red, itchy eyes and nasal congestion. The nurse in me knew I could not continue. Besides having an allergy to the rats, I had to face the possibility that the stress to my body of an allergy could throw me into a big exacerbation with my MS. It had happened before with UTIs and bad colds. The decision to quit was also reinforced by the increasing fatigue, tremors, and spasms I was experiencing with the MS since I was dragging myself to work and on my feet most of the time there.

So one day after cleaning up my work-day rat turds and getting all twenty-eight of my rodents tucked comfortably into their cages, I talked to my boss and explained I needed to tender my resignation. She looked shocked and then very put out. Her reply was, "Okay. I understand. But I took you and the staff out to lunch the other day for your welcoming meal. I thought you would stay." Thus ended my short-lived yet illustrious rat-a-tat-tat career in a medical research lab.

MY LAST HOORAH

After the rat fiasco I went back to recouping once again after abusing my stressed body. I returned to a healthier, better-managed shape of MS body. I tried my darnedest to not look in the want ads for any more jobs. And I did pretty well in that respect.

Then one day my good friend Joe, JoAnn's husband who is a barber, told me of an interesting conversation he'd had with Dr. Mullican—a longtime customer who was a local physician. Dr. Mullican owned a medical research facility in Evansville. The good doctor was opened to Joe's suggestion to check out the qualifications of his good friend Mary who was an RN with much experience that might be interested in a part-time job. Now I know Joe, being the good friend he is, tooted my horn pretty loudly that day. Thank you, Thomas Joseph Harris.

End result was shortly after that barber chair conversation I started working as a quality assurance coordinator for MediSphere. The company knew of my MS before I interviewed so I did not have to tiptoe around that land mine. And my MS had stabilized once again to a manageable state.

My job description had me working in both quality assurance and employee health. My hospital experience left me well educated in the whole OSHA (Occupational Safety and Health Administration) compliance thing and I knew all about chart reviews for quality assurance and compliance. Understanding the basics of employee health was also a part of my nurse management duties. Converting my hospital experience to fit a small research company with mostly nurses as staff was an easy leap. I hired on as an assistant to the coordinator but within that first year was promoted to oversee both areas.

MediSphere hired me with an RN salary commensurate to the office position. It was approximately half the salary I earned as assistant head nurse at the hospital, about two-thirds my salary as DON and a whopping double my salary as a rat handler. When you try to figure out how much that overpaid nurse caring for you really makes, you better consider where she is and what she does. Like everything in life, it is all relative.

The one year I was able to work part time at MediSphere was a breath of fresh air for me and I loved it. I had been given another chance to be productive, to contribute to society, to work one more time in the capacity of an RN. I read charts and I oversaw employee health. I was once again happy and fulfilled.

But as you can guess, the joy did not last. Although my boss let me set a very flexible work schedule of my choosing for the twenty hours a week I was expected to work and gave me every accommodation I needed in the office, I could not meet my obligations.

It was the perfect job for me as far as being accommodating, but I gradually got beat to a pulp again. I could not force my body to get ready with a shower and dress or to drive the thirty-minute commute to work or to sit upright in an office chair to review patient charts. I had constant pain, tremors, weakness, unsteady gait, blurred vision. Once while at work I briefly lost my vision completely and had to call Roger to drive me home. I may have still lost my vision if I'd been flat in bed at home, but the overall exacerbations were due largely to the increased activity and demands on my body and mind while trying to work twenty hours a week.

I talked to my immediate boss Dr. Steve Elliott and explained my problem. I had worked with this skilled physician at the nunnery for several years when I was DON and he was Medical Administrator for Seton. We had a long-standing professional respect for each other. Dr. Elliott knew I would not be leaving if there was any way to make my job work with the MS. And I knew he would bend over backward as long as he could to keep me in my nursing position. Unfortunately, we were in a no-win situation. There was no more room to tweak and tweak. We knowingly looked into each other's sad eyes and agreed I would need to resign. I resigned.

MediSphere was the last paying job I held and that was approximately nine years ago. At that point, I no longer denied my disability. I could not work. I had been trying to hang onto work while the MS worsened for about five years since diagnosis and had adapted to the symptoms as a hospital floor nurse for at least four years before that. I had given it my best shot. God had blessed me with so much. Now it was my turn to say thank you for everything and please show me Your Will now, outside of a nursing career.

There were still a few bumps in the road related to my leaving work. On a couple occasions, I dusted off my resume and went so far as to interview once for another nursing position in a hospital setting. That did not grow to fruition and for just cause. Since then I have turned my eyes toward new paths God has laid before me and it has been enlightening and fulfilling. There really is life after a nursing career.

HENNABABE

When I was approaching the milestone of turning fifty years old I had been dealing with the multiple sclerosis diagnosis for almost five years. Those five years held many bumpy rides, like leaving a nursing career, but God had seen me safely through all of them. So that fall season of my fiftieth year, I was feeling extremely grateful to be alive, walking on my own steam and clearheaded enough to function fairly well in everyday life. Yes, I felt that deep, warm, belt-cinching tightness of love and thankfulness toward God and the cosmic world.

So I spent some time trying to figure out a befitting celebration of turning fifty. A few things I knew for sure: no bitching, no black balloons, no assessment of wrinkles and sags, no regrets. Female friends of mine at the same half-century benchmark were making dramatic speeches about where they were in life and how expectations had fallen short and society was pigeonholing them into an over-the-hill category. There was often an unspoken sense of failure and remorse.

So I doggedly started to research what could be an opposite birthday approach for me. God's synchronicity plopped a magazine article into my lap that touched upon an old art form called Mehndi. Mehndi is the application of henna as a temporary form of skin decoration. A common term in the United States for Mehndi is "henna tattoo." Henna tattoos on average last one to three weeks. It is not uncommon to see the rusty orange-brown henna tattoos applied on sandy beaches of the Caribbean. It is very uncommon to see henna tats in and around St. Wendel, Indiana.

Now the use of henna goes way back. It was ancient practice to color nails, hair, and even beards with henna. Archeologists have found traces of henna on the nails and hair of mummified Pharaohs. And the henna body decorations varied in style geographically—Asian, Middle Eastern, and North African. Each version of the art form has a different flair, but what unites them all is the use of henna to decorate and beautify the body.

I went to Central Library in downtown Evansville and checked out every book I could find on Mehndi. It all intrigued me and I was soon hooked. It became almost an addiction for me. The more I read, the more excited I got. Learning about Mehndi was a perfect fit to turning fifty. The whole idea behind Mehndi art was to celebrate life. That captured what I wanted to see happen on November 20, 2002. I wanted to celebrate life!

Next, I zeroed in on teaching myself the art form. I quickly learned that there was no local vendor for the henna itself so I found a simple kit at a Barnes & Noble bookstore. The kit included an informative little book with designs from India and a pretty dried-up tube of henna. It got me started with some practice designs on myself and later I ordered the henna from an online supplier.

There is a henna plant that grows in arid climates. To make henna for body art use, the leaves are dried, crushed, and then reconstituted with something like my preferred aromatic eucalyptus oil.

I doodled hundreds of designs on paper with a black felt-tipped pen until I was happy with the look and practiced until I was good enough to offer the freehanded henna designs to friends and acquaintances. Eventually fate would have me presenting small informational seminars to local university students. I explained a little of the rich history of Mehndi art and then applied tattoos to the largely international students in attendance.

A moment of true joy for me with my henna body art was when I did a tattoo on the left side of the neck of a University of Southern Indiana international student from Saudi Arabia. He was so excited to get his first henna tattoo and relayed to me how his "Momma" back home had a henna plant growing in their backyard. He had fond memories as a boy watching her grind the dried leaves from the plant in the kitchen with a mortar and pestle and how good it always smelled when she made the paste for use on her family and friends. He said Momma had never really explained what she was doing and was appreciative I had shed some light on the mystery paste his momma had been making in their kitchen.

He said he never got in on the actual body designs, as it was more a woman's task in his family. After sketching me his desired design, Fizal asked me to make the cursive *F* as big as possible on his signature tattoo at the base of his neck and while the paste dried he walked around the next hour with his dress shirt collar pulled away from the staining dye. Fizal returned the following year at "international days" when I returned with my henna booth. His nod of recognition seemed to acknowledge an unspoken secret we shared. And his smile was just as broad the second time around when I wrote "Fizal" on the nape of his neck.

My unexpected, intimate connection with Fizal reinforces the magnitude of blessings multiple sclerosis has brought into my life. Had I not been forced to give up nursing and find other fulfilling pursuits, I would never have met Fizal from Saudi Arabia, explained Mehndi to him, and given him his first henna tattoo. Plus I would never have experienced the radiant warmth of his proud smile as I sent him off to show friends his tattoo.

Mehndi was the beginning of my new career as an artist. The creativity of Mehndi designs was a springboard for applying the same designs to trinket boxes. That led to painting walking canes with some Mehndi designs and branching out to acrylic paints. One thing led to another as I gained confidence and positive feedback from family, friends, and the general public.

My henna tiptoe into the art world led to bigger and bigger things. I became more daring and experimented with canvas and other art mediums like oil, charcoal, and watercolor. I took a few art classes and joined the local arts council of Southwestern Indiana. I became comfortable in the art world, took in some varied art shows, and with time developed a supportive network of artists and gleaned some insights.

Artists are no different than anyone else. They are never completely sure of what they are doing and always put themselves out there on a very vulnerable limb. Much like writing can do, painting exposes one's soul to the world and an artist must be comfortable letting the public see their underbelly. It is a daring career and a humongous gamble in regards to financial compensation. There are no guarantees as beauty is definitely in the eye of the beholder.

Now I find myself answering the posed question, "What do you do?" with "I'm an artist." It took some time for that to roll off my tongue, but it now does with ease and confidence. I own my new career as an artist.

Painter and writer are a very far cry from RN. I thought nursing was my destined lot in life. The flip from nursing to art is about 180 degrees. And I never saw that title coming. No way. The closest I came to artist growing up was doodling in my notebook margins until some teacher nun scolded me for my waste of time and made me quit. The child artist in me was definitely stunted, but adult growth at fifty was made all the sweeter for it.

We are all so much bigger in God's eyes than one chosen career. His powers are endless so He can do anything, including making Mary Ellen an artist after twenty-five years in the nursing profession. We are so narrow-minded to think we have only one big choice of career path. We don't. I believe if we honestly and faithfully follow what God places on our hearts we are on a long, windy road that leads to unimagined wonderlands. The scary part is having the blind faith that God knows what He is doing and our job is to prayerfully follow Him.

When he was at his own career path crossroads in college, I once offered my soon-to-be son-in-law Chris some advice I learned because of MS. "If you have a thought or read something and it makes your heart speed up and go pitter-patter, pay attention! That's how you know it's right. Pay attention to the heart-pounding thoughts."

I will get off my podium now as I am not a preacher and all my words of wisdom are mere ideas in my head and heart. Yet God has led me to share the wisdom he has planted inside me while on my multiple sclerosis yellow brick road. Oz is truly wonderful and magical.

RICK LEAVES THE HOSPITAL

DOC'S EXPERIENCE

Rev. Warren Weresby once paraphrased the story of God miraculously healing Naaman through Elisha in 2 Kings 5:1-19.

> Every morning Naaman would get up. He looked in the mirror as he put on his armor, arranged his medals and meticulously positioned his helmet. He strapped on his sword and would go out into the day. Everywhere he went, people would see him and say, "There is Naaman, the great general." But every night he went home and undressed before the same mirror where he saw Naaman, the man rotting away with leprosy.

In a way I felt like Naaman, but without the hope of a miracle-working Elisha. I put on my scrubs, draped the signature doctor's stethoscope around my neck, and walked into the ED. There I worked as Dr. Yeager with all the responsibilities, demands, and skills expected of an Emergency Room physician. But at the end of the shift, I would go home exhausted, knowing my body was doing less than it had a few months ago. I would look in the mirror and see Ricky Bob, the man with MS.

In 2007 I had talked with the MS specialist about when to quit. He said that should be my decision. Debbie kept encouraging me to continue. She felt that when I stopped working I would go home and become a vegetable. She had good insight. But by fall of 2008 both the neurologist and Debbie said that my days as a doctor should be ended. I knew it too. I needed to work fewer shifts and would need to rest for two to three days after a few hard shifts. I worried before starting each shift that something would happen that I would not have the strength to handle. Before shifts I would pray, "God, please give me the strength to handle these problems."

The staff had been great in creating subtle helps. Sometimes they tacitly directed me with a, "Here, Doc, is the medicine you wanted." Suturing was much harder because I could not stand well and at times my vision changes made complex injuries harder to approximate skin and underlying tissues. The nurses made sure I had a stool, which I never used before in suturing and often administered the local anesthetic. The RNs did the simple suturing and did an excellent job. When I did gynecological examinations, I would need to rest one leg on a stool to have the knee support. The staff would very quietly lift my leg up on the stool to stabilize me during the procedure without drawing the patient's attention.

Toward the end, I worried about doing an emergency delivery. I wondered if I had the strength to deliver the baby and hold it, to suture the episiotomy and care for the newborn all at the same time. Thankfully that did not occur. It was becoming harder to quickly do complex thinking. I am sure the hospital administration watched my performance. They had to in the interest of the patients. But they graciously never made me feel like my competency was in question.

Carol Godsey, the hospital administrator, made thoughtful suggestions to ease the burden of the work, like my using an electric scooter. Dr. Vaughn worked hard to make the schedule as workable as possible. He and the other ER doctors offered to let me work half shifts, even though it would have made scheduling and working those hours a nightmare for them. All the doctors offered to come in and help or work for me if I had problems. Even though I could see the end was approaching fast, these wonderful people did all they could to prevent it from arriving. I never for a minute felt I was being pushed out.

Finally my prayer changed from, "God, please give me the strength…" to an urgent prayer of, "God, please don't let this happen." On February 27, 2009, I donned the blue scrubs and draped the stethoscope over my neck for the last time.

LIFE CHANGES

DOC'S EXPERIENCE

A doctor died and went to Heaven. St. Peter met him at the pearly gates and said, "I checked and your name is written in the Book of Life. Come on in. But you need to remember that you are no longer a doctor."

The doctor said, "I understand but after all these years, could I please keep my stethoscope?"

St. Peter reluctantly agreed and the doctor went into the celestial cafeteria. Doc draped the stethoscope across his shoulders and went to the head of the line. St. Peter went over to him and said, "You can't do that now. You are no longer a doctor."

The doctor said, "Oh yes," apologized, and went to the back of the line. A few minutes later, someone came in, threw a stethoscope across his shoulders, and went to the head of the line. The doctor asked St. Peter why this could happen.

St. Peter answered, "Oh, that is God. Even God likes to play doctor sometimes."

It was months before no longer being a practicing physician began to sink in. Just a few months before, I was seeing new patients and those accompanying them as frequently as every fifteen minutes. With each encounter there were labs and x-rays to be considered, findings explained, and prescriptions to be written. I had to make sense of the patient's complaints, findings, nurses' observations, lab reports, and x-rays. Sometimes these decisions could be life-changing for the patient and had to be made quickly. Now I could go for days and only talk with Deb, Matt, and Beth after they were off work and tired. The only decisions were which news commentator was lying and could I make it to the bathroom on time.

I never used the term "retired" and tried to avoid the label "disabled." Instead I would say, "I have just stopped working for a while." Much like Mary Ellen, I reasoned, "I could have a remission. Who knows? Stranger things have happened." But inside I knew that I no longer belonged in an Emergency Department. The relief from my worries that I might hurt someone because of my illness made the transition a little more palatable. Still I missed every aspect of caring for patients, its responsibilities, and its rewards.

Early in my practice, a man came in for a routine office visit. The next day I learned that he went home, walked out to his shed, and killed himself with a shot gun. A close friend to both of us said that when he went home, he told his wife that I said he had cancer. I do not remember mentioning anything like that to him and have no idea what I said that could have been so devastating. But following that solemn experience, I have always weighed my words very carefully to my patients. I still choose my words carefully. Some old habits do not change. But now, when people talk with me, they no longer listen to me like my words have the weight of a doctor to a patient. Many times my words have no importance to them at all. Well-meaning strangers and friends often look at me and see a partial man on an electric scooter who needs their kindness instead of a patient looking up at me and searching the face of a physician walking into their exam room with clip board and tests in hand. I believe that I miss that doctor-patient interaction the most.

I enjoyed caring for patients. The staff with whom I worked did too. David Vaughn and I consistently had the highest patient satisfaction scores. Some of the patients were easy to like. Some were a pain. But it does not take long for these things to change. Once a patient came in who was a "frequent flier"—that is, she came in often with usually trivial or contrived complaints— she was often seeking "pain killers." In the past she had written at least one formal letter of complaint about her service in our department. When we saw her face at the registration, we all wished she had waited for the next shift. On one of these visits, she was to receive IV medications. The staff inadvertently gave her the wrong drug. This never happens but it did this time and to make things worse it was a medicine that could harm her. Fortunately, it caused her no ill effects. I wondered what would be the best thing to do. If I did not tell her, there would be no reason for her to ever know and she would leave the department no grumpier than usual. If I told her, she understandably could throw a fit right there and no telling what later, certainly a "The Lady or the Tiger" moment.

I stood up from the desk and walked into the treatment bay, hoping for an epiphany in route. It did not come. My mouth surprised my brain as I heard it say...the truth. "I'm sorry. We have given you the wrong medicine." Rather than being irate, screaming, and threatening, she smiled. She answered, "I know. I heard the nurse tell you at the desk." She had found a doctor and one of the few people whom she could trust. We became friends and gradually, almost begrudgingly, I began looking forward to her visits. These personal interactions were no longer to be.

The last week of practice I had an unusual phone call that led to a buffering of the transition. Several years ago, I walked into the ED and it was a mad house. The EMS team was wheeling an injured teenage girl into the ambulance for an ASAP transfer to a larger hospital for head injuries. She had been struck in the forehead with a baseball during a game. The patient was the daughter of our community veterinarian, Dr Mauck. I studied the x-rays and then asked Dr. Mauck if he would look at them with me. I wanted to talk with him Doctor Daddy to Doctor

Daddy. I showed him where I thought there might be a fracture of the frontal bone with possible displacement. I felt that the thin bone had served as a buffer and the cranial cavity and brain were intact. He and I were both a little relieved and hopeful after we reviewed the films together.

The last week of work I received an unexpected phone call. It was Dr. Mauck. He was the Health Department Board Chairman and Dr. Like was a board member. They asked me if I would consider being the Warrick County Health Officer. I had done this job about a decade before. It was not pretty. The employees had been squabbling and there were questions about the integrity of the department's actions. I had been overwhelmed trying to resolve the problems when I only had a few hours a week to be there. I resigned, leaving the department in total chaos and swearing I would never touch another community position again. But now this offer gave me the limited opportunity to still be a doctor. I jumped at the chance. Fortunately, the department had been reorganized and had become a cohesive team. I felt it was something the MS could allow me to do.

The first few months had some unusual demands. Among them was the H1N1 flu epidemic. The rush of the public for vaccinations approached pandemonium. The Health Department staff did all the work. But I felt I was an essential part of this near historic event. I thrived on the adventures of our department.

At home, the transition of going from a twelve-hour-a-day ED doc to a stay-at-home log was like the deceleration of a fast freight train striking a mountain: best expressed as, "Crash." The MS had been taking its toll and there was not a lot I felt like doing or could do. I read and caught up on subjects I had not had time for while working. I did a little work on the Cobra but did not have the strength or balance to get up or down. Anything exceeding thirty minutes of serious work expended more energy than this body could generate. The tired, Cobra Jet engine that Dad and I had rebuilt twenty years before needed another overhaul.

Because I could no longer do the work, I had to ask a professional performance engine building team to rebuild the engine. They bored the block, changed to a stroked crankshaft, and reassembled it with shiny chrome and fresh paint. It looked great but ran poorly. The first time the engine was fired, an intake valve bent. The veteran mechanics spent many hours working to make it right. They referred me to a NASCAR specialist carburetor and dyno shop to have the engine tested. Even after their tweaking, it made less than half the horsepower it should have.

I emailed Bob Walker, a Cobra guru, and asked him if he knew of anyone who was knowledgeable on this particular engine. After I shared my tale of woes with him, he surprisingly said, "No problem, just bring it over. It sounds like a simple problem with a complex presentation." It reminded me of a basic principle in making diagnoses I had used so many times when I was a physician. Bob did a complete tear down with an analysis, which would make a pathologist turn in his skull-opening saw. When the engine was reassembled and back in the car, I had to take it to him for more changes and tuning. His skills were incredible, but, more importantly, he let me watch and even "assist" him. It evoked pleasant memories of working in the garage or barn with my dad when I was a boy. Often I could only tighten a few bolts at a time and then rest. He was patient and let me feel like I could still do something. His wife Di would often join us. Bob understood my limitations and watched my work carefully. He would just laugh when I would call him and tell him I had gotten lost on the way there again and needed more directions. I enjoyed those last days of wrench turning with him. They gave me pleasure and value while I was coping with the changes in my new world.

During this transition another event occurred. My second cousin, Vinson Hendrickson, and I had the opportunity to become close after I returned to Boonville. Our time together was limited but we shared a lot of things in common besides family. He was a pharmacist. We had both lived in the south side of

Chicago. We enjoyed genealogy. Our family had been in Warrick County for six generations. They welcomed the Abe Lincoln family when they moved to southern Indiana. His eyes would light up when we began talking. In the late 1990s, he shared a personal secret with me. He had been diagnosed with multiple sclerosis. In 2001, I learned I had MS. We shared one more thing in common. During my transition from work, Vinson was found dead in his home. It called to my mind Revelation 2:10: "...do not fear the things you are about to suffer."

I was fortunate to have the support of my family during the transition and now. Debbie was always a vigilant observer of changes. Josh, a clinical neuropsychologist, was always just a listening phone call away. All I had to do was pull up the phone and the couch for a "psychology session." The MS has limited my once busy world to a windowed family room and a small bedroom cluttered with unfinished paperwork. A computer, phone, and dimensionless TV add distraction to that large, motionless room. It is Matt, Luke, Beth, and their active young friends passing through this still life painting that breathe life into my MS world. They always slap or hold my hand for an instant when going past me on the couch, sometimes a hug even. They tell me they love me and offer to help. They recount their day and special blessings. Matt and Luke ask me to help them with their business or school papers. Beth tells me about her teaching victories and problem students. Friends call and text me. Larry Powers, a longtime friend to me and the boys, calls nearly every day just to check on me. I count these folks as very special blessings. They do not abate the physical losses of MS, but interacting with their lives gives strength in this battle. They give me life.

Not all friends draw closer when one is deteriorating. Some friends will be more distant. They still care. They do not know how to deal with the changes they see in you. Mother noticed it too when she was suffering with cancer. I have heard several explanations for this phenomenon. Perhaps it is because the friend does not want to see your decline or suffering, or maybe the friend fears saying the wrong thing. It could be that seeing you causes the friend to recognize his own vulnerability to infirmities. I do not know but please be understanding. MS is difficult for friends too.

It is good that friends understand that sometimes you are stronger than others so that phone calls or visits should be fairly short or other times longer and more animated. It is also wise when visiting a patient to remember to sit down rather than stand even if it is a short visit. There is an old story passed down from senior doctors to medical students about doctors who took their hats off were better liked. In the old days, when the doctor took his hat off, it gestured to the patient he was staying longer even though it was the same amount of time. Like the story of the old doc, sitting suggests a longer visit. Another benefit to sitting is that you are looking eye to eye with the patient, not down on them. Mary Ellen remembers Dr. Reed sitting down to help her with her first IV crisis.

There is no patch for the life changes of going from a professional caregiver to a disabled patient. The two worlds are separate. Although the second world has value, its satisfaction has never filled the void left from the loss of the first world.

FEAR AND SADNESS

I cried last night and I am crying this morning and I did not know the man whose death I am mourning.

Last night I received a brief e-mail response from Rick related to my asking about his trip to Nashville, Tennessee, tomorrow to see a new doctor for his MS. We both know the seriousness of his spiral downward with symptoms and his poor response to his present line of treatment modality. We have talked honestly about it. Like I said earlier, MS seldom shortens the life span of a patient. "Seldom" is the operative word there, meaning some do die early.

Rick is a physician, me an RN. We know either of us could fall into that small percentage of MS people who die early because of systemic complications related to multiple sclerosis. We also both understand he is a prime candidate for that to happen being male, older age, and diagnosed and categorized "progressive MS." I on the other hand may be less likely to die early from MS because of my good, current function and my high, ten-year bench mark rating on the "Expanded Disability Status Score." Plus I have responded extremely well to my current Tysabri treatment for MS.

That being said, Rick's e-mail noted he'd been on the phone earlier Saturday morning talking to his brother Myron who lives in California. Their cousin Vinson Hendrickson, a few years younger than Rick, had died and they were discussing his death. The next sentence read, "Yes, he had MS."

Nothing more was said in the correspondence about Vinson's death. There was no need for that. That four-word sentence spoke volumes between Rick and me. We did not need more words. We were friends both living with multiple sclerosis and both knowing too much for our own good. We were medical professionals and it was one of those double-edged swords. We understood in our innermost, hidden spot what tsunami of emotions could come rushing forth if we let it. Vinson's death hit close to home for both of us.

My tsunami hit last night and I am picking up the pieces of devastation this morning. How cruel, how sad, how damn unfair, that this man I did not know died at fifty-nine. He was six months older than me and three years younger than cousin Rick. It sucks! And it could be me. It could be Rick. It could be anyone with MS.

I don't know if my tears are for me, for my dear friend Rick, for Vinson and his family, or for everyone touched by MS. I suppose it is all this and more.

In a most selfish way I am scared of losing someone who has quickly become my friend and confidant and support. I have no crystal ball. Rick could live to be one hundred and still be giving me a hard time and cracking one of his inane jokes. That is the vision I choose to see after the tides have ebbed from this reality shock. And that is the approach we both take in living life to its fullest with MS. Multiple sclerosis for us is like some string-tied Mt. Dew can bouncing behind a newlywed's bumper, providing sparks when the speed and friction is right. It rattles loudly and captures everyone's attention, but if you look closely it is just a cheap tin can. Empty, sticky, dented, and belongs in the trash.

After Rick's Nashville trip, he called me on the road back to Boonville. He sounded exhausted, his speech a little slow and hesitant, but he was clear. Excitement colored his voice because he liked the new doctor consult and felt encouraged that his worsening symptoms were being treated like a bad exacerbation. The new physician had ordered IV steroids and a continuation of the Tysabri IV. Yeah, we get to hang out two days later and commiserate over another IV infusion! I felt my selfish relief fully.

Rick seemed very relieved to have a definite plan of action, and, most of all, he had hope again. He had true hope that his condition might improve. I also noted great relief in his voice along with the hope. Our emotions fluctuate so extremely with MS. No matter how long we deal with the disease, it always maintains the power to knock us down and beat us to a pulp at times. Then it is up to us to suck it up, pick ourselves up once again, and somehow convince ourselves that all is well, there will be a tomorrow, and life is worth living. I appreciated that Rick was smack dab in the middle of one of these knock down moments and was trying desperately to find the strength to go on with courage and fortitude. I ached for my friend and the battle he was fighting at that moment.

Upon Rick's return, we talked more about his encouraging news of a definite treatment plan for his ever-worsening MS condition. Within this, I asked about the funeral arrangements for his cousin Vinson, who'd had MS. It seems the funeral was delayed because of family travel time from out of the country. Rick acknowledged my question but obviously did not want to discuss it in detail or certainly not how Vinson's death affected him, related to his own MS. Rick dismissed me with, "He was only a second cousin. I did not know him well." That was the end of that. I respected Rick's dismissal of the subject.

THE CHICKEN OR THE EGG

Six months after I left MediSphere I was approved for Social Security Disability. It was necessary but was still a big pill to swallow. About the same time this happened was when I had maxed out my tolerability of the Copaxone shots. My neurologist and I had agreed I would not take any of the remaining ABC drugs for MS as my skin could not tolerate any shots for the time being and there was nothing oral for her to prescribe on the market. So I had what I called my "free time" for about two years—no shots of any kind.

Next stop on the MS road to nowhere, I was prescribed Rebif. Rebif, interferon beta-1a, is another shot treatment for MS that is given under the skin into the fatty tissue, three times a week. It is touted to have a three-prong attack to multiple sclerosis that slows disability progression, decreases relapse rate, and decreases development of brain lesions as seen on MRIs. A neurologist I went to later described the potent Rebif as the elephant gun for MS patients and questioned why my neurologist at the time would put that next on my treatment agenda, so early into my diagnosis.

At the time I did not question the order for Rebif as I had had four successful years with the Copaxone she had ordered earlier and I respected her judgment. This hits upon the grayness of MS treatment once again. There is nothing black and white as far as MS treatment goes. It is very subjective and depends greatly on the individual school of thought of your physician. All the more reason we must be strong advocates for ourselves with decision-making related to treatment modalities for multiple sclerosis. The physicians do their best but there is no black and white for them either.

The use of Rebif shots for me was extremely short-lived at seven weeks. The exact length of time I gave myself these shots is a blur. All I remember is quickly becoming very depressed. Roger and I lived in Kenzi apartments at the time in Evansville. It was the extreme downsizing stage in a long string of nine moves to find the right home for us. We kept going up and down in size and upkeep partly because of my ever-changing needs with MS. Hmm, selling loved houses—another symptom of MS no one would guess to include in the long list.

I tried all the obvious tricks to snap out of the depression, LOL (learned that one from my techy Facebook stuff), like anyone can snap out of depression. Maybe a more accurate description of what I was doing at the time was trying with all my might to be proactive in fighting the depression. I tried to make myself do routine, daily activities and not cut myself off from friends and loved ones. None of it slowed down the rearview mirror scene I had of a semi descending upon my back bumper. The semi was bright orange.

The moment I knew I was in trouble and had to act quickly came early one morning after Roger had left for work and I was alone. I had been lying awake in bed trying to assess the old MS body status and figured it was time to get up and get going. I swung my feet off the edge of the bed and dangled off the right side of the mattress. I stared at the short, ecru-colored, shag carpeting below my feet and had the pep talk with myself to stand up now! Nothing moved. I looked up at the dark green drapes over the bedroom window directly in front of me and noted how dark it was in the room. I told myself to open them and let sunshine in. Nothing moved besides the raise of my head to stare at the brocade-type tan design threaded throughout the heavy-insulated material.

My butt was glued to the satin sheets and weighed a ton. My arms and legs weighed a ton. My head was too heavy to lift up one more time. The next random thought in my head was, "How many sleeping pills are left in the pill bottle stuck in the top left drawer behind my folded pyramid of underwear?" The nurse in me started to calculate strength of those pills and maybe some left over muscle relaxers and pain pills I might still have in the plastic shoe box high on the closet shelf.

Amidst the pill calculations I thought, "Face it. You are depressed. You know what this looks like. You are a nurse. Pay attention." Quick to follow behind that was, "I'm not depressed. I just don't care if I live or die. That's different, isn't it? I can't be depressed this bad. I am overreacting and being silly."

Time stood still while my head conversation ensued. I believe God intervened at that moment with the clear realization He put in my head next, "The Rebif is making you this way. You are depressed and it is the medicine. Stop it now."

A great urgency surged through my body, electrical in nature. I called Roger from the phone next to the bed and cried, "I am so depressed. I want to die. I'm scared. I am quitting the Rebif now. I think it's making me this way."

By the tense sound of his voice, Roger was scared. I hated doing this to him; he'd already endured so much with me. He talked to me a while and asked if I wanted him to come home right away. I felt better just by his asking me that question. We agreed I was okay to stay alone until he could come home for lunch. I felt relief in knowing I had made a decision and would stop the drug immediately.

I called my neurologist the next day and told her I had quit the Rebif and why. My delay in calling the following day was deliberate. I feared if I called immediately they might try to discuss giving the med a longer trial and I knew in my heart I had to quit the medicine immediately. It was literally life or death in my mind. It was one of the few things I was sure of in the moment.

I gradually felt better and returned to my normal, befuddled state of mind. A weight had been lifted off me and I counted my blessings once again.

Suicide. Now there's a nasty word we once again do not say out loud in polite conversation. It ranks high up there on the no-no list right alongside poop, pee, and sex. The only set of words that come to mind that can have a similar impact to stop conversation dead in its track is something I heard firsthand on Unit 4600 back in the mid-eighties. I can still see and hear it now. A feisty, red-haired nursing assistant asked our head nurse, "Hey, I've always wondered. Why does a woman's moose toot?" Like I said, some things you just don't say out loud in polite conversation no matter how badly inquiring minds want to know.

Suicide is no laughing matter but, uttered, it is just as show stopping as "moose tooting." Suicide can devastate any family when it happens, and, as I noted earlier, our family had experienced that phenomenon of destruction firsthand with the suicide death of my nephew Rick.

The months following Rick's death found my family in a whirlwind of emotions that included much anger, sadness, confusion, questions, and placing of blame, like we could have somehow had a crystal ball and seen the signs soon enough. It divided our family for a long time. Rick's suicide at thirty-four was not enough pain. We had to add guilt and finger-pointing to try and make sense of something that would never make sense. There are no answers in suicide.

And like I said, there is the unwritten rule of society not to say that nasty word suicide out loud in mixed company. So after coming upon Rick's bloody body, and after the ambulance stopped blaring and flashing its siren, and the coroner released his body in the black zippered bag they actually use (not just on TV), I had the job of calling the funeral home with details. My brother Verner, Rick's dad, had asked that I relay to the director his request to be tactful and not say the "suicide" word out loud or in the obituary if at all possible. Now I had found Rick in the shower, slumped over the sawed off shotgun he had used to take his life. I wondered how that could not be called suicide.

But the longtime friend of the family director guy complied. Rick was officially "found dead of natural causes" in the newspaper obituary a few days later. That same week, when trying on potential funeral clothes at a local department store, I overheard a conversation in the next stall between two St. Wendel gossipy biddies behind the dressing room door. It went something like this:

> Yeah, the newspaper read that Klenck boy was found dead, natural causes. Who do they think they are kidding? We all know what happened. Sounds just like them, trying to be all better than everybody else. Yeah, we know better. You knoooow what happened.

Like I said, suicide is one nasty word.

Multiple sclerosis studies have addressed risk factors of depression and suicide in MS. It is easy to understand the prevalence of depression, given the debilitating effects, isolation, and unpredictability of the disease.

An extensive Danish (people, not pastry) study is frequently cited to support the far-reaching effects of depression in MS. This study tracked 10,174 MS patients over a forty-five-year span. One hundred and fifteen people with MS took their own lives. The expected number in the general population was 54.2. The eye-opening conclusion: The risk of suicide in multiple sclerosis was almost twice as expected more than twenty years after diagnosis. The excess suicide risk has not declined since 1953. [1]

Twice as much! Unbelievable and scary! We cannot ignore these statistics. They are real. And we dare not say this only happens in Denmark.

There is ongoing debate with schools of thought as to how depression appears as a symptom of MS. The first logical thought that comes to mind is what I mentioned earlier. MS is debilitating, unpredictable, a financial and social burden, and can cause great grief and loss in one's life. Who wouldn't be depressed with that bag of issues?

On the flip side of that coin, MS lesions can attack the neurons of any part of the brain. If inflammatory activity produces the buildup of plaque in a part of the brain that controls emotion, is that more the precipitating factor in higher incidences of depression? The defective neurons could be causing a boatload of problems that include depression that is chemical or neurological in origin.

All this goes back to the chicken or the egg phenomenon. Which really comes first? No one can say for sure, but I believe it is a combination of both the stresses of living with MS and the physical changes taking place in our brains because of lesions. It really doesn't make much difference if you are the person dealing with depression where the origin truly lies. It's just another suckfest.

Regardless of which explanation, if you buy into any, the problem of depression as part of multiple sclerosis is something many of us must deal with. How we deal with that is up to us.

Over the years I have spent time in counseling and have made use of psychotropic drugs. Somehow I thought if I could rationalize that I needed to be on drugs because of a physical glitch in my brain it sounded so much better than being labeled "nuts." You know what I mean, Vern? The nurse in me realizes that is a poor acceptance of my depression but sometimes I need that crutch to support my decision to accept help. Just because I accept logical help with an antidepressant doesn't guarantee I will be magnanimous about using it. I only wish that were true.

Today, I see a mental health counselor I trust on an as-needed basis. Lisa refers to my visits as necessary tune ups similar to car maintenance. This is my brain maintenance. At present I also continue a daily psychotropic medication that I feel helps to keep my moods more leveled out and keeps me a little sharper in my thought processes. My neurologist and I have had to play with the strength of this med to strike the right balance for me. That too can be different for everyone. Rick and I have discussed our use of antidepressants. We both appreciate their benefits. We both know the feeling of wanting to end the pain. In the depth of depression, suicide can seem so logical and simple. We and family must always remain vigilant.

I have tried stretches without the psych drugs and can function fine, but my quality of life suffers because I have more low times that slow me down with activities and enjoyment of life. I have too much I want to do in my short life to be weighted down with depression if I have a way to minimize it that works for me. My momma didn't raise no dummy.

Increased energy also seems to be a benefit of this psych drug. Sometimes with MS a physician will order an antidepressant to treat the MS fatigue. I find this benefit a nice plus in addition to helping me feel better balanced with emotions. It is a win-win for me.

When I asked Rick for more about his experience with depression, he slowly began to open his psych world to me. Rick relayed what was in his heart on the subject.

DOC'S GRAPPLING WITH THE WORLD OF DEPRESSION

DOC'S EXPERIENCE

I began my medical practice by filling in for Dr. Jerry Like. A longtime patient of his came in complaining of depression. He had dealt with this intermittently for many years with just a simple, short course of antidepressants. We were trained to watch for suicidal tendencies with depression. So being a good new doc, I asked him if he had any thoughts about suicide. He replied, "Aw, Doc, that wouldn't help." Yes, I learned early to watch how I approached that subject.

I occasionally had problems with mild depression years before MS. Running helped it. Unlike Mary Ellen, I never sought help for depression because it did not cause major problems and I did not want on my records that I was a physician taking an antidepressant. I felt the formal nature of my mother and some of her fore family would consider this taboo. My staunch country upbringing made me feel that a "man" does not seek such things. As a physician I readily recommended psychological treatment for my patients and even friends. But as Dr. Ricky Bob, I could not accept it for myself. My years of medical training and experience made me know these objections were baseless and almost superstitious. Still those feelings were a part of my makeup and made seeking psychological help uncomfortable.

When the MS was finally confirmed, the neurologist started me on an antidepressant. I did not ask for it and did not want it, but she knew that serious depression was a part of MS. Losing one's ability to walk, or work, or think clearly is enough to depress anyone. The biochemical pathways to prevent depression are altered by the disease as well. This means one is facing a double whammy in fighting the blues. Not only does MS make enjoying life more difficult, but the neurotransmitters that oppose depression are diminished too. No wonder the suicide rate in MS patients may be twice that in the general population, like Mary Ellen noted earlier.

Often, when the MS worsens, I lose interest in everything. My world is dark and empty. Life does not seem worth the fight. Antidepressants and positive approaches help, but still some days the score is Depression 1, Ricky Bob 0. When deeply depressed, I have this odd feeling that if I were to just put a firearm against my chest and pull the trigger, I would feel better. What is difficult to understand is that for me the feeling does not represent a desire for suicide. Maybe it is a Freudian thought of blasting the problems away. Maybe it truly is a manifestation of suicidal desires. I do not know. The boys furtively locked my semi-automatic in the gun safe downstairs. I do not think that was necessary but appreciate their wanting to protect me.

My MS has taken a hard toll on our family. We seldom talk about it. I think Debbie still uses denial as part of her coping, a little like she did when I first told her. The boys and Beth see my physical losses as they develop. I have given them gentle "heads ups" on what the future may bring. But it is difficult for them to conceptualize what this disease encompasses. They have no past experiences with which to compare. They all say that they love me and are here for me. We will work together to meet the progressive challenges.

Still I have the battles with depression. Usually the deepest depression passes in less than a day. I have learned to tell myself it is the MS. If I just wait a while, life will look better. The reassurance that it will pass for me is a substantial help. As the Psalmist said, "Joy comes in the morning."

AFFRONTED BY MY FRONTAL LOBES

As you might have guessed by now, my husband Roger is a special man and after forty years of marriage I still love him dearly and that love is reciprocated in the most endearing way any wife could hope for. A good marriage takes a lot of hard work and we have paid our dues there. The result has been much happiness and many blessings in our life together.

So you can imagine the blow it was for both of us when Roger and I found ourselves separated. We were apart only several weeks but it rocked our foundation like an earthquake. After thirty plus years, we had found ourselves at a serious crossroads and felt ill equipped to handle the threat to our marriage.

I mention this most horrific and complicated time of my life because multiple sclerosis played a part in this. No, I can't prove it with certainty, but Roger and I have looked hard at the circumstances surrounding our very brief split and after careful consideration and the input of several counselors, we believe MS once again had its dirty paws in our happy life. This is not a copout or an excuse but a realistic observation.

From note of my initial MRI I knew I had lesions in both frontal lobes. Throughout the fourteen years since diagnosis I have noted symptoms that seem to fit that area of the brain. My most recent MRI noted a "moderately severe" level of noted plaque areas in my brain, again including the frontal lobes. I was never a whiz-bang with all the brain functions when taking my neuro tests in nursing school, but some basics remain in the recesses of my knowledge bank.

To give you an idea what the frontal lobes do, they are considered our emotional control centers and home to our personality. There is no other part of the brain where lesions can cause such a wide variety of symptoms.

This front part of the brain, behind our forehead, is involved in motor function, problem solving, spontaneity, memory, language, irritation, judgment, impulse control, and social and sexual behavior. Subcategories under these headings include loss of fine motor movements and loss of strength in the arms, hands, fingers, speech interference with attention problems and difficulty in interpreting feedback from the environment, noncompliance with rules, impaired associative learning requiring external cues to guide behavior. Add to that a little spatial orientation problem including our own body's orientation in space (remember my falling off cliffs sensations in the rain). And I love the fat cherry on top of this sundae: dramatic change in social and sexual behavior.

I don't profess to be a different person since MS entered my life, but I am different. The result is I have had to learn to live with the many changes in my physical body, plus the ones planted in my emotions and personality. So when I talked about depression earlier that was only the tip of the emotional iceberg.

Roger also has had to learn to live with an ever-changing Mary Ellen. I was no longer the bride he married, no spouse is after thirty-plus years, but my morphing was fueled with MS, which caused the fire to burn high and out of control.

I think one of the bigger challenges with my personality changes was occasional poor judgment. By nature I am a very logical thinking person. I get teased because I think in outline form and was always chosen in management meetings at the hospital to record brainstorming ideas on an easel flip chart. This was because I seldom balked at the railroading and I was a natural for it. Everyone loved following my organized and anal-looking outline format at the front of the room. At least I told myself they loved it.

So when I started making a few poor, illogical choices in my life, it was very noticeably out of my character. It could be big choices or miniscule in nature—made no difference in my messed up brain. The ramifications of bad choices hurt me, but, more importantly, ended up causing some fallout for Roger too and on occasion for the rest of my family. That was the hardest casualty for me to acknowledge. And this insight to my not-so-wise choices had a habit of becoming clear to me only after the fact, when I was already in the hot water. In the moment, I couldn't register how stupid I was being.

While apart from Roger, a dear RN friend solidified this observation of poor judgment. She assessed me bluntly as only a true friend can, got in my face, and said, "Something is wrong with you. You're not acting right. I don't know who you are anymore. The way you're acting right now doesn't fit the serious mess your life is in. You need to see a doctor."

My friend wanted me to talk to my doctors about this. I chose not to because I saw no purpose. Maybe I chose wrongly but my reason was the nurse in me felt there was no corrective avenue to pursue. Would I seek different medical treatment? No. Would there be a pill to fix my poor judgment? Doubtful. Would I ask for an MRI? Why? Would I talk to my counselor? Yes.

I talked and talked and talked, trying to get to the meat of what was my problem and our marriage problems. My counseling sessions were intense and wrought with tears, guilt, and feelings of failure. I sought individual counseling as did Roger and together we went to couples' therapy.

Knowledge gained over the years with MS included some scary statistics related to marriage with one spouse having a chronic illness. Again, it's easy to imagine the added stress any chronic illness can place on a marriage.

The results of one study were published in *Gender Disparity in the Rate of Partner Abandonment in Patients with Serious Medical Illness*.[2] Researchers in this study hailed from the Seattle Cancer

Care Alliance, Huntsman Cancer Institute at the University of Utah School of Medicine, and Stanford University School of Medicine. These guys sounded legit enough for me to take note.

The 515-study population consisted of both cancer and multiple sclerosis patients, followed over a five-year period, ending in February 2006. The rate of separation and divorce was 20.8 percent when the woman was the patient, compared to 2.9 percent when the man was the patient. A conclusion was a woman is far more likely to be separated or divorced soon after being diagnosed with cancer or multiple sclerosis than a man would be if he were the patient.

Now any woman reading this is going to say, "Duh, didn't need a fancy study to tell me that. Men are jerks. We are the tougher sex." Well, officially, study authors said the vast disparity can be explained, in part, by men's lesser ability to make more rapid commitments to being caregivers for a sick partner and women's better ability to assume the burdens of maintaining a home or a family. Like we said, ladies, men are jerks.

Great, now I knew not only was the divorce rate higher in couples dealing with a chronic illness, but for sure being a woman meant I had a much greater chance of losing my husband. Like I said, I'd put Roger through a lot with the many changes and demands of the MS, besides just being Mary Ellen. These frightening thoughts lingered in my mind even though we both wanted our marriage to work and were committed to doing whatever it took to save it.

Along the exhausting road to marital recovery, Roger and I incorporated a new therapeutic approach to healthy communication suggested by our marriage counselor. It is called Imago therapy. An intense Imago intervention took place, led by a wonderful counselor named Jessica, trained in Imago therapy. The long, three-day weekend session took place on a horse farm in Lexington, Kentucky, about a two-and-a-half-hour drive from Newburgh, Indiana, and we stayed at a beautiful bed and breakfast for the time there. Horse farms, B & B's all sound so vacation-like. It was not. It was intense work and emotionally stripped us both naked, but we left with much healing and many tools to repair our shell-shocked marriage.

Harville Hendrix, Ph.D., penned a very successful book entitled, *Getting the Love You Want.* The book serves as the Imago therapy guide to enriching a couple's relationship and is utilized by many marriage counselors. An underlying premise to the therapy is that we need to heal childhood wounds in our love relationships and to do so we instinctively seek partners that aid us in accomplishing that.

Imago therapy gives couples the information and tools to heal and have intentional dialogue to make a deeper connection with each other. Learning about "intentional dialogue" includes three communication steps of mirroring, validating, and empathizing. This is a very simplistic explanation of what Roger and I spent three days and a lot of money to learn. We continue to read about Imago therapy and practice our intentional dialogue on a regular basis. Our money and time were very well spent. No regrets there.

We always thought we were an exceptionally lucky couple. Love, passion, and friendship have always held a strong presence in our relationship. That obviously did not shield us from the same pitfalls other couples experience in less solid marriages. I must say this Imago approach has been a true blessing for us. It forced us to be more open and honest and vulnerable in our marriage. This has brought enrichment and new tools to continue a solid, happy marriage that has successfully withstood many crisis situations over the years.

After the miserable time apart, Roger and I were back together. We now had new battle scars but we were stronger as a team. The saying of "make or break you" was apt for that time of our lives. God once again took care of us during that ordeal. He never left our sides and for that I am so grateful.

God knows I was really ticked at Him for much of our time apart. And that's okay. He knows it is in my heart whether I speak it out loud or not. He's God! I was mad that Roger and I had worked so hard to be a strong couple, remained prayerful throughout, and we still found ourselves floundering like two beached whales on Orcas Island. That's life, right? We all get beached and start to dehydrate and can't find that sand-kicking tourist, combing the beach, to throw life-saving water upon us.

I guess it goes back to what I mentioned earlier: we all have our crosses to bear. They just all look different and the weight of them varies from day to day. Roger and I just had a stretch of really heavy crosses. What counts is God got us through and at the end of the Calvary-type trail we came out stronger and a tad bit wiser. Thank you, God.

After sludging through the debris of my unwise choices and the problems Roger and I shared in our marriage, I tried to be more aware of the personality changes MS dumped on me and that played a factor in our marital bump in the road. I wanted to be more cognizant of these risk factors in the future. It was the best I could think of to do at the time. I had been sort of in survival mode and now I wanted to be more proactive and hopefully minimize ramifications of my MS frontal lobe symptoms.

I wish I could say I came up with a great plan. I did not. I have yet to come up with a good deterrent for the poor judgment symptom. Roger and I talk a lot about this more frequent phenomenon in our married life. I try to talk openly when making big decisions and truly respect the guiding input of a select few family members and friends. Roger and I personally use much intentional dialogue learned in therapy. Sometimes just being aware of what MS holds for us and saying it out loud gives us strength to cope and adapt.

When I drive over an IED (improvised explosive device) like I just described with our time apart, Roger, my family, and sometimes my friends are in the tank with me. The best I can do is to be careful and vigilant, hope for minimal damage to life and limb, and turn it all over to God.

And there is a silver lining in this consignment store personality purse; the increased spontaneity that also comes with my frontal lobe malfunction adds to my creativity as an artist. It makes it easier to take chances and to try the unthinkable like writing a book. Thank you, God.

THIRD TIME TREATMENT'S THE CHARM—NOT!

By the time I survived the Rebif suicide boogey man and was back to my normal crazy self, Roger and I had downsized to an upstairs' apartment, then a downstairs' apartment, and then decided we had gone too far. Going from a farm, then a two-acre country home, to a tiny apartment was more than this country bumpkin couple could handle. So we went in the other upsize direction and decided to move into a patio home. It gave us a bit more room but more importantly gave us our own front and back yard again. I never knew how much my sanity hinged upon having grass under my feet that I owned. You can never completely take the country out of the girl.

We spent four happy years at the patio home until the loft area with the stairs became too much of a problem. Yes, I know a loft was not the wisest choice at the time because of my MS, but I was determined not to let MS totally control my life. And I so loved that cute loft set up.

Ideally, our bedroom should be in that big, opened area of the loft, but it meant some days I was isolated upstairs when the descent and ascent were more than my body could accomplish. It really depressed me and interfered with my quality of life so we once again moved.

Newburgh was our next stop and four years later we are still here. Our current home is a convenient one-level ranch with little upkeep that sits on a decent-sized lot in a small subdivision. Our backyard is edged with a steep hill, a lake, and a wooded area that completely blocks a northern view of any other house. We have great neighbors and developed our back patio and porch to be a cozy haven abundant with trees, flowers, shrubs, and birds. Squirrels, rabbits, and turtles also hang out in our yard, having given our abode the Good Critterkeeping seal of approval.

It is a sort of hobby for me and Roger to do landscaping together. You might be surprised to hear I landscape and have MS. I do. I am woman; hear me roar! I find I can adapt to many tasks, even physically demanding ones sometimes if I pay attention to my body, and landscaping is something that ranks high on my list of enjoyable life experiences.

Life with multiple sclerosis is all about choices, baby: "What fun thing do I want to expend my energy on?" That is the question I frequently ask myself. There is only so much energy to go around on any given day. Cleaning house has yet to make the top-ten list.

So on landscape days I take numerous breaks, drink ice water continuously, wear an old lady brimmed hat and a dorky ice bandanna, pace myself with the acuity of a marathon runner, and tell Roger *adios* when I hit the fatigue wall and it's time to call it a day.

My work day may not be as long as Roger's, nor as productive, but I like to think of myself as a wise, keep-cool tortoise who grins widely when crossing the finish line, however long it takes. Who wants to be a hare anyway? The chances of having your lucky foot cut off are much greater.

Roger and I love daydreaming about our suburban oasis. We share visions with each other and brainstorm about our plans for the yard after dinner while sipping a Pinot Noir on the patio. Eventually we make some of the dreams happen. The next one in my head takes the shape of a meditative Asian garden corner. Oh yeah, I can see the bumps in the bamboo and hear the trickle of the water now.

After taking Rebif, I had some time completely off any of the ABC drugs, which was my fun "get out of jail" time. Then door number three was opened and Monte revealed the big scarlet *A*, Avonex. Yippee coyo coyaaa!

There was great discussion between my neurologist and me before deciding to start Avonex, another interferon beta-1a drug, same as Rebif. Avonex 30 mcg is a one time a week intramuscular injection while Rebif 44 mcg is a three time a week subcutaneous injection. Rebif being more potent is why my new neurologist questioned why I was prescribed the Rebif elephant gun before trying the little bird bee-bee gun of Avonex. I had no answer to that. The nurse in me was too busy dealing with MS and life at the time to have that now obvious discussion with the old neurologist who made me cry with every visit.

The option to continue to do nothing as far as an ABC drug treatment was scary. Literature supported that long-term disability was so much greater for MS patients if one of the ABC drugs was not given. I was early fifties at the time, had a lot of living still planned, and wanted a mind and body that would cooperate with future plans. So I was back at the drawing board, chalking in once again a new MS stick figure.

Doc and I were both more than a little reluctant to try another interferon beta-1a drug knowing how poorly I tolerated the first attempt of the drug. We did our research, weighed the many pros and cons, and together agreed it was more dangerous for me to continue with no MS drug than to take another chance with the less potent Avonex. Avonex and Rebif were basically the same drug but were supposed to be two very different versions when it came to tolerance. Doc reassured me he would monitor me closely and I trusted him to do just that. It always boils down to trusting the doctor, doesn't it?

As an RN I am more than qualified to give myself a shot. Unfortunately, insurance coverage at the time I started taking the newly prescribed Avonex required an on-site injection protocol that included some post-injection monitoring time by an RN. So I scheduled to get my shots every Tuesday afternoon at 1:00 p.m.

at nearby Health South Rehab facility in Evansville. We lived in nearby McCutchanville back then, about a thirty-minute drive.

The RN who gave me the shots was a name I recognized but someone I had never met. Her husband was a local neurosurgeon I had dealt with professionally in the hospital setting. Nurses and doctors cross paths all the time, so you better not gossip too much about any of us. It will get back to someone it should not get back to. Sort of like everyone is related to everyone in southern Indiana.

The very first Avonex shot left me deathly ill within a couple of hours after receiving it. It was not uncommon to have flu-like side effects with Avonex initially, but usually with time the body became accustomed and the use of Ibuprofen or Tylenol controlled any discomfort. My good friend Billie with MS had been receiving the drug since it was first made available a decade before and followed that pattern. She had good results and happily continues the drug today. I clung to her reassurance and my neurologist's that more than likely I would get used to it and it would be very tolerable. That never happened.

The next year for me was a living hell and I do not use that phrase lightly. I would get my shot at one o'clock every Tuesday and every Tuesday evening found me in bed with a fever and chills, deep body aches, headache, eyes burning, and teeth hurting. It was flu symptoms at their worst. My body felt like one big throbbing infected tooth.

Finding a position of comfort in bed was impossible and I cried even when I promised myself I would not do so. I prayed. I would crawl out of bed, kneel next to the flowered footstool, hug it tight, and rock back and forth hoping the movement would distract my mind from the pain.

I begged God to give me strength, to heal me, to make time pass quickly. I bartered with God. If He only took a bit of my pain away I would make it to Mass every Friday morning. If He let me sleep till the pain was gone I would go to confession next week. If He took just the throbbing away I would never gossip again. My imagination created an endless list I put at God's feet. Nothing.

Then I'd switch tactics and say the rosary, meditating on the sufferings of Jesus Christ and try to appreciate the smallness of my pain, all the while asking for Mary's intercession with each Hail Mary. If Mary only asked her Son to help me He would surely not say no to his mother.

I repeated the prayerful petition from childhood by offering up my pain, "All for the honor and glory of God and for the poor souls in purgatory." The monotony of it soothed a bit but the rote prayer left me empty and forgotten, undeserving of intervention.

My doctor, nurse practitioner, who gave the shots, and my MS friend all had me trying combinations of Tylenol, Ibuprofen, and eventually some Prednisone beforehand and nothing helped very much.

My weeks became a sadistic ritual of driving myself to Health South, getting a shot, acting like it was no big deal, then going home and being sure this time would be different. The pain always followed me home.

The worst of the pain lasted about twelve to fifteen hours, followed by annoying but tolerable pain for another twenty-four or so. It amounted to what I began to budget as two lost days every week and a day of bitchiness on the third. Then I had four days every week I tried to cram every real-life activity into, all the while factoring in the MS which was the reason to begin with I was losing three days a week. What was wrong with that picture?

I could have begged for some hard drugs every Tuesday or tried something off the street. That was not me though. If I had decent results of slowing down MS progression and flare-ups with use of Avonex, and took it long term for years as Billie did, I could not get used to taking narcotics every week to make it better.

During this year of Avonex treatment for my multiple sclerosis, my loving husband did what he does best—he loved me.

Roger Edward Ziliak held me, rocked me, tucked me in with soft fuzzy blankets and gave me wet washcloths wrung out just right. No dribbling down my neck. He put straws in my drinks and held the glass to my lips. He kissed my brow.

But the best thing he did for me was to read Psalms out loud every Tuesday evening from my favorite King James Bible when he came home from work. He avoided making evening appointments with clients on Tuesdays whenever possible. Roger's resonant voice in my ear became the morphine drip that calmed the beast inside me. God answered my prayer through him. Thank you, God.

Going into my twelfth month of receiving weekly Avonex intramuscular injections, I was at one of those crossroads in life. Something had to give. In the middle of extreme distress, on a Tuesday afternoon, when pain that was escalated by Avonex, MS, and some extreme emotional events in my life at the time, I called my neurologist and told him I quit this method of treatment.

The treatment was much worse than I believed the disease to be in my case. He did not argue. Doc understood my struggles with side effects over the last year although he could not appreciate the magnitude of ramifications. Part of that I take blame for. Pride prevented me from full disclosure of my pain and it was too complicated to explain well. Words still don't capture the heat of the lava that oozed over me that year.

MAYTAG REPAIRMAN

Rick Yeager has frequently offered his big ear and strong shoulder in my processing of confusion and shameful moments with MS. It helps so much to have someone who listens, understands, and does not judge. I can tell immediately after my sharing intimacies of MS if the listener is accepting or put off by my revelations. Rick has been nothing but accepting.

One might think that a listener with MS would automatically be accepting and nonjudgmental. Not so. The listener may be in a very different place of acceptance of their illness and that skews their perception. Not accepting my quirks might keep their denial of MS secured more tightly in their hands.

In telling Rick of my difficult year of Avonex use and how poorly I handled it at times, I worried I might lose the respect of a good friend and IV partner. But in listening, Rick had an immediate good ole boy response that took me a bit by surprise, "Oh, Mary Ellen, your washing machine was overloaded."

"Whaaaat?" I asked. "You crazy man! Your MS brain is in worse shape than mine."

"Your washing machine was overloaded. It was off balance. You'd had a year of horrible reactions to the Avonex you took. Your MS was knocking you down. Your whole family was in turmoil adjusting to your worsening symptoms and changes. You had too much stuffed into your washing machine, little sister, and it was way off balance. Don't you get it?"

Well the dumb doc wasn't so dumb after all. His brain balls may have been as messed up as mine with ugly lesions, but he was right. I hated to admit he was right. Rick and I have healthy, ongoing battles of wits on the most stupid of topics, like where dinosaurs come from, and it set bad in my craw to admit this friendly adversary was right. Ah well, chalk one up for Dr. Yeager.

Now, thanks to stupid old Yeagerman, I think of washing machines at the craziest of times. The idea of having a big bed comforter in a machine has me seeing a square metal dance performer on stage hopping around on one foot with a Charo attitude of shimmy, shimmy, cocoa pop, shimmy, shimmy pop.

Today's psychologists might suggest we overloaded people of the twenty-first century revert back to a simpler yet efficient wringer washing machine. In childhood there was a healing power in Mom's washing ritual, right down to the blended basement smell of homebrew and sewer from the shower under the steps and the cool of concrete on my bare feet. And there was no shimmy because of overload.

I guess my family and friends sometimes see me and my heavy MS comforter as just too much for their modern-day washing machines. It overloads them and it is simply too much to handle. The extra weight throws them off balance.

A few friends have pulled away from me since I was diagnosed with multiple sclerosis and it hurts. Some have done so out of fear, others out of ignorance. It is difficult for them to understand how I can be all enthused about a night out of dancing or a play and then an hour or two before we are to meet up I cancel on them. It is easy to take that rejection personally. I get it.

Some family members have distanced themselves because of graduation parties missed or my not attending their daughter's baby shower. With thirteen sister and brother-in-laws, it's a challenge to attend all functions without MS. But I do miss my share of events no matter how carefully I plan to pace my energy expenditure and flat times of rest.

I have had Saturdays where I struggle all day in a constant state of angst because I am trying to decide if I will meet my commitment for the night. I try to let people know as soon as possible when I have to send regrets. But MS is so unpredictable that sometimes I call my attendance off too quickly and I get a boost of energy at the last minute and can go and other times I think I'll make it only to realize at the last minute the shower was too much and I can't sit upright in the car to travel to the dance.

Like I said, it's a balancing act. My remaining closest friends understand as best they can. A happy moment for me with friends Joe and JoAnn took place on a trip to Oliver Winery one fall. The Harrisses knew I had to pace myself and understood the phrase, "flat time." They thought nothing of me packing a big blanket in their trunk or my yoga mat to do my flat time. When it came time for me to lie flat and rest so I could finish out the rest of the wine tour, I said, "Okay. I've hit the wall. Gotta stretch out on this blanket and re-juice. You guys do your thing and I'll catch up with you in about twenty minutes."

They looked at me, and JoAnn said matter-of-factly, "Okay, Mary, we're taking a hike around the lake and we'll check back later." And off they went. No pity, no questions, no staying behind to babysit me, no guilt laid upon "poor Mary," no changing of their plans. They accepted the oversized comforter I stuffed into their washing machine. I never loved my two friends more than at that moment when they understood me, my MS, and my need to not make a big deal out of my MS quirks. I thank God for Joe and JoAnn in my life.

MONKEY DUST

DOC'S EXPERIENCE

Sandy Lamar, a tough biker chick and an insightful RN, would say that a friend will keep your secret but only a true friend will help you bury the body.

A kindly little man sat down in a restaurant and set a little box on the table. The pleasant young waitress took his order. She watched with curiosity as he took a tiny piano from the box and set it on the table. He then took a small frog and placed it on a tiny piano bench. Beside the piano he placed a beautiful white mouse. The frog played the miniature piano and the mouse began to sing a variety of songs beautifully. The waitress had moved to the next table where a rich Hollywood producer sat. She overheard him say to his wife, "That little combo is worth millions. I'm going to fleece this old fellow out of them." The producer offered the old fellow five thousand dollars for them. He refused. The producer upped the bid to twenty thousand. He refused. The waitress was in the background desperately shaking her head no. Finally the producer said, "Fifty thousand dollars and that is my top offer." The kindly little fellow said, "I have had them for years. They are my only company, but I badly need the money. I will sell you the mouse for the fifty thousand dollars but please let me keep the frog." The producer paid him, grabbed the mouse, and ran out the door with an evil laugh. The waitress looked over sadly to the poor little man. He winked at her and with a sly little smile said, "Not to worry, kind lady. The frog is a ventriloquist."

Buyer, beware. When the word of my MS spread among my friends and the community, there were many people offering to sell me products to help. They hawked a variety of health foods, supplements, and nutrients. Friends shared articles telling me to stop diet soft drinks, avoid refined sugars, or eat special foods. A longtime friend had a product in which he firmly believed and offered to even give me a month supply for free. Another friend whom I had not seen in thirty years drove one hundred and ten miles to start me on a product that he felt had saved his life. Dan, a friend in Florida, mailed me a three-month supply of a supplement that had helped him with neurological problems including forgetfulness. It was also undergoing therapeutic trials in patients with MS. I shared the supplement with a friend who complained of memory problems. She was convinced it helped her. I cannot see that it has helped me, but I have continued it because I appreciated Dan's remarkable kindness. When he asks, I do not want to disappoint him by saying I have stopped.

These folks believed in their products and were convinced that the supplements were worth the price. I do not doubt that they or their acquaintances had experienced amazing results with these agents. The friends offered persuasive physiological explanations on how their products change some form of metabolism or supplies some needed ingredient or degrades something. All these health aids were created by some insightful scientist or physician or brilliant entrepreneur, who had found something the rest of the world had missed. The literature or professional videos from the manufacturer presented lofty explanations of how it would make my life better. There were incredible testimonials from people who had been helped.

I was not sure they were for me. I asked myself, "If these products are that good, why are MS physicians not recommending them?" Are my friends offering me true helps or Monkey Dust? I was a physician and I know doctors want their patients to be better. We physicians listen to patients. When they say something is helping them, we make at least mental notes of curiosity. I have learned several things by listening to my patients. And yes, I did recommend some herbal and non-prescription medicines. But before I recommended them, I studied them.

Many of these products appear to be very profitable for the company that provides them. The literature often has colorful illustrations of how it functions and no shortage of testimonials. But it bothers me that if this company is so successful and if the product is so helpful, why weren't research double-blind studies there to support claims? The advertisement of the pills Dan sent stated that Nobel Prizes were given to the scientists who discovered it. But I could not see in the information where any of these scientists formally recommended this product as a health aid. The literature also presented a report from patients who evaluated the product. But there was no double-blind study.

Another consideration I kept in mind was to ask if the product had been recommended by conservative multiple sclerosis organizations. But even then I had to remind myself to consider sites thoughtfully. I also had to consider if the product would likely cause me any problems. None of the products offered to me by well-meaning friends seemed to have any significant downsides, but I had to check the label. If they contained calcium in large doses, it could cause bowel changes. Sodium content could be important if I had renal problems. Finally, is there any published research on these products other than what the selling company presents?

Most of the friends offering these products to me believe in them. It makes me uncomfortable to disappoint them by not using their supplements. Some become disappointed and a little offended if I refuse use of their product. I hate that but I can only do what is right for me.

RICK EXPLORES WHY

DOC'S EXPERIENCE

Weeping may endure for a night, but joy cometh in the morning.

Psalms 30:5 (KJV)

A generic middle-aged man ate a quick breakfast, washed, and shaved. He left for work just like any other day. His expectation to have a normal workday, go home, and share an evening with his family was so certain he never gave it a second thought. That afternoon a troublesome chest discomfort progressed into deadly pain. He called for help. The Emergency Services recognized the ECG changes of a life-threatening infarction. It was "the widow maker." Within minutes they had him to the trauma room table, lying on the stainless steel emergency table. After a hard fought battle for his life, all of our collective training, skills, and technology were not enough. This man slipped into eternity.

Physically and emotionally drained, it was now my responsibility to force myself to be collected and go to the family in the waiting room to tell his wife. I gestured the failure to her and she cried out, "Oh no, he can't be...dead!" But the impact of all that had happened in such a short time had hit its mark. She could not begin to comprehend all the attendant implications of this moment, but she knew he was gone. Through the tears streaming from her searching face, she asked the question, "Why?"

The omnipresent blockbuster question asked in the Emergency Department about terminal diseases and early deaths is "Why? Why did this have to be me?"

Early in MS one has to grapple with that universal question; the patient asks himself, his pastor, and loved ones, or a counselor. Others will incredulously ask the patient, "Why did this need to happen to you?" For me the question, "Why?" was posed long before MS.

When I was a young physician, I thought that surely there was a comforting, helpful answer to that question. I searched for that answer for a long time. The only answer I have found is still the very first empty answer I ever offered. "I don't know." The question is the same for MS as well as an infinite number of other forms of inexplicable sorrows. Why? And I still do not know.

It is a natural first searching for many MS patients. Why did I have to have MS? What did I do to deserve this? Why me?

I would offer two replies. Literally, you did not cause yourself to have MS no more that you chose your parents. The susceptibility for this illness is inherited perhaps from a combination of several genes. Yes, there are environmental factors that may increase the incidence like living in a cooler climate or perhaps not having enough sunlight or vitamin D. But the bottom line is that the disease chooses you. Period.

"Why?" or "Why, I don't deserve this?" or "What did I do wrong?" easily accompanies a component of guilt that occurs with misfortunes like MS. It is not a onetime question. It may occupy ones thoughts several times in a day when one cannot fix a simple meal or takes a hard fall or just has trouble with a bout of incontinence. "Why?" may have short-term answers like it is just a bad MS day or I knew I should not have reached that far or I overdid myself yesterday or... But these are just short answers. The primordial "Why?" stays in the MS soup and defies answer. Just leave it there.

Anger is the uglier twin brother to "Why?" Mary Ellen's up-front and personals with this are classic. My "heads on" with anger have been mere skirmishes compared to many of the MS folks' experiences. I think that in part, for me, anger was averted because I had the opportunity to do nearly everything longer than I should have and was a little relieved to bring my effort to conduct a normal life while grappling with MS to an end.

The first thing I gave up because of MS was working outside. Previous years cleaning the fence rows as time would allow had been hard but satisfying. I never finished one year thinking the next would be the last for that task. In the spring of 2006 I started clearing the fence rows and worked about two hours. My body just would not do it any longer. It told me very clearly to put the tools in the barn and go to the house. This is your last fence row.

Running was the same way. It became too tiresome to run and the left foot drop made running more dangerous. A near trip down a four-foot embankment was the final needed persuasion that running time was done. Sometime in the fall of 2006 I made some unceremonious last run. Quitting time for the Emergency Department was pushed past due too. There was no need for anger. I had worked as long as I could.

Faith and friends have been my resources for surviving the challenges of MS. But I had to learn earlier to use them with smaller problems before they could be deployed against the full frontal assault of MS. It is easy to say that the God who made the marvelous universe and sent his Son to die for us wants us to have good things when all is going well. But when from our vantage point things are not good, the faith can slip out the back door faster than you can say ex-spouse at the front door. "I believe but, Lord, help my unbelief."

In an early spring of my practice, things were going rough. Sick patients were coming from everywhere. I was getting little sleep and was facing a doctor's nightmare, a serious malpractice suit. As I was walking out the office door, overwhelmed, Ruth

Lutz, our office manager, reminded me of the scripture, "…in everything give thanks" (I Thessalonians 5:18, KJV). Ruth was a sharp, tireless, trusted friend and coworker, but she was not well known for her piety. But there it was, and she was right. I thanked her for reminding me and left. Where did she get off with that? After all the problems I was in, what better medals could I wear than anger and self-pity? It took weeks, even months of wrestling with that simple truth before I could finally admit that it applied to me. In *all* things give thanks.

Why should I give thanks? First, because that is what God said for us to do and that is enough. But that is the beginning of the story. When we know that the God who does all things well is watching over us, then how can we expect anything but good things? Even if He chooses to punish us for some wrongdoing with affliction, it is for our good and is done because He loves us. He is with us through every unpleasant moment. But not all bad is because of punishment. In John, chapter 9, when the disciples asked Jesus why the man was blind, He answered the man was blind so that people could see him healed. God has a better plan.

I learned to be thankful during problems because they taught me to lean on God more. When they were over, I could see how I had been cared for. And often things had worked out to be better than before. My problems encouraged others when they saw they were not alone with their problems. Troubles helped me to learn to care more for others. I could not appreciate how burdens affected others until I had similar ones myself. It gave me insight to concerns as a physician. It made me a better physician.

Challenges also made me learn to accept help from others. This is most humbling for a man who does not even want to ask for directions. These are important lessons for anyone. The lessons can only be learned with time and with more than one difficult experience.

A dear patient who was slowly losing the battle with progressive breast cancer and personal problems explained it simply:

"Imagine you are carrying a cross that has all your overwhelming struggles written on it. You are in church where the pastor invites everyone to bring their crosses forward. Each person is to lay hers or his cross down at the altar and step back. Then all could look at everyone else's crosses and pick the one that he or she liked and take that one back with them. Each would see all the others and pick their own cross back up again. She would walk away and never say another word."

What insight. I have a friend my age with advanced Parkinsonism that has entombed him. He has full thinking abilities but cannot so much as close his eyes. I have another friend younger than me, dying of colon cancer. I only have to take the quickest glance around me to see other people, undeserving people, with much worse problems than MS will ever bring to me.

Also, I can be thankful for how much I have. I have a wife to whom I have been married thirty years. The Lord has given me an opportunity to see my sons become adults and have some idea of what they are doing with their lives. I have Beth, my daughter-in-law, who warms the room when she enters it.

Few people have had the opportunity to have a job that they could totally enjoy and also feel that it was their ministry. I had that opportunity for thirty-one years. God blessed me then and I need to realize that this was what He has decided is best for me now. I do not understand it but I believe it.

When I am discouraged or down, thinking of things for which to be thankful and knowing this truly is better for me than anything else is the guide post for navigating through the fog of anger, self-pity, bitterness, and resentment. No, it does not always leave me singing through the rain and mud like Mary Poppins. But it draws me back to the realm of safe autopilot.

In the busy ED I was often reminded of the old adage, "When you are up to your eye balls in alligators, it is easy to forget that your first objective was to drain the swamp." Likewise as the erosions of MS progress it is easy for life goals to change. Mary Ellen told how she lost her professional career but gradually gained fulfillment in her new world of art. I have mentioned how MS took away my ability to work outside in the pasture and the fun of "man things" like riding the tractor or using the chain saw or even weed eating. Gradually the MS took away my ability to work in the garage too. When I was healthy and active, I would see things that needed to be done and put them on a prioritized "gotta do" list. Some things were completed. Some things were moved down the list, but there was always hope that I could accomplish these things. MS took away that hope. When I am outside or in the garage, I see the tasks I would have enjoyed doing. But now these are jobs I can never do. The thought of these projects has become burdensome and offers no pleasure.

Now I have to figure if I am going to have strength to go to the dentist or work on bills. Many of the skills I had hoped to impart to my sons will never be passed on. My goals are limited to the most essential things like just listening, making sure my will is correct, or finding strength to take another round of IV steroids. Now when I see someone running on a beautiful afternoon, I first think that I'll take a nice run too. But immediately the reality of MS squashes that happy thought. Then I am reminded that I cannot run because God has something better for me. It occasionally takes effort, but I believe it; give thanks and go on.

RICK RAMPS IT UP

DOC'S EXPERIENCE

In 2003 I was out working in the yard. An unfamiliar, badly worn, old Camaro clattered into the driveway. The tall driver unfolded out and walked toward me. His unkempt black hair morphed into a thin, straggly beard of a young man. His muscular frame suggested heavy lifting like construction rather than an athlete or weight lifter. He walked toward me with an uncertain, awkward smile. My curiosity was on point as I watched him approach. He introduced himself. "I'm Josh Nuekan and I want to apologize for running over your cat. I came back to bury it and the body was gone. Could I pay you for it?"

I had found the dead cat and buried it earlier, but I was awed at this young man's integrity. I could not think of anyone I had ever met who had exhibited that level of integrity.

"So you ran over my cat?"

"Yes, I am sorry," he replied.

I could not resist challenging this remarkable young man just a little. I responded, "How much do I owe you for killing it?"

He looked back with surprise and confusion. Enough is enough and it was time for me to be fair with this remarkable young man. Well, almost fair anyway. "Look around. Do you see all the cats running around here? People are always dumping off more. And I can't get rid of them fast enough. Thank you. By the way, if you could have hit my wife's horses I would try to help you through college."

He was quick on the uptake and smiled. I could not let him go without learning more about him. Searching for some common ground, I looked at the Camaro and made some comment. "About every young man with a Camaro would like to talk cars," I reasoned. With no more than appropriate pride, he told me it was not running when he bought it and he had fixed it. We talked on.

With just a little verbal nudging, he became more comfortable. He explained that about eight months ago he had accepted Jesus as his Savior and his whole life was changed. He no longer used drugs nor drank and it was because of this he wanted to do me right by the cat. I marveled at this man. We talked a little longer and I invited him to come back again sometime and we could just talk. He did not even need to kill any animals to have an excuse to drop in.

To my amazement, about three weeks later, the young man was back. We sat on the porch and talked a short while. He heard the boys playing their guitars and drums in the basement. He went down to join them.

By coincidence, if there is such a thing as coincidence, he was attending the same church our family began to attend a short time later. He graciously continued to let me be a part of his busy life. In time, Josh opened his own small construction business and took pastoral courses by mail. He began a well-attended, weekly counseling session at a local, upscale addiction rehabilitation center. He has married our friends' daughter and has two lovely children. He was director of a mission trip to Ecuador in which my son participated. What does this have to do with a disability ramp for an MS patient?

The Veterans Administration physical therapist had evaluated me for an electric scooter. She suggested that instead of a scooter I should consider an electric wheel chair. I resented needing the scooter and certainly did not want to be seen in an electric wheel chair.

The VA graciously provided me with the scooter and a lift in the truck. It was a tremendous aid in going places. I kept the scooter in the garage and used a walker in the house. My legs and pelvic muscles were progressively weakening. By last winter I was having difficulty walking from one room to the next on occasions. It was time to use the scooter in the house as well. The boys would lift it in and out of the house for going places. This was a fairly heavy-duty scooter. I think a smaller one would have been more helpful in the house.

Why did I not get a ramp when I first brought the scooter indoors? To me an access ramp to my front door was like putting a large electronic billboard in the front yard with flashing blue lights reading, "Attention Walmart shoppers! We have a lazy parasitic half-man living in this house." I felt anger toward the MS and shame every time I thought about a ramp.

Josh Nuekam saw that the ramp was needed. He did not know about my reservations but recognized the need. He built the ramp. When he was finished, I paid him for the materials. He would not accept pay for his labor. He said that I had stood by him over the years and he wanted to do this as a gift to me. His kindness melted my resentment of the ramp. Now when I see the ramp, I think about his kindness rather than my anger. What a blessing.

RICKY BOB'S ROAD TRIP

DOC'S EXPERIENCE

In the spring of 2010 the Kentucky Cobra Club's (KCC) newsletter announced that the club would attend the Carroll Shelby Car Show in Nashville, Indiana. The article stated (greatly paraphrased): "If you don't go Saturday you will be just another day older Sunday. If you do go, on Sunday morning, you will know that you have lived a good day Saturday."

That haunted me. MS has made "memorable days" fewer and farther between. I finally decided on "Road Trip." Yes, the last time I made a three-hour trip by myself was to the MS center. On that trip I hit a guardrail at 74 mph, did a 180-degree tailspin, and wrecked Josh's new Mustang. Since then my family has not let me make any long drives without adult supervision. Josh has been especially adamant on that subject.

So, who wanted to ride with me in an open-topped, poorly suspended, hard-seated, homemade car for a three-hour drive? Nobody! The family tribunal met and decided that in view of my determination and lack of willing guardians, I could make this trip solo. After all, what are the odds that someone would have two 180-degree tailspins in a row? Right?

My very first step was to call "Towin' Tom." I had no illusions about my car construction abilities. Tom Jamison had a local wrecker service. He had come highly rated from all my ill-fated automotive friends. He had always been gracious to pick up Cobra and me. Towin' Tom had rescued us so many times that he had taken pictures of the car on his flatbed truck to show his friends. Tom was a talkative ex-marine supply sergeant who was a world champion scrounger. As such, he was an excellent conspirator in my car forays. He never made me feel uncomfortable asking for help with even the most trivial of problems, now that I was no longer able to do things. His father had died with MS. We had gradually become friends.

I asked Towin' Tom if he would come and get the car if it broke down that far from home. He said he had just fixed up another truck and that this one had good tires and would probably make the trip, no problem. He was glad I called. He had just bought a '78 Cadillac limousine, which he was going to convert into a four-wheel mudder and he needed the money. In fact, he was going to start praying right away that my car would break down. He was even going to promise God to put a little more money in his tithe if it did. Odd, I had never thought of Tom as a tithing man. Yes, your friends define you.

Next call was to Bob Walker, "Bob the Motor Man." It had been only a few months since he had revived the faltering engine. I wanted his opinion about the car making this long of a trek. He assured me the engine would do great, but he had a little concern about the transmission. Maybe the reverse bands would give out first and I would not have to back home from Nashville. Images of Butch Cassidy and the Sundance Kid came to mind where the crack-shot posse had them trapped on a high cliff with a raging river below. One of them said, "I can't swim." His buddy answered with a big, reassuring smile, "Ah hell, the fall will kill you first."

Saturday morning I opened the door to go outside and embark on what would be my last, big Cobra adventure. The inside dog darted out the door and the outside dog rushed in. Neither had any inclination to return to their appropriate stations in life, despite my desperate coaxing. Yeah, I was already late so durn the dogs, full speed ahead. I loaded the car and finished checking its bodily fluids. I climbed into Ole #26, engine running, and did a last-minute mental check list. Cell phone, check, GPS, check, back up underwear and jeans, check and check, meds, check. *I was ready!* Ole Carroll Shelby, here I come. I went to put it in gear, looked up, and realized both the hood and trunk lids were still up. Yeah, MS, I'll show you.

A few blocks and turns and Cobra and I were on Highway 62. I glanced down at the speedometer. It registered 70 plus mph and I was passing the Sherriff's department. I'm a criminal already! Two miles later, I looked up and a brown pickup truck was pulling out right in front of me. So, what does a cool-as-cucumbers, former MP veteran-type driver, like yours truly, do in a situation like this? Panic stop, that's what! What does a 90-inch wheelbase, homemade car with an idiot driver traveling over 60 mph do? A 180-degree plus tailspin into the oncoming lane and ditch, that's what. When I realized the car had stopped, I remembered not hearing any breaking fiberglass or crashing metal or screaming. I dared open my eyes and looked around. Car and I were facing the way we came and were apparently intact. A white pickup truck had stopped and people were running out of their houses to see the sight. I had drawn more attention than a premiere showing of a new Larry the Cable Guy movie.

Feeling like a fool, I lamely waved everyone away yelling, "It's okay, everything is all right, it's okay." No, I did not see my life flash before my eyes or think that this was the end. Why? I ride with my wife Debbie. She is a traffic violation school multiple repeat offender with enough wrecks and speeding tickets to put our whole family in the high-risk insurance group. After twenty minutes riding with her, this becomes just a walk in the park. I was glad though that I brought a change of underwear. I started the car and turned it around. We headed on into the morning sun. No blood, no foul, right?

With less than four miles covered, I was a criminal and a habitual car skidder. Do you suppose the fates were trying to tell me something? Doesn't matter. When it comes to fates, I am a slow study.

The remainder of the trip up was unremarkable except the GPS and I had a major falling out near Bedford, Indiana. That idiot gismo! Fortunately, a beautiful Viking blue-white striped Shelby Mustang convertible pulled out ahead of me. I followed it to the show. Had it not have been there, I would have missed the turn. I kept wondering which category I should enter: most poorly homemade kit car or old guy with the best walker, or guy with the most recently changed pants.

Car and I arrived, tired, aching, and flat, tailgating the blue Mustang, but we arrived. The show officials saw the walker in the passenger seat and mercifully found a parking place for me close to the restrooms. When one has MS that is not a small favor. Sam Jackson, a kind member of the KCC—the club that got me in this mess in the first place—saw me checking in a Cobra and came over to introduce himself. His broad smile and quickly offered handshake made him an instant friend. I was excited but tired as I parked the car. I took some photos and met some nice folks. There was something about me that gave it away that I was not a standard, car show guy. You don't suppose it could have been the big shiny walker, do you? Several visitors stopped and talked with me. When I comfortably explained why I was using the walker, many were quick to share with me that they had friends and relatives with MS too.

The time for me to leave came all too soon, but the excitement was fast falling to fatigue and I had a long drive home with possible rain. I started to load the trusty walker when a cheery voice asked if he could help. It was Sam Jackson. I told him I could manage but appreciated his offer. He helped anyway. I wiggled my way into the tight little car under his thoughtful watch. I reached to turn the ignition and could not find the keys. Sam helped tear the cockpit and trunk apart searching for them until they were found right where I had left them. Yep, I am going to blame the MS for that forgetfulness too. One would never think that I could just be absentminded. Who knows differently?

When I left the park, it seemed that Ole #26 had developed a worsening "miss." About eight miles from the park something began to not sound right, like I was running it in the wrong gear. The tach was showing about 2,200 rpm, too slow for overdrive and too fast for third. Plus the GPS was telling me to go two different ways at once. To add to the worries there was an air lock in the gas tank that only let me pump five gallons. The car only gives eleven miles per gallon. So I didn't know if I had enough gasoline in the tank to get me home. No, not good signs at all.

By the time Car and I were forty miles from home, the transmission seemed to be slipping worse. A rough mental calculation suggested one slip in every four rotations. I was becoming a desperate man. How desperate? I thought about calling Towin' Tom and asking him about how much more he was going to tithe if the car broke down. Maybe I could make a deal with God and outbid Tom. I started making mental notes of places so that when Car broke down, I could call for help and give an exact location.

Car and I pressed on tenuously. When only fifteen miles from the safety of my garage, I reluctantly accelerated to pass a car and then returned to normal speed. Inexplicably the slipping stopped. Ole #26 got us home safely. I was tired, aching, but very thankful. The MS had sapped my strength but not my spirit.

When I had arrived at the car show, I was too tired to fully enjoy the event. That was expected. But it was never about the show. It was about the trip, the solo adventure; God's traveling blessings on a poor, dumb, undeserving hillbilly, including help from people I had never met before. It's a memory and a victory this poor mind of Swiss cheese can enjoy for years to come. Yes, when Sunday morning came, I had lived Saturday.

NURSE ZILIAK AND DOC YEAGER YACK

The last several months have been devoted to putting my thoughts about my life with MS on paper. I do not fully understand why I started this crazy project, but it has felt right since the first word written. Rick has shared a similar commitment to mine in telling his tale. When we began, the plan was for us to have approximately equal words to share on paper. We quickly revamped our approach, once again due to the realities multiple sclerosis forces upon both of us.

Rick's health has deteriorated greatly since he agreed to write this book with me not quite six months ago. He minimizes his disabilities (it is okay to say the word) as best he can to protect loved ones and to make people around him more comfortable in his presence. But this is his life right now, a rather quick slide down an icy snow-packed hill. Physical and cognitive challenges have made putting his thoughts to paper almost an impossible task. Together we have revised outlines, postponed deadlines, and tried to think outside the box as best we can. I want to help him and make things easier. Rick does not want to impose on me or be a burden. A most recent adjustment for Rick has been using a voice recognition program to capture his words, but even that proves taxing beyond tolerance for him most days. Besides weakness, fatigue, and great difficulty with ambulation and transfers, it is very difficult for him to stay focused and remember where he is with writing.

I just left Yeager World—a warm, scenic home filled with dogs and birds, a ramp and tile floors—after a book meeting there with Rick. We reviewed what he was still hoping to share with you and driving away from Boonville I realized more words from him is just asking too much. What kind of friend am I, pushing him to complete this? Part of our story is he may not be able to complete this as planned, regardless of how hard he tries. MS may not allow it.

The first hour of our meeting today was book agenda; the second was personal sharing. The personal included Rick helping me talk through some recent medical changes and a flare-up. It was time for some tough medicine and doctor decisions for me. I was helping him talk about where he is with the MS changes and how his family and he are coping right now. Difficult conversation does not begin to capture the seriousness of our discussion of life and death. Funny how you can spend an hour talking about life and death and yet never utter the two words out loud. Again, we are looking out for each other as friends do, not wanting to hurt each other with concrete talk of death. We are true friends who have unexpectedly shared intimate details of our complex lives, and the chapters of MS in our lives develop at a speed over which we have no control whatsoever. Rick and I join hands and pray before each of our book meetings. We agreed to that with little discussion. It is fitting to both our natures. It was my turn to say a heart prayer today and I prayed for clarity, strength, and guidance from the Holy Spirit to complete our book. I think as a result I am supposed to share a bit of our conversation.

I mentioned casually to Rick that I think he really needs a silver bullet right now to get better. He looked sternly my way from the other couch and pronounced, "No! That moment is gone. I am out of time. There is no silver bullet. There is nothing else." He stared at me until acknowledgement shown in my eyes. I hate when he reads me like that. The turkey. But we both knew he was right. Denying the inevitable helps no one. He was not being morbid. He was being honest.

Next I asked where Deb and the boys were in understanding his MS status, how bad he was. He was quiet beyond a comfortable interval, then replied, "I think they all have a pretty good idea of where I am. Deb wants me to stop my trips to see the MS specialist in Nashville because it takes so much out of me to make the long trips. She wants me to stay here. She has a valid point I must consider."

"And what is the status of the hospital bed in the living room you've been talking about?"

"She feels it is not necessary. That was the end of that discussion. She is depressed. I don't know if it is because of me."

"Oh, I see." I asked, "What about the boys?"

"They have a pretty good idea of how bad I am and have told me they will be here for me. We are so lucky, Mary Ellen, to both have that support."

"Yeah, you're right."

"But I don't think the boys have any idea of what follows next with me. We don't talk about it. What is the need?"

"I think talking about it can do nothing but help everyone involved. It is good to know what to expect. But then, that is just me. We differ on some of this. I know. It's okay."

"I have never asked Deb about this. I should ask how she feels. I may tonight."

"Sounds like a plan."

Rick had started the meeting making a mad dash to the bathroom on his scooter. He asked me if I needed to do bladder duty before we started. What other friends have that conversation when meeting up for a visit? He returned some time later and said, "No luck. I will probably be making a fast dash again shortly."

"Duly noted. Gottcha."

We needed to clarify the spelling of a doctor noted in one of his chapters. An easy answer to that one was a telephone book check. I wanted to Google the guy and teased him about being old fashioned when he nixed that idea. I offered to get the phone book. Rick vehemently refused my help as he does about 99 percent of the times I offer. I could walk quickly to get something and save us both time and him valuable energy. We argue jokingly, as is our norm, and I reply, "You are the most exasperating man I know. You drive me nuts! It's good we aren't thrown together more or we would both be out on the floor with the battle."

Rick's matter-of-fact response is, "If I let you get the book, I've given up. The MS wins. I can't."

Two days have passed now and I met up with Rick once again at our hang out, the Cancer Center. He is there for the monthly Tysabri IV. I am there for a JCV blood draw and to talk more with Tracey, the wonderful and knowledgeable nurse practitioner who is helping me navigate through some new developments of viral, bacterial, and fungal infections that have sidelined my IV at present, along with a new development of a small 8 mm meningioma that was noted on my last MRI a couple of weeks ago. As Rick and I have both noted, not everything that develops with our health centers around MS.

The meningioma is new but after the initial shock of it, I realize it is just another bump in the road. It is small, does not require surgery, only monitoring. Meningiomas comprise almost a third of brain tumors and are usually benign and insignificant. Should it need removing at a later date, it is in a prime location atop my left posterior parietal lobe and as Rick and my oncologist both said, verbatim, it can be "plucked right out." Doctors are so funny when they recite the common phrases meant to minimize our anxiety level. They don't realize how silly it sounds. Does any human being really think a brain tumor is ever "plucked" like a chicken feather? Geez Louise. But I feel good about the plans to monitor, and, once again, having a good friend who happens to be a physician goes a long way to helping me understand and cope.

Sitting next to each other in our matching, nondescript, gray, functional recliners, very close to the bathroom, we review our present dilemma. Reality is clear to both of us. Rick is too progressed with his MS to crank out any more words of wisdom and finish the book. His spirit is very willing but his body is not. We prayed for clarity. We got it.

We recall our first meeting here about a year earlier in the same corner of this treatment room. We have to laugh about how God threw us together. How His timing was perfect and His plans were exact for us to work together as friends and writers. This doctor and nurse suddenly becoming writers of a book still elicit a chuckle from both of us. God has some crazy sense of humor!

Rick looks at my red leather, high-heeled boots I have on today. He shakes his head and tells me the boots worry him.

"What?" I reply. "Why do my boots bother you?"

"I worry you will fall."

Okay, time to straighten out Ricky Bob. "I am not going to fall off these heels. I took a half hour walk with JoAnn this morning and I did fine. My boots are your phone book from Monday that you would not let me get, remember?"

"Yes."

"You said if I got the telephone book for you, MS won. For me, today is a decent day. I feel draggy and discouraged a bit that I am having some medical complications so I had to dress up more, get more foo-fooey and wear my high-heeled red boots. If I didn't then MS won."

Now the lightbulb went on under the gray mop head, which happened to be windblown today because of our blistery fall day in southern Indiana.

MOTHER YEAGER

DOC'S EXPERIENCE

> When I die, I want to die peacefully in my sleep like my
> grandfather. Not like the screaming passengers in the car
> with him.

Samuel Johnson once said of facing death, "I will be conquered; I
will not capitulate." Mother's way of dealing with cancer became
my example for dealing with MS. Mother, Mazol, was in her later
sixties and remarkably healthy. She was enjoying her retirement
with my dad, Bob. She had plenty of things to keep her active and
also managed to find more than enough for Bob too, though not
always to his high pleasure. Mazol had always enjoyed incredibly
good health. One pill a day for mild hypertension met her health
needs. But she began to complain of tiring easily. She was constantly on the go and it was difficult to attach significance to this
sole complaint. After all, she was approaching seventy and still
going like a house afire, as she would say. She often said that it
was a great, wide, beautiful, wonderful world if you didn't weaken.
She refused to weaken.

Mother was a farm child during the depression. She said the
family never had anything else but they always had food. She
gave her life to Jesus in her youth. Her favorite Bible verse was,
"But they that wait upon the Lord shall renew their strength;
they shall mount up with wings as eagles; they shall run, and not
be weary; and they shall walk, and not faint" (Isaiah 40:31, KJV).
She always trusted that God would keep His promise "And we

know that all things work together for good to them that love God" (Romans 8:28, KJV). That did not always prevent worry for her but was a working rudder in harsh storms. These factors make for a gentle, framed lady who inside was anvil tough.

I lived with Dad and Mother after finishing medical training until marrying three years later. Dr. Jerry Like invited me to work with him until I could open my own office. I saw patients in his office on weekdays and on weekends worked in a local, small ER. I had started working for Jerry just to cover him for a week's vacation. Almost unannounced, Jerry came back a month later. That relaxed way of doing things fit both of us well. Jerry still watches out for me.

During this time I started setting up my office. I had purchased land across from our local hospital. My parents went with me to pick out the modular building I would convert into an office. My longtime friend, John Lewellyn, was as involved in this project/adventure as I was. His dad loaned me a backhoe to dig the holes for the piers, and the utility services. Dad operated the backhoe and helped me with the necessary framing, wiring, and plumbing. As always, Dad and I enjoyed working together. Mother enjoyed the outings with me and just having the additional activity in the house. She enjoyed sharing the world of "her son the doctor."

One day Mother asked, "Ricky, would you feel this?" She put my fingers into the soft area between her right collarbone and neck. There I palpated a distinct, hard, immovable mass. I tried to hide the awful sickness that wrenched inside. I told mother I was unsure what it was and that I would like my good friend Dr. Lee, a thoracic surgeon, to look at it and maybe do a biopsy.

The biopsy revealed lymphoma. Other studies confirmed that it was stage IV, the most advanced. I helplessly watched my once very active mother succumb to the merciless adversary of cancer. She was heroic to the end in her battle.

Her first hurtle was losing her hair from chemotherapy, which was perhaps even more emotionally distressful than being sick from the treatments. Even so, she chose to be resilient. She wore the headscarves like a badge of courage. She and her hairdresser picked out the right wig. She continued to plan for Bob who was not in good health either and of course to worry about her adult sons Merlyn, Ricky, and Myron. Sometimes Mother and I would sit holding hands, saying nothing, but finding strength in each "others" touch and presence. Children are more comfortable to be touched on the trunk. Elderly are more comfortable being touched on the hand or forearms.

About two years before her death, Myron invited the whole Boonville Yeager clan to his home in Los Angeles, California. That is, Mother and Dad, Ricky and Debbie and the boys, Josh and Matthew. Josh was two and Matthew was only six months old. Yeager World was on a mission, to see Myron's home and Los Angeles, California. Mother and Dad had never flown before. The first ride was in a small, about sixteen-seat, passenger plane, and the trip was rough. Dad vomited. Debbie was sick with vertigo and I was just sick. Mother and the small boys were undaunted.

Mother made the most of every precious moment in defiance of the cancer. She made the trip to Disneyland and even rode some of the rides. With maternal instincts in full play, Mother and Dad kept six-month-old Matthew occupied and happy. She, little Josh, and I waded through the wet sand to put our feet in the Pacific Ocean. It was a fantasy come true. Mother occasionally, unobtrusively, took a strong pain medication, Dilaudid, to deal with the physical rigors of travel. She did not complain. She was focused on the miracles of the moment. When she returned home, she commented to me that she could feel more comfortable about Myron now that she had seen where he lived. Only a mother could comprehend that thought.

Two short years later I carried her frail, emaciated body from the house to the car for another trip to the hospital. She was so weak I was not sure if she noticed the sunshine as we went for her last ride. She knew she was dying. While she lay in the ICU bed, I made the final calls to my brothers. Merlyn and I were with her and I held her hand for our last time. She knew that Myron was coming. She slipped into eternity in peace. That faith in Jesus that carried her through living and dying was now to be changed to sight. Few people leave this world so fortunately.

Mother's struggle with cancer made her inner strength more visible and precious. She was objective in presenting her problems and her fears. She did not use her discomfort or weakness as means of gaining attention or special benefits. A life of faith and frequent self-denial enabled her to suffer and die with strength, dignity, and peace, leaving a precious legacy.

While caring for dying, saintly people, I occasionally asked them to say hi to Mother when they cross through the approaching pearly gates. All whom I asked were pleased at the thought and promised they would. None ever found the unusual request awkward.

I have been with many patients who have dealt with progressive, unpleasant illnesses, which have taken their lives long before their years warranted. As their doc and often their friend, I was the one to break the news of their diagnosis. Frequently I was the last doctor to make rounds on them the day they died. Sometimes I was with them when they slipped into eternity.

I saw how these patients dealt with their illness. After acceptance of the diagnosis, some were bitter and felt cheated. Others complained and let the illness own their last days. Others soldiered bravely on. Mother's example was clear. Use the time wisely, living not waiting to die.

I know that I have what appears to be a fairly rapid progression of MS to total incapacity and to an early death. I want to face it with the quiet faith, strength, forbearance, and simple honesty that my mother did. I do not want to complain unless it is for help with a need. I want my spirit to lift up others' spirits when they are around me, not to depress them. I cannot say I do not want to be a burden to others. I know I will be. I can only hope those around me will know that their help is appreciated and sought because it was needed. I do not want them feeling used.

These goals can only be obtained through a true understanding that God has chosen this path for me. It is the best one for His will, those around me, and for me. When our boys were young, I tried to teach and exhibit what were right ways for them to live as adults. Yes, I failed in many ways but still that was my desire. Now I must show them how to die. I want to do that well for them. I do not see this goal as a burden but rather a challenge. Yes, I will fail here at times too.

ASSUMPTION OF MARY

Rick has Mother Yeager for his inspiration on how to deal with MS. I have the Blessed Virgin Mary. *So...* move over, Sarah Palin, I'm going rogue! Catholic rogue, that is. This chapter is not for the faint of heart. I will be talking deep Catholic. So if you have a bone to pick with the Catholic Church, you strongly disapprove of their belief system, or you plain old hate Catholics, skip this chapter. It might get your panties in a wad.

Now I do not profess to be a good Catholic or even a smart Catholic who can spout off a long list of saints and the details of their sainthood. But I am Catholic. It is my being. It centers and roots me firmly to my world, here and beyond.

You might also note here that besides not being the best example of a Catholic woman, Mary Ellen did not pass the litmus test for the wife of a deacon role. Roger spent the better part of a year pursuing the deaconate program. He felt drawn to take on this ministry but later decided it was not the right time for him.

During the first night of deacon classes in downtown Evansville, there was a welcoming of students and their spouses. After a cold-cut dinner, the want-to-be deacon men split off for class and we wives went to a cozy fire-placed room to sit and chat and get to know each other. As my butt sank deeply into the caverns of an overstuffed wing chair, I tried to figure out what exactly the wife of a deacon looked like and acted like.

I met some very nice women that night. Many were much older than me. We did the small talk and quickly moved onto the topic of our men becoming deacons and how we felt about that. Being the feely-feely person I am, I shared my conflicting emotions and my concern for losing a part of Roger by sharing him so much with the church. I did not know if I was up for the challenge.

One wise, albeit mousy looking wife, clad in worn Sag Harbor attire, looked me in the eye and shared her heart. "Well, the way I look at it, I had Ed for fifty years now. It is my turn to give him over to God and let Him have him the rest of the time."

Well, hell's bells, that is not what I wanted to hear. I couldn't help but think this woman was damn tired of Ed and saw this as an acceptable way to chuck him. I was definitely not ready to give Roger away and I was not tired of him and I loved our life together. Then I thought, "Is this woman giving up sex with her husband? Do any of these other women have sex with their husbands? Are they clinging to the rule that if they die, their deacon husbands cannot remarry so no other woman will ever have him after her?"

Behind these rambling thoughts were the ones I had before this hen-clucking session. I had told Roger I didn't know if I could be a good enough deacon wife because I was not ready or willing to give up cursing. Four letter words just captured the moment too well sometimes and as you might know by now they sorta roll off my tongue without me even knowing they fell out.

That night I left the warmth of the fireplace and the cold looks of Ed's wife and went home with my not-yet-deacon husband to have wild and crazy sex, blow his mind, and brand him as mine for life. I was so not deacon wife material.

With time, the deacon program grew on me, and just when I thought I had a better handle on being a human and not perfect deacon's wife, Roger up and quit. I felt sad for him because he would have made a wonderful Catholic deacon and been an asset to our diocese. I also felt relief for me. The pressure was off for now.

Mary Ellen is far from being the pope's recruit poster person, but I try my best to live my life as right as I can and according to the teachings of the Catholic Church. It's all I can do and what God expects.

Today is the feast of the Assumption of Mary and I found myself at Monday morning mass at 7:00 a.m. Anymore, I seldom make weekday mass. When I was in walking distance back at our apartment, I went several times a week. I found it was so right for me then and gave me strength, support, and focus at a time in my life when the MS was doing just the opposite.

For you non-Catholic's, the Assumption of Mary is a holy day, though not a "holy day of obligation" meaning one is expected to go to Mass that day. It was made a holy day rather recently in 1950. We believe after Mary's death, her body was taken to heaven by God to end the full circle of her life on earth.

The start of Mary's life is celebrated on December 8th as the "Immaculate Conception." From her conception until she died, Mary lived without sin. God made this happen because the plan for her from day one in her Momma's womb was for her to be the tabernacle for Jesus Christ. Later He would be miraculously placed inside Mary's body to become man. The sinless tabernacle was only fitting.

Yeah, I know how funky that can sound to Protestants, but I believe that and it makes perfect sense to me. If I ponder for explanation of one detailed morsel of the whole Mary/Jesus event, I turn to faith. Faith comes into play then because faith is believing that which we cannot prove. So the pressure is off for me to prove this belief. It is a part of my Catholic faith and requires no manmade explanation to be proven by science.

Now my warped mind sees many similarities of Mary's life with Jesus and my life with MS. Please don't think I equate Jesus with MS. That is not my point. But I bet Mary had a gazillion challenges giving birth to the Savior of the World. I have a minute version of a difficult life dealing with the changes I experience due to multiple sclerosis. Hence the similarity.

Okay, bear with me here. First Mary gets pregnant as an unwed teenage girl by the power of the Holy Spirit. Imagine explaining that one to Mom and Dad. Then she tries to convince an older carpenter guy Joseph that she is a virgin and just happens to be swollen with child, and, oh, could he maybe marry her too and be the father of Jesus Christ? Oh, and Joe, JC will also be in training by God the Father to become King of the World. Today we would sorta call Joseph her baby daddy. Or is that the Holy Spirit? I lose track. So she gives birth in a barn, for crying out loud, in the dead of winter and later has to run for her Son's life. As Jesus grows, Mary has to track down her wayward child in the temple and endure his questioning of her like she is some idiot woman. He addresses her as, "Woman," yet she does not slap his smart mouth, such control. And sure enough He is a lot smarter than her and is God so what can she say in response while keeping her child in line? Then she watches her boy become a man and lead a path, destined by God, which lands Him much ridicule and mocking. And at the end she watches her Son be put to death in a most horrific way. No parent should have to bury a child. As we say, it's not natural, and it wasn't for Mary either.

So the way I figure it, if anybody knows pain and suffering, and the need for faith and flexibility, it would have to be the Blessed Virgin Mary. She is my role model. Mary understood challenges in life and knew how to adjust to anything life threw at her. All the while dignity and grace were second nature to her. Her God-child came with a heavy burden and she carried it well to her grave.

That is why I smile when I look at any statue or picture of Mary. She gets it. She gets all of it when I ask for her intercession with a problem I have. She is one smart and tough cookie. If I can be just a bit like her, I'll handle MS fine. What a woman!

JUST ANOTHER LOST SOLE

A year ago, I spent July 4th on Mt. Rainier in the great state of Washington. This was the tail end of a ten-day visit to see my daughter Liza in Seattle. After much searching I found a cheap ticket out of St. Louis, a three-hour drive from Newburgh, but the price was too good to pass up.

Do you know how stinkin' lucky I was that week? Really stinkin' lucky. I got to spend a nice, long stretch with Liza, a rarity, and got to be smack dab in the middle of the mountain gazing at snow, deer, and cascading glacier water. And the icing on the cake was Roger and the rest of my poor family was in a ninety-five-degree heat wave back home in Indiana. Yeah, I was a little bit petty and sadistic. But it tickled me all the more to know how special it was for a Hoosier to be chillin' on Mt. Rainier. Do you agree? I was the lucky one.

My diagnosis of MS was ever present on my mind when Liza and I hiked one afternoon. Yes, I *hiked!* All I could think of the whole time on the trail was that I had the upper hand on MS for that moment in time. Those moments can be one minute or in this case four hours. Anyone with multiple sclerosis will appreciate the magnitude of joy and exhilaration experienced in such a moment of activity, freedom, and non-handicapness.

Let me share this golden nugget more fully with you.

Liza happened to be moving from her rental house shared with three other women into her very own studio apartment. At age thirty-three this was her first time to live alone and not have to share space with other women. Her studio had a total square footage less than my family room space but pulsed "Sex in the City" chic. It was extremely hard work for us moving her after trying to downsize all her possessions. Then we had to factor in her limitations with rheumatoid arthritis and mine with MS, and we were one big balancing act of Waterford crystal.

By the time Liza turned in her old house key and got some modem of modesty with the landlord hanging up blinds in her bedroom/living room/entry area, we were both totally shot and grouchy. We had major meltdown July first and felt like we needed to cancel all other plans for my visit that involved unnecessary movement outside of eating and bathing. We both mourned the loss.

I had been staying with friends of Liza's, the Mechelkes, that I'd also known for years who had a one-year-old son. Elias was a bilingual German-English charmer but was still twenty-two months old with all that energy and busy stuff. The overload of my MS fatigue made living with his natural energy stimuli a challenge. So Liza and I decided to find a spot that felt like true vacation for both of us, away from everything and everyone.

We searched online and came across a great rental on Lake Union that looked available and a prime location to see the big downtown Seattle fireworks. It was on the water and had the feel of the houseboat where Tom Hanks lived in the movie, *Sleepless in Seattle*. It seemed very appropriate.

We submitted a reservation but never heard back from the owners so we went on to Plan C. We returned to our original hope of Mt. Rainier because by evening on July 2nd, we were both re-juiced enough from the move to attempt a visit to the mountain with the amenities of a lodge, real bed, and hot shower. I had never visited Mt. Rainier in the eight years I'd been coming to visit Liza in Seattle. The mountain season open to tourists is only May to October. Other months it is snowed in and inaccessible. My timing was never quite right to make the two-and-a-half-hour trip from Liza's home, which is further north in Washington.

So fate would have it that we got a room for one night at Paradise Inn and were able to borrow some great hiking gear from Liza's friend, Adrianna, from Columbia. So we packed frugally and I squeezed my five-foot-nine frame into a five-foot-one girls wicking Pacific Northwest shirt and we were on our way. Wow, it felt good.

As Seattleites say, "The mountains were out," as we drove along I5 South. Upon reaching the mountain path, snow was pushed aside fifteen feet deep along the steep, winding road. It was a full, sunny day with great visibility when we finished chugging the Honda Civic up the five thousand-foot spiraling elevation and followed through the Nisqually entrance. The inn was located a few miles past the national park stop point of entry where we were given our glossy map of Mt. Rainier.

The first close-up glimpse of beauty and grandeur of the white-capped mountains left me breathless. Prayers of gratitude and awe of God's wonder filled my heart and left hugging warmth inside me. I have often wondered how anyone can see these miraculous wonders of nature and deny the existence of God. Gazing upon the snowy peaks grows my faith with no effort. It just takes my soul captive.

Upon arrival, Liza and I checked into Paradise Inn that put me in mind of Ben Cartwright's Ponderosa Ranch with rugged log design in building and furniture and a big, opened fireplace at one end. But after a bit more consideration, I replaced the Ponderosa title with the hall from the movie *Dirty Dancing* where Baby sat in the corner before Patrick Swayze grabbed her hand and said the infamous words, "Nobody puts Baby in the corner." Even the wait staff living in dorms for the May/October season gave off the vibes of a close family-type group of young adults.

Every view from the lodge framed a snow-covered picture of mountains or piles of cleared away snow. In the cleared parking lot we passed many visitors speaking a multitude of languages we did not understand. It was about two in the ideal afternoon and we both had a good amount of energy left so we decided to try a hike.

All the trails near the lodge were still snow covered since it had been an exceptionally long winter in Seattle. Mountain wildflowers still hadn't bloomed in July because of the ice, snow, and cold temps. So we took the suggestion of driving down the mountain a bit and checking on trails at Longmire where the lower elevation had allowed some snow to melt off the trails.

Checking at the visitor's desk near the museum, we were shown two good trails nearby that were one and a half miles and six miles long. Liza and I felt pumped so we quickly opted on the longer trail. I was at the peak of my Tysabri energy from my IV received the week prior so if I were ever to scale the mountain trail, this would be the opportune time to do so.

While we marked our maps and rechecked our gear, I could not help but notice a second "Power Ranger," as Adrianna called them in her broken yet sexy Latino drawl, glance at us from behind his desk with a raised eyebrow look of skepticism. The six-miler "moderate trail" would take us along the Wonderland Trail and past Carter Falls and Madcap Falls, but it would definitely pose a major challenge for both of us to complete. Somehow that smirky guy sensed the hint of hesitation in our conversation.

But we figured, "What the heck. Worst-case scenario we make it one mile and have to turn around and go back. We had both lived that outcome before, too many times. But why not think big. We both needed a new win against our individual chronic disease." So we chose to ignore smirky Smokey and took off.

Enthusiasm propelled us through the first 1.7 rocky miles when we took a needed rest and snack break. While getting butt nestled on the downed cedar log bench, my foot got snagged and tripped me slightly. I caught myself before I truly wiped out but the end result was a tire blow out on my fifteen-year-old hiking boots. I had not realized the rubber on rugged shoes can dry rot just like anything else, and I hadn't done any real hiking for many years. So the end result was me standing there with one intact, right hiking shoe and the left one blown off down to the soft moccasin type underbelly. I was lopsided in height and had no solid protection on the sole of my left shoe. It was like I was trying to walk with one of Roger's sturdy cowboy boots on my right foot and a cushy house slipper on my left foot. Very discombobulating to say the least.

Upon realizing the full visual of this event, Liza and I sat on the makeshift log bench and doubled over with laughter all the while knocking off big black ants who were determined to crawl into our earthy looking cargo hauling pants, waist down or pants leg up. The ferocious ants didn't care which route they took. I swear those suckers were two inches long. Everything grows bigger in the lush and rainy northwest.

Then we switched to survival mode. Assess the situation like two competent women. Okay, here we were in the middle of a moderately difficult trail atop a mountain covered in snow with no other humans around. We had just had a doe and two baby fawns cross our path, but they only provided cuteness and an *awe* factor off the Richter scale.

We were 1.7 miles into the six-mile hike with three going, three coming back. Mom is laid up with one blown-out shoe and one functioning well clad foot, which upon further inspection was on the verge of blowing rubber also. What should we do? Aha! Take a picture of this Kodak moment. No one would believe this crazy story unless we had proof.

So we did just that. Liza and I posed and snapped and laughed some more and then got down to the business of deciding whether to continue forward or cut our losses and return to the post. Returning to the post would still entail a 1.7 mile return hike and worse yet would mean encountering Power Ranger Man who gave us the mute doubting assessment earlier. We did not want to hobble back, defeated, with tails between our legs, and see the smirk of "I told you so" under the tan Yogi Bear hat. Little time passed before we chose the onward Christian soldiers' option.

Trying to patch my almost worthless boot, we examined Adrianna's emergency supply stash in one of the many zippered pockets of the borrowed backpack. We had the "Ten Essentials" that is encouraged with every hiker. Unfortunately, duct tape or glue was not a part of the emergency supply. The only tape-like substance was a few Band-Aids and we decided they were worthless to tape my sole back onto my shoe. So I said, "Let's try it as is. So my left foot has moccasin strength protection. If it becomes too difficult, we turn around and leisurely do the return trek or I hop a lot on my right foot." So off we went into the wild blue yonder.

It was not until the return trek that my second shoe blew rubber and I just stowed away the shed tread in my eco-conscious, very green, carry-out refuse bag and went on my way. Carry in and carry out is the motto we honored as any good hiker. Time would prove my decision to proceed onward was *so* right. The rest of the hike turned out to be one of the most memorable of my life.

Liza and I concentrated on putting one foot in front of the other. We stopped often to consume adequate amounts of water from our camel pack, protein, and to take in the spectacular views. The three-mile hike to Carter Falls also had us gaining a gradual one thousand-foot elevation. We knew this because markers on the path and signage at the falls all noted exactly how high up we were on Mt. Rainier.

Exposed roots from mammoth-sized trees tripped us up on very steep inclines. We panted through several legs of the journey from both aerobic exertion and altitude adjustment. Smiling with pride, we stood atop the crests of mini hills, our poles in hand, feeling more like Moses with the stone tablets on his hip. The roar of the adjacent river was almost deafening at times. Breezes were refreshing and the temperature hovered in the sixties. Trees beside us were easily three feet in diameter and wood ferns were tall and dense. The trail under our feet was packed solid from thousands of other human feet before us and exuded a rich plethora of hiker memories. We were inside the belly of a garden of Eden.

The Wonderland Trail we were walking closely followed the path of the Ohanapecosh River and their beds were flowing with ice-cold glacier water that was fairly shallow in spots. This left an extremely large bed of water-smoothed rock exposed.

Now the artist in me absolutely loves stone of any kind. As I mentioned earlier, I was in the middle of painting the St. Meinrad series of stone architecture. I found myself examining beautiful stones with an array of colors that touched upon every earth tone known to man. One large granite-type stone that was white, peppered with black, and sparkled under the bright sunlight was very similar to a grave headstone and it took the shape of a curled-up woman on her side with the curve of her body perfectly arched. I longed for my brushes and paints to capture the essence of that form and color of Mother Nature. Instead, I smiled with the knowledge of seeing the essence of that one stone in the speck of this two-and-a-half-mile high mountain.

We crossed several narrow bridges made of roughhewn logs that taxed my precarious balance issues with MS. I concentrated on looking directly in front of me and not down at the rushing water below me. The rapids of the water were not deep but a fall would mean freefalling onto the rocks below. We were crossing a mountain bed, not the muddy Ohio River in Evansville that would be a little more forgiving in receiving my tumbling body.

The pinnacles of our three-mile excursion were Carter Falls and fifty yards beyond that Madcap Falls. Neither site disappointed. They were tall, white-foamed cascades of water that rushed forth to spray us with their cool mist. Time stood still as Liza and I gazed upon this indescribable vision.

My private thoughts naturally were wonder filled. But at the core of that wonder was the utter amazement that at the time I had been diagnosed with multiple sclerosis for thirteen years, had times I could not walk unassisted or roll myself over in bed. Yet at that moment in my life, I stood at 5,260 feet elevation on Mt. Rainier after having hiked the three miles, in one decent, sole-flapping boot and one moccasin soft boot, with only the assist of two hiking poles and my own steam. In my mind, I was experiencing a miracle and I wanted to record it for all time.

This was a rare moment for me or for anyone dealing with MS challenges. Fear and doubt infiltrated my courage to attempt this six-mile hike, but I did not let it stop me from trying. And the accomplishment of completing the six-mile trail would buoy me for a long time when I was feeling beat down and less than adequate as a productive human being. My hope was that others with MS would occasionally take those crazy-sounding risks and try the unthinkable. Sometimes we succeed; more times we can fail. But the hope must always be there that we have one more big one inside of us.

IT'S ALL GOOD

MS is the worst thing that has happened to me. MS is the best thing to ever happen to me. That sentiment warrants repeating for it has rung true over the last fourteen years. I hurt. I suffer. I celebrate. I love my life. I also seesaw that splintery, weathered teeter-totter board with Mary Ellen at one end and MS at the other. Some days I feel so secure on the playground with the warmth of the sun on my cheeks. I have a handle on life with this disease. Then *wham!* My butt hits the ground, dust flies, the wood plank pinches my thigh, and my teeth clang shut with bone-shattering pain.

Every day I make adjustments so as to lead my vision of a normal life. It may require balancing myself in a doorway or trying to comprehend a simple question posed to me. The family member next to me often thinks all is fine because I look fine to the outside world. But often I feel like the world is yelling, "Don't you dare limp just because you're missing a leg!" Only Joe Blow can't see my missing leg. He only sees my limp and does not understand at all.

There is so much that goes on inside the body of MS and only the person afflicted knows what it looks like and feels like. I believe that is our biggest challenge: somehow letting the people around us see inside our MS bodies and minds. Our situations are unique and ever changing so it is difficult for us to understand, so how can others understand?

Rick and I have tried to shed light on that understanding by letting you glimpse inside our lives with MS. We have tried to be forthright in our sharing. Yes, we can't help but wear the tinted spectacles of a doctor and nurse dealing with a medical problem we were both taught in medical and nursing school. Yet this book was written by one man, one woman, who are both living every day with multiple sclerosis the best way they know how. We have no answers, only our humanness.

We have tried to push our heavy red doors opened so as to give you a view of our stockpiles of gold; our long, twisty hallways to mystery rooms; and possible drop-offs into the dark hole. Our hope has been that by looking behind our red doors we have made it a little easier for the reader living with MS and the person at their side to see their own MS more clearly. Close behind clarity follows acceptance and peace. And above all, hope rounds out our goal. We so want all living with MS to have hope, a good life, and maybe even a last hoorah experience, be it Cobra road trip or Mt Rainier hike.

Rick and I are blessed to have some clarity, acceptance most days and always hope. We have good lives. Writing this book together has expanded all three of those blessings. At the same time, our friendship has grown. I also sense a friendship and camaraderie with you, the reader. You have taken the time to know me, to know my good friend Rick, and, most of all, to know multiple sclerosis. For today, that is more than enough. It's all good.

ENDNOTES

[1] Bronnum-Hansen H, Stenager E, Nylev Stenoger E, Koch-Henriksen N. "Suicide Among Danes with Multiple Sclerosis, *"Journal of Neurology, Neurosurgery and Psychiatry with Practical Neurology,* 2005 Oct; 76(10):1457-9

[2] Glanz M. Chamberlain, M. et al "Gender Disparity in the Rate of Partner Abandonment in Patients with Serious Medical Illness," *Cancer,* 2009 Nov; 115.22: 5237-5242